MEDIEVAL EUROPEAN

European Culture and Society
General Editor: Jeremy Black

Published

European Culture and Society Series
Series Standing Order
ISBN 0–333–74440–3
(*outside North America only*)

You can receive future titles in this series as they are published by placing a standing order. Please contact your bookseller or, in case of difficulty, write to us at the address below with your name and address, the title of the series and the ISBN quoted above.

Customer Services Department, Macmillan Distribution Ltd
Houndmills, Basingstoke, Hampshire RG21 6XS, England

Medieval European Pilgrimage, c.700–c.1500

Diana Webb

palgrave

First published 2002 by
PALGRAVE
Houndmills, Basingstoke, Hampshire RG21 6XS and
175 Fifth Avenue, New York, N.Y. 10010
Companies and representatives throughout the world

PALGRAVE is the new global academic imprint of
St. Martin's Press LLC Scholarly and Reference Division and
Palgrave Publishers Ltd (formerly Macmillan Press Ltd).

ISBN 0–333–76259–2 hardcover
ISBN 0–333–76260–6 paperback

This book is printed on paper suitable for recycling and
made from fully managed and sustained forest sources.

A catalogue record for this book is available
from the British Library.

Library of Congress Cataloging-in-Publication Data

Webb, Diana.
    Medieval European pilgrimage, c.700–c.1500 / Diana Webb.
        p.   cm.—(European culture and society)
    Includes bibliographical references and index.
    ISBN 0–333–76259–2—ISBN 0–333–76260–6 (pbk.)
        1. Christian pilgrims and pilgrimages—Europe—History.   2. Church
    history—Middle Ages, 600–1500.   3. Europe—Church history—
    600–1500.   I. Title.   II. European culture and society (Palgrave (Firm))

BX2320.5.E85 W43 2002
263′.0424′0902—dc21

                                                                    2001056145

10   9   8   7   6   5   4   3   2   1
11   10   09   08   07   06   05   04   03   02

Printed in China

CONTENTS

PREFACE

This book is intended for students; it is only sparingly annotated. Where dates are given for kings, popes, etc., they are regnal dates. The bibliography is divided into broad categories which, it is hoped, will make it possible to find further guidance on particular topics without too much difficulty. It is not a comprehensive bibliography of medieval pilgrimage, still less does it adequately cover the associated topics of sanctity, miracles and crusade. The books and articles listed are mostly, but not exclusively, in English, but their bibliographies and footnotes provide multiple signposts to relevant scholarship in several languages. They include a few on modern and non-Christian pilgrimage, and also some sources, where possible in English translation. A miscellany of translated sources is to be found in my *Pilgrims and Pilgrimage in the Medieval West* (1999) and some of the quotations used in the text come from that source. For the map, and a great deal else, I am indebted to my husband, Dr A. W. Webb. My other major debts are to the multitude of scholars who have written about medieval pilgrimage and edited relevant texts, and to the institutions which have made it possible to explore this literature: a special word is owed to the Institute of Historical Research of London University and, as ever, to the London Library.

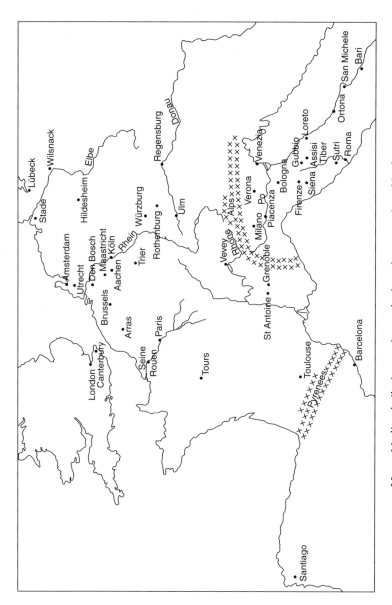

Map Medieval pilgrimage sites and other places mentioned in the text

INTRODUCTION

Pilgrimage is not a peculiarly Christian or European phenomenon, still less a peculiarly medieval one. In one or another of its many shapes, it has been a feature of most of the world's religions, and its origins probably go back long before the written record. The apparently deep-seated human tendency to locate the holy at a distance from one's everyday surroundings and to seek solutions to personal problems and the alleviation of suffering (or boredom) in a journey to such a place was clearly manifested in pre-Christian cultures. In the religions which preceded Christianity in the Near Eastern and Mediterranean region we can observe features that will persist throughout the Christian epoch. The idea that particular benefits accrued in the afterlife to those who had made the pilgrimage to Osiris at Abydos became familiar to Egyptians of the New Kingdom, and Abydos remained an important shrine in the Hellenistic and Roman epochs. Healing shrines, not least those sacred to Asklepios, abounded in ancient Greece. The 'guidebook' written in the second century AD by Pausanias mentioned many of them, as well as the great sanctuaries such as Olympia with their imposing panoply of sculptural images. Greeks practised 'incubation', sleeping at a shrine in order to obtain a cure, and medieval Christians developed their own version of the practice.

The ancient Tuscan city of Arezzo illustrates continuities and recurrences over a period of more than two thousand years. In 1869 a large haul of objects was discovered in the vicinity of a spring known as the Fonte Veneziana, in the area of the modern cemetery just east of the modern city. They included votive offerings such as bronze models of body parts (eyes, legs, arms) dating from the sixth century before Christ. On the hilltop known as Castelsecco south-east of the city, there are remains of a theatre and a temple which is thought to have been sacred to an Etruscan goddess, later equated with the Roman Juno, who was invoked by pregnant women. Here terracotta models of swaddled babies have been found, dating from the second century BC; these may have been left in petition for a safe delivery or in thanksgiving for one. Other finds at Arezzo, as at other Etruscan and Roman sites, include little models of horses, cows and other animals, some with loops for hanging them up. *Ex votos* of similar types were deposited at the Christian shrines of medieval Europe.

The Fonte Veneziana remained in use until about 1500 and another spring to the south of Arezzo, known as the Fons Tectus or Tetta, was also still frequented in the early fifteenth century. The Franciscan preacher Bernardino of Siena heard about it when he preached in the city in Lent 1425, and identified it as a 'pagan' sanctuary, which he tried to have destroyed, but the local nobility opposed his efforts and drove him out of town. On a second visit in 1428, he was successful. Bernardino consecrated an oratory of the Virgin on the site, and after his own death and canonisation a chapel in his name was added to what is now the elegant Renaissance church of Santa Maria delle Grazie. By 1482 a superbly graceful portico had been built to accommodate the pilgrims who now flocked to the church in honour, not of a holy well, but of the Virgin and Bernardino.

For at least two thousand years successive generations of Aretines had been frequenting local shrines, and some of them undoubtedly made longer journeys in the hope of reaping bigger rewards. They also expected, or hoped, to play host to pilgrims from elsewhere. In the fourteenth century the city statutes proclaimed safeconduct for 'those who are visiting the shrines of any saints reposing in the city of Arezzo or its district', or who were passing through on their way to St James of Compostela, to Rome or to the shrine of St Michael the Archangel in Apulia.

Christians, like the adherents of other religions, sought in particular places the visual and tactile embodiment of a reality other and higher than themselves, not just in a generalised sense of 'the holy', but in the form of contact with the continuing presence of the great departed. These impulses are very far from extinct, as any observer of modern tourism will instantly recognise. The visitor to Paris may choose to satisfy them by visiting the Père Lachaise cemetery or Napoleon's tomb, or he may fight to get a glimpse of the Mona Lisa behind its bullet-proof shield, even though a good reproduction would serve the purposes of study just as well or better. The point of this last exercise is that the tourist can say that he or she has seen the 'real thing', however fleetingly and imperfectly. Nearly seven hundred years ago Dante imagined his emotions on finding himself in conversation with the soul of St Bernard of Clairvaux (*Paradiso* XXXI, 103). He felt 'like a Croatian, perhaps' who beheld at Rome the veil of St Veronica on which Christ had impressed an image of his face, and exclaimed in wonder, 'Was this, Lord, your real semblance?' The 'Veronica' was one of the exhibits pilgrims to Rome most yearned to see, and Dante's Croatian was expressing a double sense of wonder: that the object itself was a true image of the Saviour's countenance, and that he himself was there to behold it. This sense of both personal participation in an experience and the supreme reality of the object being experienced – the image, the relic, the place – was and is still integral to pilgrimage both religious and secular. What is absent from the mere tourist's experience is the sense that the real thing, really perceived, may be the means of obtaining a blessing or even a miracle.

Many of the great cults and temples of Egypt, Greece and Rome had less to do with the wants and problems of humble individuals than with the requirements of the rulers or 'state'. Provided that the individual fulfilled any ritual obligations that might be laid upon him by the state (particularly the Roman state), he, with his family and neighbours, was more or less free to worship such gods and construct and frequent such shrines as he thought fit, in the home and in the locality. It was at this level that personal and familial wants were catered for. This distinction between levels was of course by no means watertight. Facilities were provided in some Egyptian temples for the individual pilgrim to petition the god, and many Greek shrines catered for both official and popular needs.

On the face of it, the scriptural religions, Judaism and Islam as well as Christianity, did not distinguish levels of access to the divine. Emperor, king and caliph, peasant and artisan, alike subscribed to the same creed and in their various degrees participated in its prescribed rituals. The pilgrimage to Mecca was and is an obligation on the Muslim of every social rank. Christian churches, it has been pointed out, became distinctive in that they united under one roof the functions of the sanctuary, the holy of holies, and the congregational meeting-place; they even permitted burial within the same building, thus departing from the ancient custom which segregated the dead from the land of the living. Some distinctions however, both spatial and social, persisted. In most societies the powerful have been identified with ritual spaces which are acknowledged to be peculiarly their own, and this was true of medieval Europe. Rulers might encourage their subjects to enter these spaces in a reverent manner, as the kings of England encouraged pilgrimage to the Confessor's shrine in Westminster Abbey, but that was intended, at least in part, to promote an association in the public mind between the saint, the god behind the saint, and the ruler whose piety and patronage were on display at the shrine. Furthermore, like many other repositories of celebrated relics, this was a monastic church, to which the ordinary lay person had restricted access. To maintain that Westminster Abbey fulfilled the same functions and attracted the same congregation as a wayside chapel of the Virgin Mary would be a misrepresentation.

Far below this exalted level swarmed thousands of healing and problem-solving shrines, some of them, at least in origin, of doubtfully Christian character, with which the secular and ecclesiastical hierarchy had relatively little to do. A complete picture of medieval European pilgrimage must include both these levels and all the ones in between. Some shrines more than others straddled the divisions. The tomb of St Thomas Becket at Canterbury was at one and the same time the scene of great public occasions, the receptacle of opulent benefactions from the great, and a healing shrine and objective of popular pilgrimage. The distances traversed by pilgrims also varied greatly. Long-range pilgrimage – from Scandinavia to Rome, from Hungary to Compostela or St Patrick's Purgatory, from Scotland to the Holy Land – understandably impresses the modern observer who has any imaginative picture of the difficulties of medieval travel. The effort and endurance involved bear eloquent witness to the faith that made such journeys possible, and we are struck that women and the elderly also attempted them.

That these were not the only, nor perhaps the typical, pilgrimages of the middle ages is, however, sufficiently obvious to the English reader who thinks of Chaucer's pilgrims. For some of these characters, for example Harry Baily the Southwark landlord, Canterbury was not all that far to go. Canterbury was first and foremost a shrine for the inhabitants of southern England, not least for Londoners, but it can also be classified as a European shrine of the second rank (behind Jerusalem, Rome and Santiago), attracting both a local and regional public and a considerable number of longer-distance pilgrims. Everywhere in Europe there were shrines with comparable pulling-power, such as the shrine of the Three Kings in Cologne Cathedral, which drew pilgrims over distances that varied from a few miles to several hundred. For all its obvious uniqueness, Rome too possessed this double aspect; it attracted Italian as well as non-Italian visitors. Many shrines of middling importance lay en route to another and perhaps 'greater' one, and drew a substantial proportion of their clientele from what might be termed the passing trade. This could be said, for example, of several of the southern French shrines – St Foy at Conques, Our Lady of Le Puy or of Rocamadour, St Gilles du Provence – which lay along the roads to Santiago de Compostela. If shrines of this intermediate magnitude were numbered, perhaps, in the hundreds, there were thousands which were known as places of pilgrimage only to dwellers in the immediate locality.

There was no rule which stated that a journey had to be of a certain minimum length, in terms either of distance or of duration, in order to qualify as a pilgrimage. Most practitioners of long-distance pilgrimage would also have gone during their lifetimes to the shrines which were most nearly accessible to their homes. The individual pilgrim would have been aware of the existence of a number of holy places both near to him and far away. The mental shrine-maps entertained by different individuals featured a number of places in common, Rome, Jerusalem and Compostela doubtless among them, but the dweller in England, Saxony or Calabria added to this common core a list appropriate to his or her own circumstances. A complete map of medieval pilgrimage, were such a thing conceivable, would have to consist of a number of maps, on very different scales, superimposed on one another or visualised simultaneously.

The key point is that at all times, from the beginnings of Christian pilgrimage to the present day, these different levels have coexisted. Historians have debated when it is legitimate to speak of the first Jerusalem pilgrims, but we can be sure that these pioneers, whether in the third or fourth century or even earlier, had contemporaries, beyond all reasonable doubt much more numerous, who were seeking comfort and healing at local shrines such as had existed for centuries in the Graeco-Roman world. The spread of Christianity north and west from the Mediterranean, accompanied by the creation of new saints and the movement of relics, brought into being a host of shrines which rarely had more than a local or regional clientele but did have the indispensable merit of being accessible to the relatively poor and humble. A member of the Spanish community in north London today may contemplate joining an expedition to Rome, Lourdes or the Holy Land, but he or she can with rather greater ease get on a coach to the Carmelite friary of Aylesford in Kent for a Sunday excursion which may not seem particularly arduous but is none the less advertised as a pilgrimage. The coaches did not run in the fifteenth century, but Margery Kempe of Kings Lynn only had to expend a little more energy when, at the suggestion of certain priests of her acquaintance, she went 'on pilgrimage' to a church of St Michael the Archangel two miles away. This was a woman who in her lifetime went to the Holy Land, to Rome and Compostela, to Wilsnack in Prussia, to Aachen and Assisi, and to the major shrines of England. She had no hesitation in using the same word to describe all these expeditions.

Are we to believe that pilgrimages over such very different distances, to such very varied destinations, were all undertaken for the same reasons? Although there is no neat and tidy way of assigning one type of motivation to the long-distance pilgrimage and another to the short journey which might not even involve an overnight stay, some broad distinctions are possible and have been observed in other pilgrimage cultures. For good practical reasons it was unlikely that a pilgrim would go to Jerusalem to seek a cure for a sore throat or a solution to some mundane problem. The very greatest shrines were not, generally speaking, places where cures were sought, although they might be places where thanksgiving was rendered for benefits already received, perhaps in consequence of a vow. They tended to be associated with the quest for a special devotional experience, and, especially in the later middle ages, for especially large quantities of indulgence. Limited means or restricted personal circumstances might dictate that some people had to seek both their indulgences and their devotional experiences closer to home.

Pilgrims may be classified, then, by where they went, and by their reasons for going. Another important distinction can be made between pilgrims who made their journeys voluntarily and those who went involuntarily as penance for their sins or even as punishment for secular offences. Pilgrims may also be viewed as belonging to an age band, an occupational or religious grouping, a social class and (not least) a gender. Different groups disposed of different resources and also different degrees of freedom, both of which affected the capacity to make long journeys. Female participation in pilgrimage was, of course, conditioned by all these variables.

All the indications are that men considerably outnumbered women as long-distance pilgrims, but the picture at many local shrines was very different. Were men and women expressing different sentiments or fulfilling different purposes when they went on pilgrimages long or short? If women were more likely to frequent accessible shrines which specialised in routine problem-solving, did that mean that as pilgrims they were more concerned than male pilgrims were with other people's problems, those of children and husbands foremost among them? All of these questions of motivation, purpose and participation form part of

the still larger question of the place occupied by the practice of pilgrimage in the culture (in the widest sense of that word) and the web of
social and personal relationships which characterised medieval society at
different periods and in different places. This is a subject with a hundred
facets.

Pilgrimage was, obviously, a religious activity, but this is neither an
easy category to define nor one that excludes others. As a form of travel,
of physical exertion, it required many types of infrastructural support
from the upkeep of roads and bridges to the provision of victuals,
accommodation and sometimes, regrettably, burial. From this point of
view, and also from the standpoint of the custodians of shrines and
relics, it was an economic activity, which on the one hand required
investment and expenditure and on the other produced income. The
material objects which can be seen in some sense as either products of or
stimuli to pilgrimage varied from the monumental and more or less
enduring to the tiny and ephemeral.

At one extreme stood the churches themselves. Not only did their
internal design reflect the need to control or facilitate access to shrines
but their larger setting, the lay-out of the roads and gates which led to
them, and the disposition of neighbouring buildings, might also reflect
the same preoccupations. Within the churches shrines possessed their
own architectural and sculptural features, and there were numerous
other significant elements in the accompanying decor, including
images, which increasingly became the objects of pilgrimage in their
own right in the later medieval centuries. At a lower level of permanence
and aesthetic pretension were the badges and other objects which functioned not only as souvenirs, but also as amulets and even, sometimes, as
the instruments of miracles. The ubiquity of pilgrimage, in terms of both
its geographical and its social impact, is paralleled and given expression
by the sheer variety and wide distribution of these artefacts.

It finds expression too in numerous other cultural forms. Music was
produced and performed by and for pilgrims (much of it now recon-
structed and available in modern recordings). The vigilant gallerygoer
will discover in both painting and sculpture images of pilgrims and of
saints garbed as pilgrims, not least St James, 'Santiago' himself. A wide
range of literary forms either describe pilgrimage or draw from it meta-
phors and images evocative of the human condition. Chaucer famously
makes an imaginary pilgrimage party on the road to Canterbury the
vehicle for a motley collection of stories and story-tellers; the rascally
Reynard the Fox garbs himself as a pilgrim with dubious intentions;

Dante sprinkles throughout his work haunting images of the pilgrim's mental and physical displacement. On what is usually a much lower level come the guidebooks and individual pilgrimage narratives, which vary enormously in length and religious sophistication, some revealing devotional responses and an interest in scenes and people, others doing little more than enumerate indulgences acquired and expenditures incurred.

There are few if any activities which elicit total unanimity of opinion and participation from all the members of a given society. Pilgrimage was no exception. Not everyone was or could be a pilgrim, for reasons of physical or economic incapacity or other constraints, and not everybody approved of pilgrimage. Pilgrimage was never, in principle, indispensable to the practice of the Christian religion and it could be argued that it was an irrelevance or worse, a distraction from true interior devotion. The Lollards of fifteenth-century England and their Protestant successors rapidly identified pilgrimage and the idolatry which they closely associated with it as prime targets for their criticisms, but in some respects these criticisms echoed fears and hesitations which had been expressed from the early centuries of Christianity by thinkers of unquestioned orthodoxy and austerity.

Pilgrimage became popular partly because it spoke to impulses that were deeply ingrained in humankind, and which were both older and wider than Christianity. Radical reformers who saw it as a pagan activity were in a sense quite right. The clergy, for the most part, shared in the emotions and beliefs of their fellow-Christians. They did not constitute a smooth and homogeneous mass: they varied considerably in their social origins, their wealth and their education, and different groups of clergy might well be found pursuing their own agenda. It is therefore insufficient to say blandly that 'the clergy' controlled and manipulated pilgrimage, for the question 'Which clergy?' may need answering. Monks (important custodians of relics, especially in the earlier middle ages) were not always amenable, or even subject, to the control of diocesan bishops, and it was far from unknown for parish clergy to encourage popular pilgrimage cults in defiance of directives from the upper levels of the hierarchy. Standards were laid down at the highest level by which sanctity and miracles were to be authenticated, but pilgrimage was never confined to saints and cults that had received the seal of official approval. Even when bishops, including the pope himself, encouraged pilgrimage by the grant of indulgences, this was often, indeed usually, simply in response to petition from the custodians of relics or images.

The clergy, at all levels, had economic incentives to encourage the devotion of the faithful in all its various forms, but there were other reasons for doing so and for accommodating the needs and beliefs of the people among whom they lived and on whom in a very real sense they depended. Rigorist reservations about the propriety of certain popular devotions often gave way before these other imperatives. When criticism became too vociferous and spread beyond the circles of the teachers and preachers who were entitled to express it, the church scented danger, not merely to the income generated by shrines, images and relics, but to the social consensus on which the authority of the church rested.

It would be foolish to suppose that any of these aspects of so ramified a subject, let alone all of them, could be adequately surveyed in a book of this length. I am not an historian of art, literature or music. The book's geographical scope, as already indicated, is limited to western Christendom; the Orthodox world presents its own special features. The homogeneity of the medieval west was only relative, but in so far as it existed in the limiting conditions of relatively primitive transport and communications, the more or less universal official acceptance of Catholic Christianity under the direction of Rome was an important part of it. The chronological weight of the book falls in the central and later middle ages, the period when the commonwealth of Latin Christian nations which accepted papal headship had expanded beyond its historic Mediterranean core into northern and eastern Europe. Englishmen, Scandinavians, Germans, Poles and Hungarians expressed their sense of membership in this commonwealth in many ways, and pilgrimages to Rome, to Compostela, to the Holy Land were among them.

It would be surprising if this society had not undergone very considerable change during the twelve hunded years which separated the Emperor Constantine from Luther, the Christianisation of the Roman Empire (and the beginnings of Christian pilgrimage) from the Protestant Reformation (and the end or at least interruption of pilgrimage in some parts of Christian Europe). This book begins with a chronological survey of the broad phases into which the history of medieval Christian pilgrimage can reasonably be divided. It was not, originally, by conscious design that the first chapter should address the question 'When?', and the second, third and fourth the questions 'Why?', 'Who?' and 'Where?' but that is the pattern which has emerged. Some overlapping of subject-matter between chapters has proved inevitable, but it is to be hoped that the material presented cumulatively achieves an effect which is both comprehensible and enlightening.

The final chapter attempts a survey of the manifold ways in which pilgrimage left its mark on the culture of medieval Europe; no one can be more conscious than the author how tentative and incomplete that attempt is. Part of the fascination of medieval pilgrimage is that it has left its traces everywhere in Europe during the history of a long period. If the reader obtains a sense of this omnipresence and an interest in seeking out the evidence for it, the writing of it will have been justified.

In memory of
a much-loved mother-in-law
Hilda Ethel Webb
(1905–2001)

1

MEDIEVAL PILGRIMAGE: AN OUTLINE

Pilgrimage before the First Crusade

Scattered testimonies suggest that Christians may have been paying religiously motivated visits to Palestine before 300, or even 200, but there has been debate as to whether their motives identify them as pilgrims in the sense familiar later.[1] Eusebius transcribes a letter from Melito of Sardis (d. c.190), who had taken the opportunity of a visit to the Holy Land to compile an authoritative list of the books of the Old Testament for a friend. To Melito this was the place where the biblical events had taken place and the 'truth' had been revealed. Any attempt to disentangle 'devotional' motives from the more academic quest for information on the part of such visitors may be doomed to frustration. Why, after all, were Christians interested in the scriptures if not for devotional reasons? When describing Holy Land topography Eusebius repeatedly uses language which implies that biblical sites were 'shown' to visitors. Clearly the long process of identifying them had begun by the early fourth century.

The identification of Roman pilgrims raises similar problems. Early in the third century, again according to Eusebius, the theologian Origen gave as his reason for visiting Rome that he wanted to see 'the ancient Roman church'. Throughout its history, Rome's unique position within western Christendom has made it a magnet for visitors both lay and clerical, but for this very reason it is sometimes difficult to discern whether a particular visitor went there on ecclesiastical business or as a 'pilgrim' motivated primarily by devotion in the sense of the desire to venerate the apostles and martyrs.

1

Christian pilgrimage, at least over long distances, was probably relatively uncommon before the reign of Constantine.[2] Apart from the various difficulties which at all periods attended the Holy Land journey and those resulting from the intermittent persecution of Christianity, acceptance of the idea of pilgrimage itself took time to become widespread among Christians. The concept of 'holy places', of sanctified earthly locations of peculiar Christian significance, was in important ways at variance with beliefs in which Christians had been schooled from the first days of the church. Christians were true *peregrini* in the original sense of the Latin word, 'strangers' or 'foreigners' in the midst of a sometimes hostile society, spiritual pilgrims between earth and heaven, between physical birth into this world and spiritual rebirth into eternal life. It has also been argued that the long process of distancing Christianity from Jewish belief and practice delayed the moment at which Jerusalem, which had become the Holy City of the Jews and central to the practice of the Jewish religion, could be appropriated as the Holy City of the Christians. Its virtual refoundation as a Christian city by Constantine and his successors, which included the building of the Church of the Holy Sepulchre, provided the physical setting in which Christians could manage this transition, just as the ending of the persecutions, the adoption of Christianity by the emperors and the progressive conversion of the upper echelons of imperial society provided the political setting.

Initially, at least, Christianity challenged the apparently innate human inclination to believe that certain places are holier than others, either in their nature or because they have been specially sanctified by mythic events or by ritual. From the beginning there were those who remembered, in the words of St John's Gospel (4:24), that God was to be worshipped in the spirit and in truth, and that this could not be done more (or less) effectively in one place than in another. A first step in the opposite direction was taken almost as soon as the *ecclesia*, the assembly of the Christian people, moved out of private houses and clandestine meeting-places into purpose-built churches, and the buildings themselves came to be designated *ecclesiae*. The sense that these places localised holiness was strengthened when they were built around the tombs of Christian martyrs or sanctified by relics brought from elsewhere. In effect, if without any such conscious intention, Christians increasingly conformed to patterns of belief and behaviour exemplified by their pagan ancestors.

If it is difficult to set a precise date on the beginnings of Christian pilgrimage to the Holy Land, there can be little doubt that it flourished in the fourth century. Pilgrims from the more westerly parts of the Roman Christian world began to flow to Palestine. The Bible was their guide-book and the Old Testament bulked large in their concerns alongside the New. Among the pilgrims who left some report of their travels were the 'Bordeaux Pilgrim' and the nun Egeria or Aetheria from Spain or southern Gaul, who toured the Holy Places late in the century. In Egeria, devotion was combined with an insatiable curiosity to see more and more, which prolonged her travels indefinitely. Some Christians took up residence in the Holy Land for lengthy periods of prayer and study, believing that a superior quality of spiritual life was, ideally, attainable in this favoured setting. The most celebrated and learned of these was St Jerome (d. 420), a Dalmatian by birth. After education at Rome, a period as a hermit in Syria and sojourns at Constantinople and again at Rome, he settled at Bethlehem in 385 and stayed there for the rest of his life. Among the disciples who followed him there was a noblewoman, Paula, who founded a community of nuns in the vicinity. Possessor of a famously tart tongue which helped to keep him on the move, Jerome was quite well aware of the dangers of mere religious tourism. His aphorism that it was 'not sufficient to have seen Jerusalem, but to have lived well at Jerusalem' was much quoted in later centuries.[3]

Alongside Jerome we should remember the 'Desert Fathers', men who cut themselves off from conventional urban existence to live as hermits in the deserts of Syria and Egypt (although they were often not all that far from civilisation). The more celebrated of these holy men were sought after by other aspirants to a more rigorous spiritual life, including visitors from Rome, as well as by ordinary people who sought their aid and counsel, and they thus became the objects of a kind of pilgrimage in their own right. The most celebrated of these individuals, Antony of Egypt (d. 356), not only became famous in the west when the *Life* of him written by Athanasius of Alexandria was translated into Latin, but was destined to become one of the most widely venerated of medieval saints and an object of western pilgrimage after his relics were allegedly brought from Constantinople in the eleventh century and installed at La Motte in the Dauphiné.

For every pilgrim who made the arduous journey to the Holy Land in these early centuries there must have been many more who frequented shrines closer at hand. This more localised form of pilgrimage can be seen as growing from two roots. The first was the cultivation within early Christian communities of the memory of their honoured dead, the martyrs whose lives, and still more deaths, had borne witness to Christ.

The second was the already established custom, known all over the Roman and pre-Roman world, of recourse to particular hallowed places for curative and sometimes divinatory purposes. As the martyrs became not only exemplary figures but wonder-workers, these growths rapidly became intertwined.

This does not mean that all the old gods turned into Christian saints or that all pagan cult-sites were resanctified, but rather that the habit of seeking healing, for example at springs, and of keeping seasonal festivals at special sites, was a deeply ingrained form of behaviour, attested all over the pre-Christian world, which readily took on Christianised forms. The number of holy wells which became and remained associated with Christian saints speaks for itself. One such, in the Auvergne, was associated with the martyr St Julian; a native of the region, Gregory, bishop of Tours late in the sixth century and a voluminous hagiographer, remembered annual family pilgrimages to St Julian at Brioude and credited the saint with cures of himself and other family members. New springs marked places of martyrdom, like the one which supposedly appeared at Verulamium at the spot where St Alban's head was cut off.

Wherever Christianity had existed in the Roman world there had been potential martyrs, although in Britain only the memory of Alban was preserved with any clarity. For as long as the church's only saints were the martyrs, undisturbed in their original burial places, the scope for pilgrimage to their tombs was limited. Early Christians performed miniature pilgrimages to the *memoriae* of the saints in suburban cemeteries, thus traversing the physical and spiritual distance between the dead and the living, to commemorate the anniversaries of their deaths, which became the feast days of the later church.[4] The erection of custom-built shrines, sometimes large churches with elaborate decoration and provision for visitors, represented a considerable development, not to say transformation, of this idea. The impulse sometimes came from personal patronage and enthusiasm such as that of the Gaulish nobleman Paulinus (d. 431) who settled at Nola in the Campagna where the third-century confessor Felix was venerated, and devoted himself to the cult, building and decorating a new church in the saint's honour and providing for the needs of travellers and the poor nearby.

Such churches rapidly came to be found everywhere in the Christian world, in Syria, Egypt and North Africa and in Europe from Gaul to Austria. The Constantinian basilicas in the Holy Land and at Rome provided models for emulation. In the early eighth century Bede described the splendid church which had been erected, presumably in the fourth century, over the burial place of St Alban, and which he believed had been continuously frequented ever since. We know the name of one early pilgrim to St Alban: in 429 Germanus, bishop of Auxerre, came to Britain to combat the Pelagian heresy and visited St Alban to give thanks for the success of his mission, endowing the shrine with further valuable relics.

As relics emerged into the full light of day and generated public cults, they even began to migrate around the Christian world, creating new shrines. Early prohibitions on the disturbance of burials broke down earlier in the Christian east than in the the west (Constantine endowed his new capital on the Bosphorus plentifully with relics). In the west they were maintained longer at Rome itself than elsewhere, until about 600, but St Augustine a century earlier witnessed translations and miraculous cures in both Italy and North Africa. In 386 his elder contemporary Ambrose of Milan brought the relics of the local martyrs Gervasius and Protasius from their original burial place to the church which he was building for his own tomb (now the great Romanesque church of Sant' Ambrogio). Augustine noted how well publicised the event was; relics of the two saints became widely distributed over Christendom and numerous churches were dedicated to them. The bringing of the relics of the protomartyr St Stephen to Utica in North Africa after the discovery of his supposed tomb in 415 resulted in the foundation of several secondary shrines, which included one at Augustine's own episcopal seat, Hippo. These had therapeutic properties and attracted local and regional pilgrimages. Augustine describes cures that he had seen with his own eyes at Hippo and makes interesting observations about the records that were kept of miracles, and the measures taken to publicise them, both there and elsewhere in North Africa.

A development of equal significance was the multiplication of saints made possible by the recognition of 'confessors', men (most often) and women who bore witness to the faith not by their deaths but by their labours and sufferings in life. Antony of Egypt and Felix of Nola, both already mentioned, belonged to this category. In the west, the extension of Christianity into regions ever more distant from its Mediterranean heartlands was accompanied by the appearance of other saints of this new type. Pre-eminent among them was St Martin, who abandoned the life of a Roman soldier to become a monk and bishop and died at Tours in 397. He was a hero of the long-drawn-out struggle to bring Christianity into the rural hinterlands of late Roman Europe, taking vigorous measures to extirpate pagan worship. Not only did Martin's tomb, enclosed in a large basilica decorated with mosaics depicting his miracles, make Tours one of the most considerable pilgrimage destinations in medieval Europe north of the Alps, but relics of him and church dedications to him multiplied throughout western Christendom. The Venerable Bede believed that it was in the ancient church of St Martin just outside Canterbury that Bertha, the Frankish Christian queen of the pagan Aethelberht of Kent, worshipped before the conversion of her husband and his kingdom at the end of the sixth century.

Missionaries carried relics and knowledge of the saints with them into new areas of Europe, and like Martin, themselves frequently became saints for the ecclesiastical communities they founded and subsequently for the peoples they evangelised. Despite the transportation of some bodily remains from place to place, the relics which accompanied the dissemination of cults in the early medieval period were often not skeletons or even fragments of human bone. 'Secondary' relics, sometimes called *brandea*, might consist of pieces of cloth which had been in contact with the relics or even just with the tomb, or of chippings or dust from the tomb itself. Most relics of Christ and the Virgin were necessarily of this 'secondary' type, including alleged garments and girdles, and also innumerable fragments of the True Cross, which the Emperor Constantine's mother, Helena, had unearthed at Jerusalem.[5] Holy Land pilgrims later coveted fragments of stone from the Holy Sepulchre.

References to the relics eagerly collected in Rome by such luminaries of the English church as Benedict Biscop of Monkwearmouth (d. 689) and Wilfrid of York (d. 709) are almost certainly to relics of this kind. Any of them could breed further 'relics', which were believed to have the same value for body and soul. Steeped in water, for example, they created home remedies of great efficacy and convenient portability. Belief in their effectiveness remained alive even in later periods when the movement of body parts was more common. Not only books and relics travelled back to northern Europe from the Mediterranean: so too did architectural styles and techniques and ideas for the arrangement and decoration of churches and shrines.

In the fifth century a people who had never been subjected to Rome entered into the ranks of Christian countries. Irish Christians, predominantly monks, had a profound effect on the Christianity which was introduced or re-established in many regions of barbarian Europe between the sixth century and the ninth. The norms of life followed by these men (and women) differed from Roman models in several respects. Pilgrimage, as practised by Irish monks who aspired to a more rigorous spiritual life, was less a simple journey to a shrine than a process of alienation, in many respects resembling the self-exile of the Desert Fathers in a rather different geographical environment. The pilgrim sought literally to make himself a *peregrinus*, a stranger or foreigner, voluntarily cut off from home and kin, which was normally an undesirable and dangerous thing to be, whether in Roman, Germanic or Celtic society. Having thus cast himself adrift on the world for the love of Christ, the pilgrim did not necessarily become a holy vagrant, but might well spend time practising the monastic life in a foreign community under the leadership of a distinguished teacher, or himself found a monastery in a foreign land. This option often merged insensibly into missionary enterprise. When in the ninth century Walafrid Strabo wrote a life of St Gall (d. *c*.630), whose wanderings took him into what is now Switzerland, he remarked that the custom of pilgrimage had virtually become second nature to the Irish ('*quibus consuetudo peregrinandi iam paene in naturam conversa est*').

In Ireland as elsewhere, however, pilgrimage also took the forms that were becoming increasingly familiar in the rest of Christian Europe. Shrines were established around distinguished relics, which became objects of devotion not only to monks but to neighbouring laypeople. One of the most notable grew up at Kildare around the burial place of St Brigid, who died early in the sixth century and took on some of the attributes of an earlier Celtic protectress of animals. In the mid-seventh century the monk Cogitosus described in some detail the arrangement and decoration of her church and also the rather mixed crowds who frequented the shrine. Some people came because of the abundance of food there was to be had there, others were in search of cures, and some bore gifts to the saint's solemnity on 1 February; some, he said, just wanted to look at the other people. Similar crowds must have assembled at popular shrines throughout Christendom.

By a variety of means, therefore, the supply of relics and shrines was augmented over an ever wider area of Europe. 'Translation', the transference of a holy corpse to a new and usually more elevated and conspicuous shrine, became an important element in the public recognition of sanctity both before and after the development of a formal system of canonisation. With increasing frequency it took place shortly after the death of a man or woman who was believed within his or her community to have been a saint. St Cuthbert of Lindisfarne (d. 687) was a case in point; his translation in 698 was attended with a splendour and ceremony supposedly unprecedented in England. Like his near contemporary Etheldreda of Ely (d. 679), Cuthbert derived his reputation for exceptional sanctity not just from the holiness of his life but, in large part, from the incorruption of his body. Etheldreda's sister Sexburga brought her body from the cemetery at Ely into the monastic church in 695, sixteen years after her death; her remains were installed in a Roman sarcophagus, a not uncommon way of distinguishing an elite burial in different regions of the former Roman Empire. A saint's burial, thus presented, was quite simply more visible than other men's (or women's). In the tenth century, Bishop Ratherius of Verona remarked that the common people paid more regard to a holy body if it was elevated above the ground in an honourable position.

The burial place of St Chad at Lichfield was clearly highly accessible. According to Bede it was a wooden coffin shaped like a house, with an aperture in the side which enabled suppliants to reach their hands in and extract a little of the dust, which could be mixed with water to make remedies for men and cattle alike. Another means of obtaining a cure was to spend the night by the tomb, as a wandering madman did who entered the church unobserved by Chad's custodians. This practice bore some resemblance to the ancient custom of incubation, well known to the Greeks, during which the god would appear to the patient with instructions as to how to obtain a cure, rather than effecting it then and there, as the saints sometimes did. Throughout the history of Christian pilgrimage suppliants tried to achieve this overnight closeness to the saint, although it was not always conceded.

There was often a tension between the desire to permit or even encourage the close approach of suppliants to the tomb and the need to preserve a reverent decorum, a sense of rarity value, or the seclusion of the saint's custodians (often monks), which the saint, frequently a monk himself, might well desire both to protect and to share. St Oswald's tomb at Worcester was in fact moved to a less accessible location, somewhere around the year 1000, because it was thought unfitting that it should be too easily approachable by all and sundry. Oswald's relics could be brought out into the town to quell fires or epidemics, but, as both a saint and a monk among monks, he was entitled to rest in dignified seclusion. It might be particularly necessary to keep women at arm's length, for their intrusion would seriously compromise the integrity of the monastic life.

Saints were in the first place the possession of their communities, which, whether they were monasteries or cathedral churches located within small early medieval cities, had property interests and sometimes predatory neighbours. Early medieval miracle collections frequently reflect the belief that the saint's wonder-working power was used primarily to protect the community, its members, friends and property, both during and after his or her lifetime. The saint's protection was needed above all against the assaults of the devil but secondarily against outsiders incited by the devil: thieves, brigands and sometimes simply the neighbours, especially violent and greedy nobles. Like an effective abbot or abbess the saint needed to be able to manage these outsiders, and in the longer term this was best done by offering physical and spiritual benefits, healing and comfort, to the wider world, as well as by threatening punishment for infractions of the community's property rights or for breaches of ecclesiastical discipline. This was increasingly the point of the posthumous miracles that were attributed to the saint. The more widely known this thaumaturgic power became, the more impressive the saint, and the more clearly his or her enemies were identified as being the enemies of the whole Christian community. With respect and gratitude came gifts and, often, pilgrims.

Miracles done in the saint's lifetime (*in vita*) were important in creating an initial reputation for supernatural power, but pilgrimage generated (and was generated by) posthumous miracles. Increasing weight was given to posthumous miracles as formal systems of canonisation developed, for, if well-attested, they were thought to be independent of any suspicion of magic or contrivance. This helped to focus the attention of the custodians of relics on the public performance of their saints. Religious communities did not always rely solely on their original and native saints, and new supplies of relics were always welcome. Saints both major and minor changed hands. In the seventh century the abbey of Fleury laid claim to the relics of St Benedict (hotly disputed by the monks of his original foundation and burial place, Monte Cassino), and the Lombard king Liutprand is supposed to have brought the relics of St Augustine to Pavia from Sardinia.

Fresh acquisitions created local excitement. The arrival of new relics at Fleury early in the ninth century attracted mixed crowds, which were so importunate that special arrangements had to be made to permit women limited access to these new treasures. Visits to shrines formed only part, however, of the reciprocal relationship between the saints and their churches and the wider world. Relics were often brought out to be carried in solemn procession around the church or even around the locality, both on festive occasions and also in times of emergency, invasion, plague or fire, flood or drought. The saints, in the form of their relics, witnessed the proceedings at councils and assemblies, adding their weight to demands for peace and an end to wrongdoing. In all these manifestations, they functioned for the most part as local or regional patrons, although some enjoyed greater fame and attracted a wider public than others.

The persecutions had ended, but for some centuries there was continued scope for recruitment to the ranks of the martyrs. Newly Christianised or unChristianised regions could still be dangerous for missionaries such as the Englishman Boniface of Wessex, who died at the hands of the Frisians in 754, and the Vikings made martyrs in the ninth century, most notably Edmund, king of East Anglia, whose murder in 869 ultimately led to the creation of one of the major pilgrimage shrines of medieval England. In the mid-seventh century a violent upheaval of quite a different order transformed the environment of pilgrimage in much of the Mediterranean. The forces of Islam erupted out of Arabia, swept Christian rule from the eastern and southern shores of the inland sea, and early in the eighth century overran most of the Iberian peninsula. From Syria to Spain, this disaster undoubtedly resulted in the obliteration of some Christian shrines and the displacement of relics. Muslim piracy in the western Mediterranean down to the tenth century created an atmosphere in which stories of the 'rescue' of relics from exposed situations to safer locations flourished.

Unquestionably and obviously, however, the most significant consequence of the Islamic conquests for the history of Christian pilgrimage was the end of Christian control of the Holy Land itself. This did not mean the obliteration of Palestinian Christianity, but it did mean that between the mid-seventh century and the end of Ottoman power in modern times the Holy Places were under Muslim control, except for ninety years between the conquest of Jerusalem by the First Crusaders and its reconquest by Saladin, and for a much briefer period of truce, negotiated in 1229 by the Emperor Frederick II. Christian pilgrimage did not cease, but pilgrims could face additional hazards. The Anglo-Saxon Willibald, who went to the Holy Land from Rome in the 720s, later remembered that although he and his companions experienced difficulties from the Muslims, some at least of the latter viewed Christian pilgrims with equanimity, assuming that they were 'obeying the dictates of their law' in wishing to see Jerusalem, as Muslims did when they performed the pilgrimage to Mecca.[6] There is later evidence that Muslims regarded Christian pilgrimage as not only comprehensible but profitable. A trickle of western pilgrims to Jerusalem continued, some of them even conveyed from the Italian coast by Arab merchantmen.

The Holy Land pilgrimage can never have been performed by more than a tiny minority of western pilgrims, and it is unlikely that the Muslim conquest was solely responsible for the surge in the popularity of pilgrimage to Rome which is evident by around 700. Roman pilgrimage was not simply a substitute for the more hazardous journey to Jerusalem. Its enhanced popularity, attested by the Venerable Bede among others, had a great deal to do with the entry of the northern European peoples into the Christian commonwealth. English Christians, and the Germans who were in part evangelised by English and Irish monks, were very conscious of the ties that bound them to Rome and of the debt they owed to the popes who had authorised and even inspired the missions to them. Bede reported that several seventh-century English kings retired from the turmoil of earthly politics to seek shelter with the prince of the apostles at Rome. Churchmen too, such as Wilfrid and Benedict Biscop, went to Rome for a variety of ecclesiastical purposes, and Englishmen and women in general were increasingly eager to set the seal on their profession of the Christian faith by taking the road to Rome. According to the collective papal biography known as the *Liber Pontificalis*, the first Bavarians to offer their prayers at St Peter's shrine were Duke Theodo and his entourage in 716.

The power of the Carolingians who took control of the Frankish kingdom in the mid-eighth century rested primarily on their strong right arms, but their alliance with the papacy, which began when Stephen II sought Pepin's help against the Lombards and was cemented a few years later when Zacharias in effect ruled that the new dynasty had the right to supplant the Merovingians, imparted a special character to the authority claimed by Pepin and his successors. This was Christian, Roman and universal in scope. The Carolingians associated themselves with the missionary enterprises of Willibrord, Boniface and others in Frisia and Germany, and looked to extend their own authority over the lands and men thus Christianised: where Frankish arms went, Roman Christianity went too. Charles's own visits to Rome (on one of which, in 800, he received imperial coronation) may look more like demonstrations of power than pilgrimages, but such ambiguities were inevitable when great men, lay or ecclesiastical, went to Rome, for their visits almost invariably had more than one purpose.

Franks of lowlier rank became familiar with the road to Rome, like their English coevals. The result was a multiplication of hospital and other facilities for pilgrims both at Rome itself and along the roads that led to it from north-western Europe. Even before the Frankish conquest of northern Italy the Lombards, now converted to Catholic Christianity, contributed to this improved provision. The Carolingian rulers from the middle of the eighth century endeavoured to ensure protection, freedom of toll and the provision of hospitality for pilgrims to Rome or elsewhere. At Rome itself, both the popes and other Christian benefactors of various nationalities were involved. When Pope Leo III returned to Rome in 799 after a temporary exile he was greeted by the inmates of four 'colonies' (scholae) of foreign residents in the city: Franks, Frisians, Saxons and Lombards. The population of these scholae at any one moment comprised persons of the relevant nationality whose business, including pilgrimage, happened to have taken them to Rome.[7]

The Carolingian kings were also aware of possible abuses of pilgrimage. In 789 the royal proclamation known as the Admonitio Generalis suggested that certain 'rascals' festooned themselves with chains and claimed that they had been sent on a penitential pilgrimage; it would be better for guilty persons to be kept at home to work off their penance under supervision. According to canon 45 of a council held at Châlons-sur-Saône in 813, too many Christians, clergy and laity alike, believed that the mere act of going on pilgrimage was sufficient to relieve them of the burden of sin. 'Powerful men' levied taxes from their inferiors on the pretext that they were undertaking a pilgrimage; poor men used alleged pilgrimages as an excuse for begging. Pilgrimage was to be commended to those who had confessed their sins to their priests in the regular manner and had received advice from them; it was acceptable as part of a general reformation of life and conduct. The canon mentions only two pilgrimage destinations by name, Rome and Tours.

The fact that pilgrims, penitential and otherwise, by now had a distinctive appearance is implied by the eighth-century story of a robber who garbed himself as a pilgrim in order to investigate the lay-out of the church of St Trudo (Sint-Truiden in present-day Belgium). In a letter to Offa of Mercia, written in 797, Charlemagne complained that merchants were concealing themselves among bona fide English pilgrims in order to avoid paying tolls. Sometimes motive, rather than identity, was dissembled. In 788 Pope Hadrian III warned Charlemagne that the widow of the Lombard duke of Benevento was planning to make a pilgrimage to the Archangel Michael in Apulia together with her two daughters; he clearly believed she was up to no good.

In the ninth century a newcomer to the select ranks of the very greatest shrines made its appearance in a remote corner of north-western Spain, although its greatest development awaited the generally expansive years after 1100. There are still unanswered and probably unanswerable questions about the genesis of the belief that the body of St James the Great was brought to Galicia by his disciples after his martyrdom in Jerusalem. Improbable in itself, it seems to have originated as a pendant to the equally unlikely belief, attested already in the late seventh century, that St James had preached in Spain, returning thence to Jerusalem and martyrdom. It is not known when pilgrimage to the shrine began, but the long-reigning Alfonso III, king of the Asturias (866–910), with Sisnando, bishop of Iria (c.880–920), actively promoted its fortunes, and a new church was consecrated to the apostle in 899. If it is true that Alfonso was in touch with the clergy of Tours in the early years of the tenth century, seeking to exchange information about Spanish saints for information about Martin, this suggests one possible channel by which the shrine was publicised beyond the boundaries of Spain. The earliest named pilgrims to Compostela came from France. The first certainly identified was Gottschalk, bishop of Le Puy in the Auvergne, who went there in 951, and he was followed within a few years by Raymond II, count of Rouergue, and Hugh of Vermandois, archbishop of Rheims. The fame of the shrine spread sufficiently far and fast to attract a wandering hermit called Simeon, a native of Armenia, who went from Italy to Compostela and Tours in about 980.[8]

The genesis of the cult of St James in Spain coincided, chronologically, with the Islamic occupation of much of the peninsula, and the pilgrimage stirred into life as Christian resurgence gained strength, but it is more difficult than might at first sight seem likely to establish causal connections between these phenomena. There is little clear evidence that St James was hailed as the champion of Spanish Christianity against the infidel before the mid-twelfth century, when, in a forged diploma of King Ramiro I of the Asturias (842–50), he was associated with a victory supposedly won by the king at Clavijo in 844.[9] In April 1024 it was recorded in the cartulary of the Catalan monastery of Sant Cugat des Vallés that Seniofredi Flavi, presumably a local man, had made his will at the monastery on his departure for Santiago; on his return from the pilgrimage he had gone 'to Spain' to fight the Saracens and there received wounds from which he had died. No explicit connection is made between the two events, although it is clearly possible that they were connected in Seniofredi's own mind. It is certainly not apparent that the pilgrims who in the late tenth century began to make their way to Compostela from outside Spain viewed St James in this 'crusading' light.

In accounting for the immense success of the Santiago pilgrimage, some weight must obviously be given to the sheer magnitude of the claim that the relics of so great a saint were available in the far west. Compostela was not alone in this period in laying claim to apostolic relics. The stories that the Venetians had obtained the relics of St Mark from Alexandria and the somewhat less plausible idea that the priest Regulus, or Rule, had brought St Andrew from Constantinople to the east coast of Scotland both originated in the ninth century. Such legends exemplified the popular genre of *furtum sacrum* or 'holy theft', in which the theft or looting of relics was represented as fulfilling the saint's own desire to be transferred to a better resting-place. The Christianisation of transalpine Europe had created a demand for relics of antiquity and worth which could not be met by local saints and secondary relics from the churches of Rome. Where it was not possible to obtain a reasonably well authenticated parcel of relics from Rome or elsewhere by means of imperial or papal favour, a *furtum sacrum* was a useful device, making possible the establishment of new pilgrimage attractions or the refurbishment of old ones. It was not always necessary actually to perform a theft, still less to lay hands on the 'real' relics of the saint in question, although the perpetrators may often have believed that they had done so. The beauty of the motif, which could be adorned with all manner of picturesque and plausible detail, was that it made it possible to claim both that one had obtained possession of prestigious relics and that the saint had set the seal of his (or her) own approval on the transaction. A well-known example of the genre was the supposed theft of the Gaulish child-martyr Foy by the monks of Conques in 866. Foy's martyrdom had taken place at Agen and there she had rested since the fourth century. The acquisition of her relics was a shot in the arm for Conques, which had fallen on difficult times after some of the monks moved, in the mid-ninth century, to a new site at Figeac. In the course of time, Conques became a stopping place on the road which led from Le Puy (an important shrine of the Virgin Mary) towards Santiago de Compostela.

The story of the coming of St James to Galicia was of a rather different order. Like both the Venetian and the Scottish fables it appropriated apostolic patronage for a church which was most unlikely to have any such thing. Elsewhere in western Europe there was a busy industry in the fabrication of pseudo-apostolic foundation legends for local churches. These usually took the form of a claim that legendary companions and disciples of the apostles had become the first bishops of certain sees (most frequently in France) where they had personally implanted the faith and not uncommonly suffered martyrdom. One example was St Denis of Paris, who was mistakenly identified with Dionysius the Areopagite, mentioned in the *Acts of the Apostles* and subsequently regarded as a disciple of St Paul. By the eleventh century the monks of Vézelay in Burgundy were laying claim to the relics of St Mary Magdalen, whose house in Bethany became a popular stopping place for Holy Land pilgrims. According to the elaborate legend which was developed to account for the Magdalen's presence so far from home, the saint had come to Provence by boat from the Holy Land, with her sister Martha, during the persecutions which followed the death of Jesus. In one version of the legend, a host of pseudo-apostolic saints now venerated in southern France had accompanied them. Mary died in Provence and was buried at Aix, but a *furtum sacrum* rescued her relics when Provence was devastated by the Saracens, and brought them to Vézelay. However preposterous, the story and the resultant pilgrimage prospered until the clergy of St Maximin at Aix exploited the legend to their own advantage and put in a successful counter-claim to the Magdalen in the late thirteenth century.

Among the stimuli for all this legend-mongering was the desire to emulate the example of Rome, to invest local saints with the authority that derived from an apostolic pedigree and also to establish linkages with the east at a time when interest in Holy Land pilgrimage was growing. The account given in *Acts* of Paul's missionary journeys in the west was influential, as the story of Denis and other saints suggests. Many of the saints thus invented or rebranded became objects of at least a modest pilgrimage: St Martial of Limoges (first heard of simply as a third-century missionary bishop) was a noteworthy example. St James, in both stature and success, was by far the greatest of them all.

It has been suggested that a contributory reason for Santiago's rise to prominence was a relative downturn in the contemporary popularity of pilgrimage to Rome, caused above all by the insecurity of the Alpine passes which pilgrims from France and elsewhere in north-western Europe had to traverse. Certainly there were nests of Saracens infesting the Alps when the noble Gerald of Aurillac (d. 909) made the numerous Roman journeys which are recorded by his biographer Odo, abbot of Cluny, but so imposing was Gerald's reputation that they merely hastened to act as his baggage-handlers.[10] In the last decade of the tenth century, probably in 993, Sigeric, archbishop of Canterbury, made the journey to Rome to receive his *pallium* from the pope. We have a list of the overnight stops (*mansiones*) he made on his return journey, but this does not indicate whether or not he encountered any special hazards along the way. In about 980 the Armenian Simeon traversed some of the same ground on his way from Rome to Santiago, but his biographer makes no special comment on the dangers of the road. The Frankish pilgrims, who, it seems, were going in gradually increasing numbers to the Holy Land in the later tenth century, certainly went by way of Rome and southern Italy.

There is, then, no very compelling reason to suppose that the road to Compostela was so much safer and easier as to seem a preferable option for that reason alone. In its remote corner of Galicia Santiago was not in the front line against Spanish Islam, but it was not immune from threat. In 997 the town was sacked by the redoubtable Al-Mansur, who carried the bells off from the apostle's church. Thirty years earlier the province had been terrorised by a band of Vikings, who killed the bishop in 968. For the first long-distance pilgrims to Santiago the journey may well have seemed a leap into the unknown rather than into a haven of security.

The pilgrimage to Santiago did not gather momentum in isolation; it shared in a general quickening of pace and enlargement of interest in pilgrimage. Gerald of Aurillac, indefatigable pilgrim though he was, seems not to have looked beyond Rome; the only other destinations mentioned in his *Life* are St Martin of Tours and St Martial at Limoges. The horizons of men of his class, it seems, broadened in the next century. Abbo, abbot of Fleury (d. 1004), once gave advice to Bernard, abbot of Beaulieu, when, wearied by the cares of this world, the latter wanted to give up all his possessions and go to Jerusalem. Had he done so, according to Abbo's biographer Aimon, he would have been following in the footsteps of his father Hugh, a noble of Aquitaine, who 'almost before any of the inhabitants of Gaul in this age, vowing penitence, had undertaken and completed that journey'. Abbo in fact forbade Bernard to go to Jerusalem, but permitted him to go instead to Rome and to the shrine of St Michael the Archangel in Apulia. In 986, Gerald de Avelena, who held land in the Dordogne, was reflecting on the inevitability of death and the importance of rendering his dues to God. He wanted to go to Jerusalem, and with the consent of his wife he made over certain properties to the abbey of Tulle and gave his son Adhemar to the abbey as a monk.

In a famous passage, the early eleventh-century chronicler Ralph Glaber described what he thought was a significant increase in Holy Land pilgrimage from the west around the year 1000. The Holy Sepulchre was attracting such crowds of the faithful as to provoke the envy of the devil, who engineered a conspiracy among the Jews of Orleans to provoke the Caliph Hakim of Cairo to destroy it. One indication of some lower-class traffic to the east, though not necessarily a trustworthy one, is Glaber's belief that the Jews employed as their agent a vagabond monastic serf who passed himself off as a pilgrim. Hakim, the son of a Christian mother, did in fact destroy the Church of the Holy Sepulchre in 1009, though undoubtedly not as a result of this alleged conspiracy. Benefactions flowed in for the rebuilding, which seems consistent with an already high level of interest in the western world. Richard II of Normandy (996–1026) sent one hundred pounds of gold to the Holy Sepulchre and subsidised pilgrims who wished to go there, most notably the mass pilgrimage led by Richard of St Vannes, abbot of La Chaise-Dieu, in 1026–7. Robert I, the father of William the Conqueror, went to Jerusalem to expiate his crimes, dying on his way back in 1035, and the notorious Fulk Nerra, count of Anjou, went three times to Jerusalem, in 1003, 1010 and 1038 or 9. Glaber had earlier eulogised the Norman dukes for their care of the poor and of pilgrims and related how every year monks came from Mount Sinai to Rouen to collect gifts of gold and silver; it was around relics brought by these monks that a subsidiary cult of St Katherine grew up at the abbey dedicated to her in Rouen.

Whatever the level of traffic to the east had been before 1009, it intensified thereafter. According to Glaber, the first to go were people of low estate, and then the middling sort, and only then the powerful and high-ranking. An unprecedented development was the participation of women of all ranks in this pilgrimage. If Glaber is to be believed, there were even people who were so 'vain' as to make the journey solely for the sake of saying that they had been. Much of this traffic went as it had always done by sea from the ports of southern Italy, and this was to the benefit of shrines to the south of Rome. The sanctuary of St Michael on Monte Gargano, to which Abbo of Fleury directed Bernard of Beaulieu, was one of many dedicated to the warrior archangel in early medieval Europe.[11] One version of the story of the beginnings of Norman involvement in southern Italy begins with a party of Norman knights making a pilgrimage to Monte Gargano, and the miracles of Dominic, abbot of the Calabrian monastery of Sora (d. 1031), include two stories of pilgrims who were diverted to Sora from San Michele. One of them is simply described as a *Francigena*, the other was a French knight of the count of Segni. Some patrons of the shrine were pilgrims on their way to or from the Holy Land. In 1087 the foundations of a flourishing cult were laid at Bari, recently conquered by the Normans, when the relics of St Nicholas, a fourth-century bishop of Myra, were allegedly brought there from Muslim-occupied Syria. Nicholas, who had a special tenderness for children and seafarers, became one of the most universally popular saints throughout not only the Norman domains, including England, but all Europe. Pilgrims who embarked for Palestine from the Apulian coast frequently called at Bari, as they did at San Michele.

Meanwhile an alternative land route had been opened to the east. Glaber associated this development with the conversion of Hungary under St Stephen (1000–38). The establishment of Christian kingdoms, in Bohemia and Poland as well as in Hungary, was significant because it facilitated the flow of traffic across the region but also because it increased the total European public for pilgrimage. Not only did the natives of these regions join in pilgrimage to the great Christian shrines, but domestic pilgrimage networks developed which implicated the cults of both native and imported saints. St Martin of Tours, by birth a native of Pannonia, was a particularly suitable candidate for veneration in Hungary, where churches were dedicated to him from the early days of Christianisation.[12]

Opposition provoked by the process of Christianisation in eastern Europe, as also in Scandinavia, also helped to make martyrs out of several rulers, even when it was doubtful whether their violent deaths were in fact suffered in defence of the faith. Wenceslas of Bohemia (d. 929) was one example, and Olaf of Norway, who died fighting to regain his throne at the Battle of Stikelsted in 1030, was another. Later kings of Bohemia and Norway assiduously cultivated their memory and both became the objects of important regional pilgrimages, at Prague and Trondheim respectively. Olaf in his early life had been a Viking chieftain; others of his type, habituated to the rigours and risks of overseas travel, took readily to Holy Land pilgrimage, in the eleventh century and later. Harald Hardrada, fated to die in battle with his English namesake at Stamford Bridge in 1066, went to the Holy Land while he was a member of the Varangian guard of the emperors of Constantinople and was recorded as the first Scandinavian pilgrim to perfom the standard rituals such as bathing in the Jordan. To such men the long sea journey through the narrow seas and round the Iberian peninsula into the Mediterranean held no special terrors.

Whatever the absolute dimensions of Holy Land pilgrimage in the eleventh century, there can be little doubt that it helped prepare the way psychologically for the extraordinary armed pilgrimage which was launched in 1095 by the preaching of Urban II at the Council of

Clermont. Doubtless, many of those who took the cross in 1095 knew, or knew of, individuals who had already taken the road to Jerusalem; they were more likely, perhaps, than their ancestors a century previously to have heard stories, alarmist or otherwise, of the hazards of the road and to have developed ideas about the state of the Holy Land and of the eastern churches. Importance must also be accorded to the close relationships that often ran in families and linked fighting men to neighbouring monasteries, and the associated habit of local and regional pilgrimage.

It was not uncommon for landholders to enter into agreements with neighbouring monasteries before they departed on pilgrimages of any magnitude (and 'crusades'). These agreements often combined practical and spiritual objectives. The prospective pilgrim settled any outstanding causes of dispute there might be between him (or her) and the monks and, in consideration of the gift or restoration of parcels of property to them, might receive a cash subsidy to assist the journey. Published charters reveal such agreements made before departure not only to Jerusalem but to destinations within western Europe. The negotiations were not always entirely amicable. When a knight called Guicherius asked the monks of Holy Trinity at Vendôme for financial assistance for his pilgrimage to Rome in 1075, they tried to make it a condition that he should cease to make unjust exactions from the peasants of Chateaurenard, but he would do so only on consideration of an outright gift of twenty pounds. Women consented to agreements made by their male kin and also made them themselves. In 1067, for example, a Catalan woman called Michell made her will with the monks of Sant Cugat del Vallés before she set off for Le Puy and Conques.

The individuals involved in these transactions were conscious of the inevitability of death and their own sinfulness. Those who made crusading vows in and after 1095 were embracing a supreme remedy for sin, but they did not know that they were proposing to go 'on crusade'. The First Crusade, to contemporaries, was a *peregrinatio* (or, simply, a journey, *iter*) and the participants were *peregrini*. The 'crusades' continued to be so called into the thirteenth century and even beyond, although the term *crucesignatus* (one signed with the cross) came into use in the later twelfth century, deriving from the practice, inaugurated in 1095 on Pope Urban's directions, of sewing a cross to one's garments in sign of the vow. The rather differently motivated 'crusade' against the heretics of southern France, early in the thirteenth century, was called a *crozada* or *crozea*, but so slow was a specialised terminology to establish itself that participants in the crusades against the pagan Baltic peoples were still sometimes called *peregrini* in the thirteenth century.

There are several versions of Urban II's appeal at the Council of Clermont in 1095 and possibly none of them accurately reflects what he really said. Guibert of Nogent's account lays some stress on the alleged sufferings of Jerusalem pilgrims at the hands of the Muslims. The story of the great German pilgrimage of 1064–5 led by Gunther, bishop of Bamberg, suggests that pilgrims sometimes aroused the interest of robbers by travelling with undue pomp, but also that where brigandage occurred it might be due to the local breakdown of law and order. The governor of Ramleh came to the rescue of the German party, reasoning that if word got around that the roads to Jerusalem were not safe, a profitable traffic would be cut off. To underline the point, he forced the rescued pilgrims to spend two weeks in Ramleh although they were anxious to get on to Jerusalem.

Christian pilgrimage to Jerusalem may sometimes have been difficult in the eleventh century, but it was clearly not impossible. The establishment of Christian rule in the Holy Land, for as long as it was effective, none the less clearly brought about an improvement in conditions and may conceivably have distorted perceptions of how things had previously been. William of Malmesbury, writing in the 1120s, recalled a penitent who had been sent to Rome and Jerusalem by Archbishop Atto of Cologne (d. 1075) but had ultimately come to Malmesbury and received relief from St Aldhelm. William thought it remarkable that he had managed to get to Jerusalem before the forces of Christendom had 'liberated' the Holy Land.

The Age of Indulgences, *c*.1100–*c*.1500

By 1095 pilgrimage had a long history as a remedy for sin, either as a penance imposed by ecclesiastical authority, or undertaken by the sinner of his or her own free will. Already by *c*.800 churchmen were expressing their concern that the requirements of penance, notably genuine contrition, were being misunderstood. The same difficulty later attended the understanding of indulgences. Indulgences rested on a number of concurrent developments in thinking about penance and about the mechanics of the forgiveness of sin. The rigours of early medieval penitential systems, in which the penance enjoined by the confessor had to be completed before absolution could be granted and the sinner re-admitted to communion, had by the tenth century largely given way to an arrangement more accommodating to human weakness and the brevity of human life. The priest imposed a penance, but granted absolution once he was satisfied of the contrition of the penitent. By implication, this procedure distinguished between forgiveness of the guilt involved in the sin (culpa), signalled on God's behalf by absolution, and the punishment of it (poena), embodied in the penance, which had still to be performed.

What, however, if the penance – perhaps a lengthy pilgrimage – was not in fact completed? The crystallising notion of Purgatory made a space available for this to be done even after death, and for satisfaction to be made for sins forgotten, unconfessed or otherwise unaccounted for. All but a very few choice spirits could expect to spend a greater or lesser time in Purgatory, enduring exquisite torments, which differed from those the damned suffered in hell because, however long they lasted, they were finite. All those admitted to Purgatory had the ultimate guarantee of salvation.[13] Still, it was not something to look forward to, and the indulgence offered remission of at least a proportion of the pains to be expected after death. In 1343 Pope Clement VI spelled out the theological rationale underpinning indulgences in the bull Unigenitus, by which he proclaimed the second Roman Jubilee, to be held in 1350. The Church was enabled to offer remission to the sinful on the strength of the inexhaustible Treasury of Merits bestowed on it by Christ through His sacrifice on the Cross, supplemented by the merits of the saints and the Virgin.

Because Purgatory, unlike heaven or hell, existed in time, indulgences were frequently expressed in terms of days, weeks or years, although vaguer expressions are found: for example, a half of all the penance enjoined on a given individual. There was another possibility: that the Church might grant remission of all the penance so far incurred by the sinner. It appears that a 'plenary indulgence' was first offered to Christians by Urban II when he preached the First Crusade, or so it rapidly came to be believed. Robert the Monk and Fulcher of Chartres have him speaking simply of 'remission of sins', and Fulcher seems to imply that this was available only to those dying on the journey, in battle or in captivity. William of Malmesbury's version was that the journey, properly motivated, should serve instead of 'all penance'. Later popes gave more precise expression to the grant, underlining the theological requirement that it applied only to sins confessed and sincerely repented. This was, and for a long time remained, a crusader's privilege, awarded to those who took up arms against the Cathar heretics of southern France or the Emperor Frederick II before it was extended to other types of *peregrinus*.

The First Crusade and its successors were pilgrimages, and their participants were visually distinguished not only by their crosses but by the insignia which were already associated with pilgrimage, notably the staff and satchel. Ceremonies existed before 1095 for the liturgical blessing of the departing pilgrim and his (or her) insignia, and this can be seen as yet one more sign of the ever greater integration of pilgrimage into the fabric of Christian life. A chronicler observed that the blessing ceremony was now extended to include the pilgrim's sword. Just as 'crusaders', including Richard the Lionheart in 1190, were invested with the staff and satchel, non-military pilgrims, going without any military intent, adopted the sign of the cross, as Raimondo Palmario of Piacenza and his mother did when they made their pilgrimage in the 1150s.

The foundation of the orders of the Hospital of St John of Jerusalem and then of the Temple in the wake of the First Crusade were designed to improve conditions for travellers to and in the Holy Land, and many non-combatants took the opportunity to undertake a journey which was somewhat more secure than it had been, and to enjoy a religious experience enhanced by the development of a Latin liturgy and picturesque ceremonial in the churches of the Holy Places. The period produced numerous Holy Land pilgrimage narratives and itineraries compiled by pilgrims from many parts of Europe, north and south of the Alps. In the 1140s or early 1150s Niklas, abbot of Munkathvera in Iceland, made his way via Norway and Germany to Rome and on by sea to the Holy Land, leaving a detailed account of his itinerary, and there is another, anonymous Icelandic account of *c*.1150; the very full descriptions by the Germans John of Würzburg and Theoderic were written about twenty years later.

Already in the eleventh century, pilgrims had recorded intensely emotional reactions to what they saw and did and heard in Palestine; now more and more people brought back with them a store of images and emotions (as well as souvenirs), which contributed to the intensification of Christ-centred cults in the west. Raimondo Palmario presumably derived his nickname from the palm which returning pilgrims brought back to the west with them; Theoderic notes that they were blessed on Palm Sunday by the Patriarch of Jerusalem. Visual reminiscences of the Holy Places that were rather more substantial than palm fronds included churches built in imitation of the form of the Church of the Holy Sepulchre, such as the one still to be seen at Eichstätt in Bavaria, a place already hallowed by association with the eighth-century Holy Land pilgrim St Willibald and his sister Walburga.

Relics and images too flowed west, a process which culminated in the infamous Fourth Crusade in 1204 and the sack of Constantinople, while the impoverished rulers of the failing Latin kingdom of Jerusalem were forced to dispose off their relic collections in the course of the thirteenth century. By these varied means innumerable relics of the saints and of the Passion enriched the pilgrimage patrimony of the west. They included the Crown of Thorns itself, acquired by Louis IX of France and enshrined in the Sainte Chapelle at Paris, and samples of Christ's blood, such as the one installed by Henry III in Westminster Abbey in 1249. There were also innumerable Byzantine icons of the Virgin and Child, some of which came to be venerated as 'images not made with hands' and endowed with miraculous properties. The Volto Santo of Lucca, the most celebrated of a number of crucifixes depicting Christ clad in a tunic (a motif of Syrian origin which had fallen out of use in the west), probably originated in the eleventh century, but legend attributed it to the disciple Nicodemus and dated its miraculous arrival in Lucca to the eighth century.

The Santiago pilgrimage also entered on its great age in the early twelfth century, thanks in no small measure to the activities of Diego del Gelmírez, bishop, and later archbishop, of Compostela between 1100 and 1140. He solicited the favour of Pope Calixtus II (1121–4) for his church, and this pope's name became indelibly associated with Santiago. A manuscript compilation of texts and documents produced at Compostela c.1140 came to be known as the *Codex Calixtinus*; it contained a collection of the miracles of St James, attributed to the pope, and also a lengthy sermon, *Veneranda Dies*, in which the pseudo-Calixtus eulogised Santiago and denounced all those who defrauded and preyed upon pilgrims in general and St James's pilgrims in particular. If the author was to be believed, virtually every other well-known shrine in Christendom was a school of fraud and rapine.[14] The Compostela pilgrimage may well have benefited from the increasing European publicity given to the wars of reconquest which were intermittently waged by the Christian kings of Spain against the occupying Muslims. Those who joined in the Spanish struggle were awarded the spiritual privileges of 'crusaders', Spanish knights were encouraged to give priority to their domestic crusade, and, as already noted, the first unequivocal evidence for the presentation of St James as an active champion of Christian Spain against the Moors appears in the mid-twelfth century.

The most celebrated part of the *Codex Calixtinus* is the fifth, the so-called *Pilgrim's Guide*. Written apparently by a Poitevin, perhaps called Aimery Picaud, it describes four main roads across France, which converged across the Pyrenees in a single route to Compostela, and ends with a description of the shrine of St James itself. The author gives valuable but rather uneven information about the shrines that the pilgrim should visit along the way, such as St Gilles du Provence. The *Guide* suggests that a host of shrines, some of them (such as St Martin of Tours) much older than Santiago, and many of them the foci of regional pilgrimages of some consequence, such as Conques or St Gilles, were being increasingly linked into an interconnected network. New shrines too arose to form part of this network. Rocamadour, north-east of Cahors, an important shrine of the Virgin Mary, came to prominence in the middle of the century, after the *Pilgrim's Guide* was compiled: its first famous visitor was Henry II of Anjou and England, who apparently went there twice, in 1159 and 1170.

Inadvertently, Henry himself helped to create another major new shrine, when Archbishop Thomas Becket of Canterbury was murdered in his own cathedral on 29 December 1170 by four knights who thought they were carrying out the king's wishes. Pilgrims had been going to Canterbury for centuries, if in small numbers, to venerate saints such as Augustine, Alphege and Dunstan, but it was Becket's cult, created by his widely publicised death, that made Canterbury's fortune. The shrine of the Three Kings, or Magi, at Cologne, established after the supposed translation of their relics from Milan in 1164 by the imperial chancellor, Rainald of Dassel, was another in this class, attracting pilgrims from beyond the boundaries of the Empire. Rocamadour, Canterbury and Cologne all proved long-lasting recruits to the upper ranks of European shrines.

Some shrines of ancient origin meanwhile continued to prosper and others fell into relative or total obscurity. Rome scarcely fell into obscurity, but the city experienced some difficult times during the twelfth century. There were several antipopes during the century, notably (at the instigation of the Emperor Frederick Barbarossa) between 1159 and 1178. Some of them commanded little support, but their existence was symptomatic of division and instability, in which the Roman nobility as well as the German emperors played a prominent part. According to William of Malmesbury, Calixtus II, who for the first two years of his pontificate had to contend with the antipope Gregory VIII, took steps to counteract the limitless cupidity of the Romans and was at least temporarily successful in improving conditions for pilgrims. However, because of the rapacity of the Romans, he discouraged the English from making the journey to Rome and decreed that the value of two pilgrimages to St David's should be regarded as equivalent to that of one to Rome (an example, if authentic, of a very imprecise form of indulgence). Roman pilgrimage none the less generated a considerable twelfth-century literature. William of Malmesbury incorporated a brief 'guidebook' to Rome, consisting essentially of a catalogue of churches and relics, into his *History of the Kings of England*. Niklas of Munkathvera, who visited the city on his way to the Holy Land *c*.1150, was also interested only in the Christian sites; he remarked that persons worthy of belief had said that no one was so learned as to be certain of knowing all the churches of Rome. There was, however, another way of viewing the city. In the 1140s the citizens of Rome sought to emancipate themselves from the tutelage of the popes and proclaimed a commune, recalling the glories of their ancestors. In the same decade a canon of St Peter's produced the *Marvels of the City of Rome* (*Mirabilia Urbis Romae*), much of which is devoted to the pre-Christian ancient monuments (often misidentified and misinterpreted). This antiquarian emphasis was even stronger in the somewhat later work of an Englishman, Master Gregory, whose *Account of the Marvels of Rome* (*Narratio de mirabilibus urbis Romae*) deals almost exclusively with the 'Roman remains'.

The Holy Land too had its pre-Christian attractions, but the Old Testament was an integral part of the Christian story; the pre-Christian past of Rome had to be co-opted for Christian purposes by rather different means. Many medieval chroniclers emphasised how the Roman Empire, by imposing universal peace and the rule of law, had prepared the way for Christianity. The popes, as rulers both of the city of Rome and of the universal church, laid claim to imperial insignia and attributes. The guidebooks hinted, however, that the monuments had their own fascination. Henry of Blois, bishop of Winchester, was even observed during a visit to Pope Eugenius III in the 1140s haggling for ancient statues in the marketplaces.

In 1191 Philip II of France passed through Rome on his return from crusade and, according to an English chronicler, was favoured with a special exhibition of the 'Veronica' by Pope Celestine III. This was a cloth, preserved among the relics in St Peter's, on which Christ had miraculously impressed an image of His face; its name, taken to be an anagram of *vera icon*, 'true image', was also supposed to be that of the woman to whom He had given it. Celestine III's successor, Innocent III, was responsible for bringing the Veronica further into the public domain, when in 1207 he instituted an annual procession to the hospital of Santo Spirito in which the relic was carried. In the course of the thirteenth century the relic attracted more and more attention. It seems appropriate that, in an age in which the popes were laying claim to the title 'vicar of Christ', an image of Christ Himself should have come to play an ever greater part in the Roman pilgrimage. Indulgences for venerating the Veronica headed a list of those available at St Peter's in 1289, and in the 1290s Dante remembered seeing pilgrims in Florence who were on their way to Rome to see the image. Exhibited on Fridays and major feast days, it was a big draw for the crowds who flocked to Rome in 1300. In the fourteenth century, there were prescribed times for the exhibition of the Veronica, which were extended by Urban V; important visitors were granted private views, and the image was reproduced as a souvenir in a number of materials, tin, cloth and paper.

In February 1300 Pope Boniface VIII learned that pilgrims arriving in Rome were expecting something special to be made available to them at the turn of the century. The result was the proclamation of the first Holy Year or Jubilee, and Boniface made a plenary indulgence available to pilgrims who visited the basilicas of the apostles. In the course of the thirteenth century, the popes had increasingly exceeded previous limits on the quantities of indulgence available at St Peter's and the Lateran basilica. When in 1291 Pope Nicholas IV listed the indulgences available at the Lateran, the tariffs varied from one year and forty days on any day of the year to a maximum of seven years and seven quarantines[15] at certain major feasts, for pilgrims who had come from beyond the Alps or over the sea. Romans and inhabitants of the adjacent regions got a maximum of only four years and four quarantines, Tuscans, Apulians and Lombards five years and five quarantines.

This differential principle was perhaps as significant as the overall rise in the level of grant. It was applied in 1300, necessarily in a different form, when the Jubilee indulgence was made available to the 'foreigner' after fifteen days' attendance at the basilicas of the apostles while the Roman had to devote thirty days to the task. Numerous accounts survive which testify to the success of the Jubilee. A north Italian chronicler recorded that parties of knights and ladies of France passed through Parma on their way to Rome, providing a source of income for anyone who could sell them food, drink and lodging; a few individuals, at least, came from as far afield as England.

The popes' control over Rome had continued to be menaced by the turbulence and factiousness of the nobility and the rest of the population, as well as by their own conflicts with the Emperor Frederick II in the first half of the thirteenth century. For much of the fourteenth century they were entirely absent from the city. Between 1309 and 1377 they resided at Avignon in Provence, and in 1378 the outbreak of a new schism, which was destined to be of unprecedented duration, created fresh turbulence. It was not until the middle of the fifteenth century that the papacy was more or less securely reseated in Rome. Intermittently, none the less, the popes took advantage of opportunities to encourage pilgrimage to the city of the apostles and to associate themselves with it.

In 1300 Boniface VIII had envisaged that Holy Years would occur only at intervals of a century, but in 1343, Clement VI, who had no intention of returning to Rome in the near future, yielded to the representations of the Romans and proclaimed that Jubilees would in future take place every fifty years; given the brevity of human life, individuals now had a better chance of availing themselves of the Jubilee indulgence. Urban VI (1378–89), the first Roman pope of the Great Schism, decided that it would be appropriate for Jubilees to take place every thirty-three years, in commemoration of the life-span of Christ, and he announced that one would take place in 1390. In 1400 public demand effectively ensured that an unofficial Holy Year took place at Rome, with the appropriate indulgences. Subsequently there was a reversion to the idea of a fifty-year interval and 1450 was, accordingly, a Holy Year. Then the decision, still in force, was taken to reduce the interval to twenty-five years; a Jubilee took place in 1475.

The Jubilees demonstrated, with considerable success, the power of the popes to promote pilgrimage to the city by the exercise of their unique power to award plenary indulgences. Naturally they would use their powers in the first place for the benefit of their own churches, and initially the only way of earning the Jubilee indulgence was to go to Rome. Clement VI initially resisted persuasions to make it available even to those who were prevented from going for legitimate reasons. Very soon, however, he was permitting the retrospective grant of the indulgence to certain people in return for a cash payment and compensatory good works, and this became normal practice thereafter. It of course remained a condition of the efficacy of the grant that the beneficiary was contrite and confessed, and the development was not without parallel or precedent. Since the early thirteenth century it had been possible to obtain the benefits of the crusading vow by making a contribution to the financing of a crusade; it made sense to be able to mobilise the resources of those such as women, monks and invalids who could not go east as combatants. In a similar manner, Jubilee indulgences became fund-raising devices for the general needs of the church, including the crusade, as the menace of the Ottoman Turks intensified after the mid-fourteenth century.

In common with the rest of Christendom the Holy Places acquired their indulgences, which were listed in the guidebooks and pilgrim narratives that multiplied in the fourteenth and fifteenth centuries. The conditions of Christian pilgrimage inevitably changed after the fall of Jerusalem to Saladin in 1188. For a century the position in the Holy Land deteriorated, until the last Christian outposts were lost in 1291. There were impassioned and complex debates about the right strategy to adopt in face of this disaster. Attempts were made from the later thirteenth century to undermine the economic power of the Egyptian sultans, overlords of the Holy Land, or at least to prevent the dissipation of Christian resources, by imposing an embargo on trade with the Muslims in certain goods. This policy was accompanied by a prohibition on unlicensed pilgrimage to the Holy Land, in case this should lead to illicit trading or otherwise to the profit of the infidel.

From the mid-fourteenth century a new normality took shape, although it remained necessary to seek permission to make the pilgrimage. The Franciscans were re-established in the Holy Land and took on the role of guardians of the Holy Places, in effect responsible to the Muslim author-ities for the behaviour of pilgrims, who were directed to them on arrival. They provided information (including guides and guidebooks) and organised hospitality. The Venetians took care of the business end of the traffic, which, thanks to the incursions of the Ottomans in south-eastern Europe, now once again had to be conveyed by sea. Inclusive packages of varying degrees of elaboration, depending on the depth of the pilgrim's purse, were obtainable by negotiation with licensed shipmas-ters at Venice. Numerous narratives and diaries left by late medieval pilgrims depict vividly the conditions they experienced both on the voyage to the Holy Land and back and during their stays there.

Innumerable late medieval shrines were associated with the Virgin and with Christ Himself. Rome, with its churches and relics, and the Holy Land, with its biographical and topographical associations, were both well-fitted to cater for the demand for Marian and Christ-centred devotions. Many pilgrims to Compostela took care also to visit the Virgin at Finisterre and the shrine of the Saviour (St Salvator) at Oviedo, as the pious goldsmith Fazio of Cremona already did in the thirteenth century, and we know of later pilgrims who visited Our Lady of Montserrat near

Barcelona. For those who could not or would not make lengthy journeys there was no lack of provision closer at hand. Although the Prussian mystic Dorothea of Montau venerated the Virgin at both Aachen and Einsiedeln, she also went several times on pilgrimage to the Virgin at Koszalin in Pomerania, about a hundred miles west of her home in Gdansk. The shrine of Our Lady of Walsingham originated in the twelfth century but began its rise to pre-eminence among the shrines of England in the mid-thirteenth century, aided by royal patronage which lasted until the Reformation; it catered almost entirely for a British clientele. The Virgin's house at Nazareth, which according to legend was miraculously transported to Loreto, near the east coast of central Italy, in 1294, ultimately enjoyed considerable fame, but solid evidence for its popularity within Italy dates only from the later fifteenth century.

Hundreds, or more probably thousands, of local and regional Marian shrines all over Christendom were focused on an image, often a miraculous image, such as that of the Annunziata in Florence or of Our Lady of 's-Hertogenbosch in the duchy of Brabant, which performed numerous miracles in the 1380s. Miraculous crucifixes and relics of the Holy Blood played a similar role in creating shrines of Christ-centred devotion. There were prominent shrines of both types in pre-Reformation England. The Holy Blood venerated at Hailes Abbey in Gloucestershire was an example of the older style of Holy Blood relic, purportedly consisting of blood shed by Christ on the Cross. The Holy Rood of Boxley Abbey in Kent was a remarkable contrivance, mercilessly exposed by Thomas Cromwell's commissioners as a fraud (like the Blood of Hailes). In the fourteenth and fifteenth centuries sacramental relics became common, for example consecrated wafers which resisted destruction by fire or the alleged attacks of heretics or Jews, and sometimes also produced fresh blood. The Holy Blood of Wilsnack in Prussia, which acquired an international following in the fifteenth century after initial attempts by the ecclesiastical hierarchy to suppress the cult, was perhaps the most conspicuous example.

There were innumerable similar cults with more limited drawing power. In 1345 a native of Amsterdam received the last rites but vomited the host out into the fire: the host remained undamaged, and the miracle generated a eucharistic pilgrimage which enjoyed some celebrity within the Netherlands and is still commemorated by an annual 'silent procession' in Amsterdam in March. To survey all the late medieval European sites that are known to have attracted pilgrims out of devotion either to Christ or to the Virgin would require volumes. For some of them the surviving evidence is slight and fortuitous, perhaps consisting of no more than the grant of an indulgence. Many locally and briefly popular shrines must have gone altogether unrecorded, which compounds the intractable problem of determining whether pilgrimage overall became a more or a less popular activity in the later middle ages.

Indulgences were undoubtedly a popular means of promoting pilgrimage, especially on major feast days and notable anniversaries. Churches and chapels all over Christendom petitioned their bishops for forty days' worth of indulgence, or even less, in order to enhance their appeal to an essentially local public, but many also appealed to the popes for larger quantities, including plenary indulgences. The popes perceived advantages in generosity: promoting attachment to Rome might mean attracting pilgrims to the city itself, but it could also mean spreading the benefits of papal largesse abroad. Numerous churches all over Christendom took to celebrating their own Jubilees, soliciting the appropriate indulgences from the pope. The cathedral of Canterbury celebrated its Jubilees to mark every fiftieth anniversary of the original translation of Thomas Becket on 7 July 1220, and these seem to have attracted considerable crowds. During the Great Schism Boniface IX (1389–1404), Urban VI's successor in the Roman line, was particularly generous in his awards to churches both great and small within his obedience. In 1420, after the ending of the Schism, Martin V angrily rebuked the Canterbury authorities for celebrating a Jubilee indulgence without papal permission; the indulgence was successfully negotiated in 1470, but in 1520 negotiations broke down because, it was claimed, the pope was demanding an excessive proportion of the takings.

Pilgrimage in a Developing Society

It seems a reasonable contention that pilgrimage became quantitatively more popular as European society expanded in size and level of development in the eleventh and twelfth centuries. It is generally accepted that the population of Europe increased markedly between c.1000 and c.1300. Among the effects were not only a more densely populated countryside and the expansion of the cultivated area into previously wooded and marshy territory, but a process of urbanisation (even if most medieval towns were by our standards extremely small), involving both the enlargement of ancient settlements and the creation of new ones.

There are several indications of a numerically enlarged audience for the saints in the eleventh and twelfth centuries. In 1018 the press of people wanting to enter the church of St Martial at Limoges for the nocturnal vigils before his feast was such that more than fifty men and women were trampled to death. While accidents of this magnitude seem to have been rare, the weight of numbers experienced in certain churches at major festivals provided one incentive for not only rebuilding and enlarging but redesigning the setting in which relics were venerated. The people whose physical presence threatened both the structure and their own safety were also the source of offerings which would first help to make possible and then reap a return on the heavy investment in reconstruction. The classic description of such an undertaking is the one given by Suger, abbot of St Denis (1122–51), whose rebuilding and adornment of the great royal abbey was a landmark in the development of the early Gothic style. Suger mused that the small church built by King Dagobert in the sixth century had perhaps been big in its day, but it had been overwhelmed by the increasing numbers of the faithful who wanted to seek the intercession of the saints. He gives a vivid description of the suffocating crush on feast days as thousands pressed forward to see the relics: people were penned in, unable to move a muscle, women went white and screamed and had to be lifted out over the heads of the crowd, and the monks who were displaying the relics sometimes had to escape through the windows. In the lower church too the crowds of pilgrims threatened to overwhelm the brethren during Mass, and 'little women' struggled to get close to the altar by walking over the heads of the men, not always successfully, for they sometimes had to be rescued and helped out into the cloister.

Popular demand for access to relics prompted varied reactions. In the very early years of the twelfth century, an author probably to be identified as Bishop Rangerius of Lucca described how a previous bishop, Anselm I, who had retained control of the see of Lucca when he became Pope Alexander II in 1061, had disposed the relics of one of the church's principal patrons, St Regulus, in the crypt. As Rangerius explained:

> It seemed to this wise man that this treasure should be bestowed in this more removed setting, so that, the more uncommon and difficult access was, the more welcome and useful the sight [of it] would be, because everyday scrutiny, available at the first time of asking, begins by removing wonder and finally generates boredom. But this holy intention was undermined by the negligence of the custodians and the

importunity of those demanding access. The place became not so much a rarity for the pious, as frequented and open for the vain. It seemed therefore to those in charge to remove these opportunities for secret conversations and bring the holy body back from the shadows into the light.

Rangerius therefore decided, as part of his general rearrangement of the cathedral in 1109, to bring Regulus back into the upper church. It was not uncommon, however, for the patron saint to remain in the centre of the crypt, as can still be seen for example in Modena Cathedral, San Zeno in Verona and Santa Maria della Pieve in Arezzo. Access was to left and right under a raised chancel.

There had always been a demand to 'see' relics, as at Fleury in the early ninth century, and the practice of carrying them in procession, whether within a church or outside it, required portability and some-times the division of relics between containers. Giving pilgrims the kind of contact with the holy that they desired could be problematical. If relics were taken out of their container for exhibition, damage or irreverent treatment of them might ensue. Abbot Samson of Bury St Edmund's related how this had happened late in the eleventh century when a misguided monk encouraged an importunate crowd of pilgrims not only to see the bloodstained vestments in which St Edmund had met his death but to touch and kiss them. Responses to perceived demand included not only the enlargement of the space allocated to shrines, so that a better circulation could be achieved, but the provision of formal 'exhibitions' (*ostensiones*) of relics at stated times. In the twelfth century the monks of Limoges developed the practice of exhibiting St Martial's head ('discovered' and separately housed in 1130), which continued at irregular intervals throughout the medieval period. The Limousin Pope Gregory XI (1370–8) gave a golden cup for the keeping of the relic, which was opened at the beginning of the 'indulgence period' and closed at the end. In 1388 the *ostensio* was the occasion of many miracles, which were recorded by a monk of Limoges.

In 1215, as part of an attempt to prevent the abuse and fabrication of relics, canon 62 of the Fourth Lateran Council prohibited any public exhibition of relics for payment and any removal of them from their containers. Although this decree was widely incorporated into synodal legislation throughout Christendom, punctilious observance of it was another matter. The synod of Budapest in 1297 recapitulated canon 62 verbatim, but added to it the words 'except on principal feast days and for pilgrims who have assembled for the purpose, as the praiseworthy custom of certain churches requires'. It is noteworthy that the Lateran prohibition was accompanied by a restriction on the quantity of indulgence that could be granted by mere bishops to no more than a year on the occasion of the consecration of a new church and forty days on all other occasions; the pope himself, it was said, normally observed these limits (which at the time was true). If canon 62 itself was a commentary on the sometimes excessive measures that had been taken to satisfy (and perhaps also to stimulate) public demand for access to the saints in the century before 1215, the Budapest amendment and the actual practice of certain churches indicate that the exhibition of relics was sometimes deemed essential to the maintenance of popular devotion.

One very influential exhibition took place at Aachen, where it seems that the principal relics were taken out of the new shrine of the Virgin, completed in 1238, for exhibition. These relics included the shift the Virgin had worn on the night of the Nativity, the swaddling-bands of Christ and the loincloth He wore at the Crucifixion. Pieces of fabric, which it was certainly not wise to permit the faithful to touch, were especially suitable for veneration at long range, for they could easily be hung from a window or gallery. The first reference to such an exhibition of the Aachen relics from the tower of the church occurs in 1322. It is not entirely clear when this *ostensio* began to be held at a regular seven-yearly interval, but it may have been from 1349, the year of Charles IV's coronation at Aachen. The Aachen exhibition became the model for several other churches, especially in the Rhine–Meuse region. By this time, the practice of exhibiting another cloth relic, the 'Veronica', to pilgrims to Rome had become well-established. Such exhibitions were never riskfree, and accidents continued to happen when eager crowds pressedforward to get a better look. In 1300 William of Derby, a monk of St Mary's, York, died after he was crushed in the crowd at an exhibition of the Veronica, and at Limoges, the *ostensio* of St Martial's head which marked the visit of the Black Prince in May 1364 resulted in a crush that killed eighteen people.

The development of markets in the vicinity of pilgrimage churches, often held on major feast days, was a parallel and inseparable phenomenon. Already in the eleventh century Bernard of Angers told lively tales of merchants who came to do business in the shadow of the church at Conques. Historically bishops and other ecclesiastics had important investments in urban real estate and the licensing and taxing of market traders was an extension of old activities. The development of pilgrimage to the Magdalen at Vézelay and the growth of a small urban community alongside the pilgrimage church had numerous parallels in eleventh- and twelfth-century Europe. Domesday Book provides vivid evidence of the eleventh-century expansion of the settlement around the church of St Edmund at Bury in Suffolk, and settlements along the Via Francigena to Rome and the roads leading to Santiago de Compostela similarly flourished.

It was befitting, therefore, that the saints should sometimes take account of the needs of a humble clientele engaged in petty economic transactions. Around the year 1170, a poor woman came to the market at Chartres to buy wool, but went first to the tomb of St Gilduin in the abbey church of St Pierre to pray and specifically to ask that she might make a good bargain that day. Of the ninepence she had in her purse she offered one halfpenny to the saint and gave another to a poor person. Seeing the fleece she wanted in the market she learned that the price was an immovable nine pence; but the seller was willing to accept St Gilduin as surety for the missing penny. The woman now discovered that there were more than eight pennies in her purse and she gave the seller the full amount; counting what remained she found that she still had ninepence. Her reaction was instructive: 'Oh, if only I had given more to God and the saint, I believe I would have got more interest (*plurimam usuram*) from them!'

Obviously this pious woman might have given more, but there are numerous indications that it was normal to make offerings at a fixed rate, and it was even possible to get change. During the 1388 *ostensio* at Limoges a Breton pilgrim tried to palm a false coin off on St Martial. If real, the coin (an *albus*) would have been worth fivepence, and the pilgrim duly asked for fourpence in change. He did not of course get away with it, for the saint visited him with a burning heat and he repented of his deception. The story suggests that the custodians of shrines were organised to administer what might be termed a fixed admission charge which was affordable by the humble. A monk of Worcester, testifying at the investigation into the sanctity of Thomas Cantilupe of Hereford in 1307, reported that pilgrims calling at Worcester on their way to Hereford made offerings that totalled ten pounds annually, made up of farthings, halfpennies and pennies. Early in the twelfth century William of Malmesbury expressed the spirit of these transactions when he said that suppliants to St Aldhelm at Malmesbury sought to obtain a 'sum of many vows' for the outlay of a penny or halfpenny. William also remarked that the institution of a fair of St Aldhelm was intended to ensure that those who were not attracted by devotion might be lured by the desire for goods.

Another indication of the position occupied by the saints and their communities in an expanding society is the manufacture and marketing of 'souvenirs' of pilgrimage. Among the miscellaneous items of information included in the Santiago *Pilgrim's Guide* is a reference to the sale of souvenirs in the market in front of the saint's church, the earliest known evidence for this trade in the Christian west. By the end of the century souvenirs are known to have been on sale also at Rocamadour, at Becket's shrine at Canterbury and at St Peter's in Rome. In 1199, Innocent III granted the rights over the trade in badges of the apostles to the canons of St Peter's, in terms which suggest that it had been in existence for some while. These 'souvenirs' had several properties. The ampullae[16] sold at Canterbury were made to contain a solution of the martyr's blood in water and were responsible for several cures at long distance from the shrine; a Rocamadour badge, similarly, effected the cure of a priest from Chartres. When worn round the neck or on the clothing, these very portable and relatively cheap objects identified the bearer as a pilgrim and simultaneously publicised the shrine.

That pilgrim souvenirs had an economic aspect is obvious: they had to be made and marketed, and at several shrines in the later middle ages there were sporadic disputes over the rights in the trade, which suggests at least a modest profitability, even when allowance is made for the medieval predilection for litigation on points of right and honour. It was common for the clergy who controlled a shrine also to control the pilgrim-badge trade, but for practical reasons they frequently granted the franchise to lay artisans. Disputes arose when these craftsmen attempted to trade independently, and hard bargaining could then result. At Rocamadour a prominent local family claimed the hereditary right to the manufacture. In 1354 the king and queen of Naples, as rulers of Provence, intervened to uphold the right of the Dominicans, who controlled the church of St Mary Magdalen, also to control the pilgrim-badge trade. Badges were pirated by craftsmen dwelling on the roads to Compostela and elsewhere, and it is doubtful how effective attempts to stop them were, even when backed by the pope.

At Canterbury in the 1170s there seems to have been a workshop within the cathedral precinct where ampullae could be purchased, but it is not made clear whether monks or hired craftsmen were producing them. In an urban environment it would have been natural for them to be made by artisans who were in the business of producing other metal knicknacks and items of ironmongery, like the badges of entirely secular, and sometimes even pornographic, character which were also made both as personal ornaments and as signs of allegiance. The badge-makers of Mont St Michel in Normandy who in 1396 pleaded poverty to King Charles VI of France were probably workers of this kind. Their over-heads, they claimed, were so high and their returns so low that they were quite eaten up by tax. Easily broken or lost, some of these objects turned up as scrap; a Becket miracle story concerns a London craftsman who tried without success to melt a Canterbury ampulla down with other metal for reuse.

Impressive figures have been quoted for the sale of pilgrim badges. A sudden surge of pilgrimage to a miraculous image of the Virgin and Child at Regensburg in 1519 took the authorities by surprise, and although they hastily arranged for the manufacture of badges and sold over 12,500 during the year, they were nowhere near meeting demand. In the following year 109,198 pewter badges were sold, in addition to 9,763 *de luxe* models in silver. This was presumably a worthwhile busi-ness. One much-quoted proof of profitability, however, seems to rest on a misreading of the Latin text. In 1483, the parish priest of Bollezeel in Flanders was showing off his handsomely rebuilt and enlarged church, now complete but for the tower, which was currently being renewed. He said it all came of 'the oblations of the people who flock here every day and receive cure and consolation (*medelam et consolationem*) in this place'. The word *medela* in fact means 'remedy' or 'cure', not 'medal'.[17] The priest may have been selling badges, but miraculous cures were more impressive and probably just as profitable.

Many different interests were involved in the provision of access to relics and shrines and the servicing of pilgrims. Landlords lay and eccle-siastical built, owned or rented out inns and other accommodation and levied taxes on the hotel and catering industries. Custodians and patrons of shrines took steps to direct the flow of pilgrims along the desired pathways, not only within churches but in the larger urban space. A well-known example is the order of Ferdinand II of Castile in 1168 that the established pilgrim itinerary through the city of Leon should be so modified as to arrive at the church which his predecessor Ferdinand I had rebuilt to receive not only his own burial but the relics of St Isidore of Seville, brought there in 1063. Having venerated St Isidore, pilgrims now left the city by a newly built gateway. In 1365 Queen Joanna of Naples received a complaint that the citizens of St Maximin had disregarded the wishes of her grandfather Charles II of Anjou that the main gate of the town should be built immediately opposite the church where the relics of St Mary Magdalen were venerated and had in fact built it so far away that pilgrims had to take a weary detour to reach the church. The probable incentive, from the citizens' point of view, was not to permit visitors instant access to the church but to lead them past alternative attractions, such as taverns or shops (perhaps selling pirated pilgrim badges). Petty local disputes over offerings and the profits of pilgrimage, between different members of the clergy and between clergy and laymen, were common.

Although it is hardly possible to calculate what proportion of the total travelling public consisted of pilgrims, it must have been high over certain routes at certain times, and here pilgrims may perceptibly have increased the demand for goods and services, the provision of accommodation and food, the upkeep of bridges and ferry crossings. A number of saints owed their reputation in large part to their constructive labours on behalf of pilgrims. St Domingo de la Calzada (d. 1109) dedicated himself as a hermit to the service of pilgrims to Santiago, building a road between Nájera and Redecilla and also, according to tradition, a bridge over the Oja.[18] Slightly later a Tuscan holy man, Allucius of Pescia (d. 1134) built a hospital on the 'public road' near a part of the Arno where many pilgrims came to grief, probably the present Ponte a Signa. When he asked the bishop of Florence to build a bridge, he discovered that certain people in the locality were running a profitable ferry service and he had to use emollient words to persuade them to withdraw their opposition. Raimondo Palmario of Piacenza later in the century gave up his life of pilgrimage and spent twenty-two years in charitable labours which centred on hospital provision in his native city; Gualtiero of Lodi, himself an active pilgrim, trained in Raimondo's hospital and then founded several of his own, especially in remote places where help for the traveller was hard to come by.

Governments from time to time intervened in an attempt to improve the state of the going on major routes. Edward III ordered the inhabitants of Strood, which the traveller from London to Canterbury along Watling Street reached just before crossing the Medway to Rochester, to remedy the appalling condition of the roads through the town; around 1330 the rulers of Modena ordered that houses should be built along deserted stretches of the Via Emilia, for the better security of pilgrims. The Bolognese authorities were intermittently concerned in the fourteenth century with the state of the roads, bridges and bridge hospitals used by pilgrims on their way to Rome. It was drawn to their attention in the Jubilee year of 1300 that the road to Rome was impassable by foot or on horseback; repairs were undertaken and the management of the bridges and hospitals in the vicinity was rejigged. Eighty years later the bridge hospitals were found to be badly understaffed and ill-run, and the idea of bringing them under a single management was discussed. A distinction was made in these Bolognese deliberations between the hospitals presumably used by pilgrims and those intended for the sick in the city itself. Pilgrims were never the sole and often not even the principal beneficiaries of medieval hospital foundations. Over 60 fourteenth-century hospitals have been identified in what is now the province of Lucca, obviously an area much frequented by pilgrims, but the extent to which they catered for travellers varied, naturally, with their location. The care of the sick and the destitute was their major preoccupation; pilgrims who fell into either of these categories would have recourse to them, but the able-bodied were often permitted to stay only one night in a hospital, as at the Eastbridge in Canterbury, which also specialised in provision for 'lying-in women'. The well-off would anyway prefer, and be expected, to use inns. Accommodation of all grades was naturally especially plentiful where there was a constant flow of merchants or pilgrims or both. On special occasions, such as Jubilee years, private accommodation was pressed into service all along the roads to Rome and householders turned their hands to providing food and drink.

The development of western society had institutional as well as economic aspects which affected, and in many ways benefited, pilgrims. The basic protection of persons and property, which early medieval rulers had tried to enforce, took on more elaborate forms. As legal systems developed, so it became common to permit parties to lawsuits stays of action if they were already engaged on or vowed to a long-distance pilgrimage at the time the action was brought. Departing pilgrims (and crusaders) not only enjoyed the protection of the church on their property and a moratorium on their debts, but increasingly registered the appointment of attorneys to handle their business in their absence. The principle of the pilgrim's freedom from commercial tolls continued to be upheld: in 1251 Pope Innocent IV asked Queen Blanche, regent of France, to ensure that prelates and clergy travelling from Denmark to Rome were exempted from all such payments, as French officials had been attempting to tax them as if they were businessmen.

Despite the best efforts of churchmen and lawgivers to extend protection to pilgrims and to insist on their rights to alms, hospitality and security of property, however, pilgrimage was never and could never be a completely secure activity. Brawls and improprieties around shrines themselves were far from uncommon. Pious women, especially, were subject to insult when visiting shrines, and even great pilgrimage churches occasionally had to be reconsecrated because violence, even rape or bloodshed, had occurred within them. Christian writers railed against the depredations of the Saracens on Holy Land pilgrimage, but lawlessness and brigandage, much of it perpetrated by individuals and groups who eluded the control of public authority, were a perennial hazard for the pilgrim within Europe. In 1333 the government of Siena received a petition for redress from two citizens who had gone on pilgrimage to Rome at Easter of the previous year, relying on the safeconduct proclaimed by the Roman authorities (the pope himself was absent at Avignon). They had none the less fallen into the hands of the henchmen of Jacopo Savelli, a prominent robber baron, and had been imprisoned and forced to buy their release. When conflicts occurred between the rulers who were themselves supposed to guarantee the security of the roads, the hazards were compounded.

Such conflicts were hardly new, but their frequency and duration in many parts of Europe in the later middle ages may have deterred some pilgrims from long-distance travel. Preparing for the Jubilee of 1350, Clement VI was anxious about the obstacles that both the conflicts within Italy and the wars between the kings of France and England might put in the way of pilgrims to Rome. The Anglo-French wars impaired the security of communications over a wide area in the fourteenth and fifteenth centuries. Pope Clement had to order the seneschal of Rodez to release some supposed *anglici* who had been seized on their way to Rome in 1350, and the overland routes to Compostela and access to southern French shrines such as Rocamadour were also affected. One mariner of Bordeaux thought better of going to Rocamadour and sent his offering by the hands of a merchant. The miracles which accompanied the exhibition of the relics of St Martial at Limoges in 1388 included several performed on behalf of pilgrims to the shrine and other local inhabitants who had suffered at the hands of English troops; the saint also delivered a Compostela-bound party from the 'robbers and murderers' who haunted one particular forest along the way. The truce made in 1440 between the kings of England and France included provision for the free movement of pilgrims between their jurisdictions.

Such difficulties were aggravated by the divisions consequent upon the Great Schism between 1378 and 1415, in which of course the English and French monarchies took opposing sides. According to the English chronicler Thomas Walsingham, Leopold II of Austria, 'a cunning and greedy man', who was opposed to Urban VI, imposed heavy taxes on pilgrims to Rome, in an effort to deter them altogether. Rather than put up with this and other insults, the pilgrims preferred to make a lengthy detour and go by a different route. The duke's subjects, 'seeing the roads deserted and weighing the losses that they suffered as a result', begged him to permit the traffic to resume, but he rebuffed them contemptuously. The 'communities of the region' took counsel together to plan rebellion, but the duke got wind of this and took an army against this 'vulgar crowd', inflicting severe damage on them. This merely provoked further resistance and in the end the duke and all his nobles were killed in battle.

This was at Sempach on 9 July 1386 against the Swiss. In the previous year, the city of Lucerne had rejected Leopold's overlordship, and Berne too had been enlarging its territories at Hapsburg expense. Walsingham's account gives none of these details, but it seems that the reports which were reaching him at St Albans connected the Swiss struggle for independence specifically with the desire to tap the profits of the pilgrimage traffic across the Alps. It is in fact well known that improvements to the St Gotthard pass in the early thirteenth century had stimulated economic development in the Swiss cantons which lay to the north of the pass and en route to the Rhine valley, and that the traffic was disrupted in the fourteenth by the Swiss–Hapsburg conflict.

One pilgrim who was destined for spiritual distinction was caught up in the Swiss travails of 1386. In the autumn of 1385 Dorothea of Montau visited Aachen with her aging husband and their small daughter and went on with them to the shrine of the Virgin at Einsiedeln, very close to the war zone. The journey took nine weeks; sometimes the dangers of the roads forced them to take refuge amidst herds of animals or in cemeteries. Once they were robbed of all their possessions and Dorothea's husband was severely wounded. They came at last to Einsiedeln, and spent a year and a half there, during which their sufferings, including hunger, were increased by the warfare in the neighbourhood. Dorothea regarded these privations as blessings in disguise, but pilgrims made of less stern stuff, forewarned of such hazards, might well have been deterred.

Death on pilgrimage was a not infrequent occurrence which had to be provided for. In 1169 Pope Alexander III complained that the clergy and people of Benevento were complicit in the evil custom of confining the sick merchant, pilgrim or other traveller to the house and dividing his property, if he died, among themselves.[19] A number of late medieval rulers legislated to safeguard the right of a moribund pilgrim to make his will freely and to choose his place of burial. When pilgrims died abroad, there might be long delays before confirmation of the news reached home, and a variety of complications could ensue. In 1363 arrangements had to be made to reclaim forty gold ducats from Venetian merchants with whom a Scot, Alan de Winton, had deposited them before departing on a pilgrimage to Sinai, on which he died. The same melancholy reality entailed the provision of burial places for pilgrims; charitable brotherhoods often established them alongside the hospitals they ran, but they were bound to accept only outsiders for burial and not to infringe the burial rights of the parish in which the premises lay. According to the statutes of the Eastbridge Hospital at Canterbury, revised in 1340, pilgrims were buried in a plot in the cathedral cemetery, which had been allocated long ago for the purpose.

We have little idea how many people went on pilgrimage at any period. Chroniclers' figures for the numbers attracted to Rome in 1300 are often regarded as wildly inaccurate, although Giovanni Villani's estimate of 200,000 in the whole year, over and above the Roman population itself, is not impossible.[20] Seemingly precise figures, such as the numbers of pilgrim badges sold at Regensburg in 1519–20, or the 147,000 people who are supposed to have been counted entering Aachen during the fifteen-day indulgence period in 1496, cannot provide the basis for global estimates of the volume of pilgrimage earlier, or later, or in other places at the same period. Regensburg enjoyed a brief flurry; Aachen might conceivably have flourished while other shrines declined, although there is evidence that it stimulated subsidiary pilgrimages in its vicinity. No single set of figures from one shrine can furnish a guide either to chronological change or to a general European pattern. It is possible to compute the numbers that English shipmasters were licensed to carry to Compostela during the fifteenth century or the numbers of permissions to travel to Rome which were issued by the English government, but it is not so easy to be sure how complete the records are or how big a proportion of the real total of pilgrims they represent, nor of course would English figures necessarily offer any yardstick for the numbers going to these shrines from other parts of Europe.

Perhaps there was some decline in the relative popularity of old-style relic-based cults associated with individual saints, but, like all generalisations, this would require the most careful scrutiny. New saints, often assiduously publicised by the orders to which they had belonged, could achieve quite farflung popularity. The appeal of such cults was often geographically focused on a number of centres: the actual burial place attracted one clientele, while devotees in other regions established altars and obtained relics, around which subsidiary shrines were established. The canonised saints of the Franciscan order, for example, had principal shrines at their burial places (Francis at Assisi, Antony at Padua, Bernardino of Siena at L'Aquila) but also generated subsidiary pilgrimages, as Francis did in company with Elizabeth of Thuringia at Marburg. A local, unofficial saint, King Henry VI of England (d. 1471), was venerated at a number of places in England. St George's Chapel, Windsor, became the major focus after the king's remains were taken there from Chertsey Abbey, and it was here that his miracles were recorded, but there were subsidiary centres at a number of places, in Yorkshire, East Anglia and the west Midlands, and few pilgrims came from these areas to Windsor.

Analysis of surviving records of offerings in the major English churches has suggested that they hit a peak in the later fourteenth century, a period of plague and falling population levels, but were declining by 1500, when population was recovering. The decentralisation of devotion, however, makes it difficult to know whether, or to what extent, pilgrimage and offerings to small, locally popular shrines which have left no records may or may not have compensated for any downturn at greater or older shrines. That some individuals continued to make lengthy pilgrimage journeys on the eve of the Reformation is clear. It is hard to know whether there were fewer of them, or fewer pilgrims overall, than there had been, either in absolute terms or as a proportion of the total population. Critics of the later medieval church, such as the Lollards in England, were usually also critics of pilgrimage, and Protestant reformers later abolished the practice where they had the power to do so. Criticism does not of itself, however, prove that the practice being criticised is losing popularity; it may even suggest the opposite.

That there was a shift towards shorter-distance pilgrimage is a distinct possibility. Proprietors and patrons all over Christendom sought and advertised indulgences, which may tell us that they entertained high hopes of attracting pilgrims and funds to their churches, but it does not of itself tell us how successful their efforts were. By 1400, anyway, a pilgrimage was only one way among several of obtaining indulgences, plenary and otherwise. It was, for example, possible to petition the pope for the right to choose a confessor who was authorised to grant plenary remission (with all the appropriate safeguards) on one's deathbed.

Contributions to road and bridge building, almsgiving to the poor and to hospitals, prayers for the dead, were other means of obtaining indulgences. Whether the attractions of pilgrimage were diminished as a result depends on how important indulgence-seeking was among the motives for undertaking it, and this must be a subject for later discussion.

2
MOTIVES FOR PILGRIMAGE

Whan that Aprill with his shoures soote
The droghte of March hath perced to the roote,
And bathed every veyne in swich licour
Of which vertu engendred is the flour;
Whan Zephirus eek with his sweete breeth
Inspired hath in every holt and heeth
The tendre croppes, and the yonge sonne
Hath in the Ram his half cours yronne,
And smale foweles maken melodye,
That slepen al the nyght with open ye
(So priketh hem nature in hir corages),
Thanne longen folk to goon on pilgrimages,
And palmeres for to seken straunge strondes,
To ferne halwes, kowthe in sondry londes;
And specially from every shires ende
Of Engelond to Caunterbury they wende,
The hooly blisful martir for to seke,
That hem hath holpen whan that they were seeke . . .

The famous opening lines of Chaucer's *Canterbury Tales* repay repetition when we ponder the question of pilgrim motivation. Here the poet is rooting the human impulse to pilgrimage in a context of nature and season. The sap is rising, crops and creatures are astir, and Chaucer's characters, because they are Christians, express their participation in the general ferment by going on pilgrimage. Because they are also English, many of them choose to go to Canterbury, but others seek out distant shrines, and for these 'palmers' the very 'strangeness' of such places is important. The only specific pretext for domestic pilgrimage to which Chaucer refers is the desire to give thanks for delivery from sickness; he assumes that the saint's 'help' has already been received.

This piece of scene-setting directs our attention to one important fact, that pilgrimage meant travel, and provided an excuse for travel in a period and society in which opportunities to get away from the daily and domestic setting were limited variously by wealth, class, gender and religious status. Critics of pilgrimage were only too well aware that it could be used as an excuse to evade discipline and duty by a wide variety of people, from monks and nuns who should have stayed in the cloister to fugitive serfs, beggars and vagabonds. The *Formulary of Marculf*, a collection of model letters compiled *c*.700, includes a testimonial for a pilgrim which assures the reader that the bearer is not motivated *vacandi causa*, that is by the desire for mere recreation. Interests more usually ascribed to the modern tourist were clearly not unknown. Early in the twelfth century, the writer often known as Honorius 'of Autun' remarked that if pilgrims were prompted by 'idle curiosity or a desire for human praise, let this be their reward, that they have seen pleasant places and beautiful monuments and have heard the praise which they love'.

That 'curiosity' might be part of the psychology of an otherwise unimpeachable pilgrim is indicated by the account of St Willibald's pilgrimages to Rome and the Holy Land, which he related to his kinswoman, the nun Hugeberc, in his old age, around the year 780. The title by which Hugeberc's retelling of his story is usually known, the *Hodoepericon*, means a travel narrative and indicates that this is not a conventional saint's life. To Hugeberc, recounting Willibald's travels in the Holy Land was of prime importance; for her as for her putative readership and of course for Willibald himself, seeing the places of Christ's birth, death and resurrection was an experience of incomparable spiritual value. Willibald, she said, had dauntlessly surmounted all perils, and sought out and saw everything. It is hard to know whether she was reinterpreting or simply transcribing what Willibald told her about his motives for his wanderings, or how well he remembered them fifty years later, but we can presumably take it that the account of both events and impulses that she gives in the *Hodoepericon* was intelligible and acceptable both to herself and to Willibald.

Willibald, who was a kinsman of another famous native of Wessex, St Boniface, embraced the monastic life as a youth at (Bishop's) Waltham in Hampshire, but soon he longed for something more rigorous, which involved the rejection not only of the earthly riches consequent on his birth, but of home and kin themselves. This was a common reason for *peregrinatio* among monks, both Irish and English. Detachment of the self from the familiar and the comfortable represented a path to an otherwise unattainable perfection, even to salvation itself. Willibald therefore decided 'to venture upon the unknown roads of pilgrimage and to visit and explore remote foreign parts of the world'.[1] He prevailed upon both his father and his brother Winnebald to accompany him, working on his father's reluctance to abandon his domestic responsibilities with stick and carrot, fears of damnation and hopes of salvation.

Up to this point in the story there has been no mention of a destination, but it was in fact to be Rome. Willibald's father died at Lucca on the way and was buried there in the church of San Frediano. When the brothers reached Rome they gave thanks that they had been enabled to surmount all perils and deemed worthy to see St Peter's and the Scala Santa.[2] Given the popularity of Roman pilgrimage among the Anglo-Saxons as Bede describes it, Willibald and Winnebald may well have known something about the various attractions of Rome before they left England, but their ostensible objective was not sacred sight-seeing but the pursuit of monastic perfection, which could best be sought in certain specially favoured environments. It was revealing of Willibald's temperament that Rome did not suffice. After a winter which the brothers passed in 'leading a life of monastic discipline' only to fall seriously ill during the heat of summer, he decided that he wanted a still stricter observance, only to be found in a less well frequented place than Rome. Now he looked forward to gazing with pleasure on the 'pleasant and hallowed walls' of Jerusalem, and he made his way there via southern Italy, Sicily and Cyprus.

There is in fact little specifically about monastic discipline in Willibald's reminiscences of his time in the Holy Land, but there is a great deal about the sights and experiences that were on offer to the Christian visitor. Willibald went to the Jordan and bathed in it, remarking that the 'infirm' came there on the feast of the Epiphany to immerse themselves in the waters; so too did childless women. Later he describes the church built on the spot on the Mount of Olives where Christ prayed on the night before His passion. The church was open to the sky and inside it were two pillars, one against the northern wall and one on the south. Willibald noted that any man who could squeeze his body between these pillars and the wall was (it was believed) freed from his sins. He personally experienced a cure when he lost his eyesight during the celebration of mass in the church of St Matthias at Gaza, but regained it when he entered the basilica of Constantine in Jerusalem, where the True Cross of the Lord had been found. Fifty years on, he also remembered more trivial oddities such as the cattle near Caesarea, which were dark red all over, long in the back and short in the leg.

From the Holy Land, Willibald went to Constantinople, where, as he recalled, Sts Andrew, Timothy and Luke reposed in one altar and St John Chrysostom was buried before the altar at which he had officiated as priest. Willibald spent two years here, occupying a special place in the church whence he could gaze every day upon the resting-places of the saints. From Constantinople he made a special journey to Nicaea to see the church where the great council had been held in 325; he reported it was just like the church on the Mount of Olives whence Christ ascended to heaven. When he eventually returned to Italy and came by ship to Calabria, he very much desired to inspect the volcano on the small island of that name, where legend had it the Ostrogothic king Theoderic had been cast into hell, but he was unable to make the ascent to the crater because of the burning ashes and had to content himself with gazing upon the smoke and flames that issued from it. Willibald now spent ten years living according to the Rule of St Benedict (which enjoined stability) at Monte Cassino. He then went again to Rome, in the company of a Spanish priest, and was summoned to the presence of Gregory III, who wanted to know how he had managed to survive seven years of travel in the east and to evade the wickedness of the 'pagans'. From Rome Willibald's path now led to Germany and to his death, still far distant, as bishop of Eichstätt in Bavaria.

The *Hodoepericon* bears witness to the many layers of pilgrim culture and motivation that had already been laid down by the early eighth century. Overall, Willibald's lengthy pilgrimage bears little resemblance to the relatively simple there-and-back journeys made by ordinary pilgrims throughout the medieval period (and later). His original inspiration was drawn from current monastic ideals, which made ample room for the wanderlust that characterised his own personality. In principle, a precise geographical destination was irrelevant, for the real objective was a greater perfection of the inner life; but in fact Willibald sought to go to school in particular places, in Rome and the Holy Land. Here he observed and participated in pilgrim rituals designed to meet a variety of physical and spiritual needs. After a period of contemplation of the remains of the saints at Constantinople, his own *peregrinatio* culminated in a prolonged period of stable monastic life and a still longer period as missionary and bishop.

Many other pilgrim monks directed their steps to favoured destinations such as Rome or to famous monasteries – schools of spiritual instruction where great teachers were to be found. In the sixth century, St Columba (d. 597) played host to a stream of visitors to Iona who were drawn by the fame of his holiness. Just before his death, Columba told his disciples that 'Today is the thirtieth anniversary since I began to live in pilgrimage in Britain'. Pilgrimage in this sense was not a journey but a condition, and women too could enter into it, with certain limitations. Hugeberc had done so, like Walburga and another female member of St Boniface's extensive kin, St Leoba, who answered his call to the German mission-field and was buried with him at Fulda. This did not mean that such women would be endlessly peripatetic. In late sixth-century Ireland, a female recluse from whom St Columbanus sought counsel told him that had it not been for 'the fragility of her sex' she would have gone overseas to find 'a more suitable place of pilgrimage'.

Complete isolation was, however, sometimes sought, either temporarily or permanently, somewhat as the Desert Fathers had sought it in Egypt. Among Columba's visitors on Iona was St Cormac, who made repeated efforts to find an ocean retreat among the Atlantic islands. The hero of the most celebrated of all narratives of this maritime *peregrinatio* was St Brendan, whose death in around 575 was noted by Adomnan, Columba's biographer. The *Voyage (Navigatio) of St Brendan*, which survives in over a hundred medieval manuscripts, tells how Brendan set out to find 'the Land of Promise of the Saints', which had actually been visited by his kinsman Barinthius. After many adventures, observations of marine natural history and an encounter with Judas Iscariot, he and his companions found it. It seems both too fanciful and too prosaic to identify it as Greenland. Brendan was a native of Munster, and he may well have travelled quite widely as a monastic founder, but the spectacular sea voyage described in the *Navigatio*, which was probably composed around 900 by an expatriate Irishman in the Rhineland or the Low Countries, seems to represent a late embroidery of the tradition. It was certainly still alive at this date: the *Anglo-Saxon Chronicle* records that in 891 three Irishmen set out from Ireland, with food for seven days, in a skin boat without any oars, not caring where it took them. In fact it took them to Cornwall and they immediately made themselves known to King Alfred. Such a seaborne 'pilgrimage' would usually result in a more or less prolonged period of eremitical residence, as it did for the monks who perched precariously on the rock of Skellig Michael. Family, friendship and monastic networks all provided means by which knowledge of shrines and routes could be transmitted. Willibald's Holy Land pilgrimage was, to Hugeberc as to Gregory III, the most remarkable thing about him and deserved publicity. The Venerable Bede inserted into his *History* some excerpts from Adomnan's book on the Holy Land, which was itself based on the account of the Frankish bishop Arculf, who had been blown a long way off course on his return from Palestine and ended up narrating his travels on Iona. Bede regarded this as a most useful work for those who would never themselves behold Jerusalem. To what extent such travellers' tales, whether transmitted orally or in writing, furnished an incentive for actual pilgrimage is impossible to know. To the public they reached it is a fair assumption that (like the *Navigatio* of St Brendan) they were both inspirational and entertaining for their marvellous qualities. The roads to Rome were better known and information was relatively easy to obtain. The Kentish abbess Eadburga sought St Boniface's advice about a pilgrimage to Rome and he in turn quoted the counsel of another pious Anglo-Saxon woman who was currently in residence there.

Penance

Willibald's departure from England (like his brother's) was by all accounts entirely voluntary, and did not rule out a subsequent return, for Winnebald came back to his homeland at least once. Columba was well-connected by birth to the ruling lineages of Ulster, and it is debated whether his departure from Ireland was an enforced or a voluntary exile in difficult political circumstances. Clearly *peregrinatio* bore some formal similarity to exile, and it is not surprising that, as penitential systems developed for the correction of sin among both clergy and laity, pilgrimages came to be imposed as penance (or punishment) for certain offences. One of Columba's visitors on Iona was a clerk from Connaught who had made the journey, he said, 'in order to wipe out his sins on a pilgrimage'. When he confessed what these sins were, Columba instructed him to spend seven years on Tiree in penance; only then was he permitted to receive the sacrament. Popularised in the first instance by the Irish and the Anglo-Saxons whom they so much influenced, this use of pilgrimage was destined for a long future, although penitential practice was, as already explained, changing its shape markedly by the year 1000.

In the later middle ages, the ecclesiastical tribunals of bishops and inquisitors and also secular courts in the cities of northern Europe employed a more bureaucratised version of this penitential procedure, often demanding that the penitent or miscreant should bring back a certificate of performance from the shrine to which he or she had been sent. Such penitential pilgrims were not always guilty of spiritual or moral offences of the kind normally reserved to ecclesiastical jurisdiction. A bishop in his capacity as 'lord of the manor' could impose pilgrimages (often very local ones) for poaching or similar infringements of his rights, and almost any temporal offence, from slander and trouble-making to homicide, could be thus punished. The distance, frequency and arduousness of the pilgrimage to be undertaken was normally proportional to the offence. A short local pilgrimage was a form of public penance which exposed the offender to the scrutiny of people who knew him; a lengthier pilgrimage preserved something of the character of exile, and might be imposed where the offence was not merely severe but made it desirable to remove the offender from circulation for a prolonged period. In 1283, John Pecham, archbishop of Canterbury, commanded an incorrigibly fornicating priest of the diocese of Chichester to go to Santiago, Rome and Cologne in three successive years. In 1366, Pope Urban V wanted soldiers who had incurred excommunication as members of the dreaded 'companies' during the Anglo-French wars to spend as long in pilgrimage to the Holy Sepulchre as they had spent as members of the companies, and to fight the infidel if the opportunity arose. Alternatively they were to go to Rome and visit the usual shrines for a year, going afterwards to Compostela. Some secular sentences were frankly political and arbitrary and amounted to exile: in 1400 Giovanni Bentivoglio, *signore* of Bologna, sent one of his enemies to Compostela and another to the Holy Sepulchre.

Sometimes it was possible to buy off a penitential pilgrimage; alternatively, it might be possible to employ a substitute to undertake the pilgrimage, just as someone who had taken the crusading vow might be permitted to send a deputy. Such stipendiaries in a sense occupy a middle ground between the purely voluntary pilgrim and the involuntary penitent. They were available for hire and were frequently employed by executors to carry out pilgrimages for which deceased persons had allotted funds. Women as well as men are documented in this employment. Testators often, however, stipulated that pilgrimages should be carried out by 'honest priests', who had the advantage that they could say masses on behalf of the deceased at Rome or wherever they were sent. Occupying another place on the spectrum were friends and relatives who undertook to fulfil the wishes of the dying, sometimes purely out of good will, although often they were to be remunerated from the estate, and it was not unknown for sons to be required to carry out the designated pilgrimages before they could enter into their inheritance.

Compulsory, involuntary pilgrimage was an identifiable category, but throughout the middle ages, penitence or self-inflicted penance remained an important motive for pilgrimages which were by any reckoning voluntary. This element could in fact be described as inseparable from authentic pilgrimage, including pilgrimages undertaken in order to obtain a cure for infirmity or a solution to a practical problem. Given the prevailing tendency to attribute disease and misfortune to sin, only penitence could secure a remedy. The rigours of travel in medieval conditions inevitably imparted a penitential element to pilgrimage, which could be aggravated by additional requirements imposed either on oneself or by superior authority: these might include going barefoot, in scanty clothing or in fetters, and abstaining from certain foods. To this were added the pains of separation from hearth and home, although it must not be forgotten that medieval individuals, like their descendants, sometimes chafed under the restrictions of the domestic routine and the horrors of dysfunctional families and sought escape from them.

Bereavement (whether this was experienced as loss or as liberation) and other personal crises could trigger the impulse to lose oneself in pilgrimage, as of course they also triggered religious conversion. In practical terms, widowhood or the removal of paternal authority could open up the opportunity of travel. In the mid-twelfth century Raimondo Palmario of Piacenza took the opportunity to go to the Holy Land with his mother, after his father's death; later, when his wife and all but one of his children had died, he set out on what he intended to be a career of lifelong pilgrimage. Two hundred years later, John Rivers, who had served Edward III, went to the Holy Land when his wife died and sub-sequently became a Dominican friar. The Prussian mystic Dorothea of Montau persuaded her husband to join with her in a stricter religious observance when they had lost all but one of their children; they marked the transition by making a pilgrimage to Aachen in 1384. To Dorothea, the privations they suffered in 1385–7 on a second pilgrimage to Aachen and Einsiedeln were so many blessings, which facilitated her longed-for shift from the mundane condition of wife and mother to a greater intimacy with God. In Rome, early in 1390, she was so ill that she was unable to stand and was left in the middle of the road by two strong men who had unavailingly tried to help her to St Peter's to see the exhibition of the Veronica. Christ Himself explained to her why He had permitted this illness. When she was ill at home she had the benefit of the ministrations of family and servants, and therefore would think relatively little of it; 'in exile', as He significantly said, it was a different matter and enforced a greater sense of dependence on God alone.

Cure and Devotion

The radical self-abnegation of religious adepts who abandoned the norms of family life and did not return to them was never the pattern followed by the generality of pilgrims. For many of them, the local or perhaps the regional shrine provided for their needs for both 'devotion' and healing. Our knowledge of these shrines and of people's specific reasons for going to them is, however, limited. Narratives of visits to Rome, Jerusalem or Santiago often mention other shrines in passing, but we are less well informed about the details of journeys to Aachen, Canterbury or Tours. Where shrines had an important healing aspect, collections of miracle stories in part plug the gap, but there are problems involved in using miracle stories as a guide to the motivation of the average pilgrim. There are many shrines about which we would know little if it were not for miracle stories, but many others never generated a miracle collection, and miracle stories anyway have little or nothing to say about pilgrims who neither sought nor experienced a miracle, who must surely have been in the vast majority. In so far as they do appear it is as supernumeraries, conventionally very numerous, serving as background and audience for miracles.

With all these reservations it has to be acknowledged that throughout the medieval period it is from miracle collections that we derive most of our information about the operations of the 'average' shrine and the nature of the public it attracted. In the sixth century the numerous hagiographical writings of Gregory of Tours (d. 594) are of particular importance. After he became bishop of Tours in 573, Gregory was naturally particularly attached to St Martin and he compiled a collection of his miracles, but he preserved an earlier family attachment to St Julian. He had made regular pilgrimages with his father and brother to Brioude, and his *Life* of St Julian gives vivid testimony to the operations of this essentially regional shrine.

This was one of many associated with a holy well, in which, it was said, St Julian's head had been washed after his execution. A large church had been built on the strength of the numerous cures that took place, and it was not uncommon for the incurably sick to be left there to live on the alms of the faithful. One such woman, reposing in the colonnade attached to the church, was cured in a dream during the night between Saturday and Sunday, always a popular time for miracles. Persons possessed by devils accused Julian in their ravings of inviting other saints, including Martin, to his festivals just to increase their sufferings. Visitors took away relics – a drop of wax, water from the spring – which carried with them the therapeutic values of the original shrine and gave rise to miracles and secondary centres of devotion to the saint, at Saintes, Limoges and Tours itself, where Gregory, newly made bishop, installed threads from the altar-cloth at Brioude in the basilica of St Martin. In 571, Gregory made the pilgrimage to St Julian to obtain protection from plague. On earlier occasions the motive of the family pilgrimage to Julian's annual festival was simply devotional, but it was sometimes accompanied by sickness, as when Gregory's brother Peter, severely weakened by fever, asked for dust from the tomb to be hung about his neck or given to him in a drink. In the following year, Gregory himself was afflicted on his way to the shrine by sunstroke and a violent headache, which was alleviated at another holy well a few miles from Brioude. This one was sacred to St Ferreolus, also a martyr and an associate of St Julian.

Gregory's account of the miracles of St Martin at Tours sheds additional light on pilgrimage practice. Here too the poor were sustained by the alms of the faithful and a register (*matricula*) was kept of them. A woman who had herself received a cure stayed for the rest of the day preparing drinks and thereafter returned every year bringing food. On several occasions cures were performed while stories of Martin's miracles were being read aloud. There were custodians stationed at the shrine who were supposed to inform the bishop about miracles, but they did not always give him full particulars. The more assiduous pilgrim might perform a sacred itinerary, venerating the saint's tomb in the bishop's church and then crossing the river to Marmoutier, where Martin had lived as a monk, to visit every single place that he had sanctified with his presence. The place of his death, at Candes between Tours and Poitiers, was similarly venerated. Here the 'bed' on which the saint had lain, which in fact consisted of cinders with a stone for a pillow, was protected by a railing. A blind woman from Tours received her sight there and was so inspired by faith that she never left the place again. Many of the features of the cults of Julian and Martin as Gregory of Tours describes them have echoes and analogues down the centuries. One entirely typical characteristic is their modest catchment area. Martin was unquestionably a saint of European celebrity, but with rather few exceptions the pilgrims mentioned by Gregory came from central southern and south-western Gaul; there is only one explicit reference to a pilgrim from Paris. His clients, like Julian's, were frequenting a local or regional saint; if they were in need of cure they did not cover excessive distances in search of it. Few pilgrimages involving a journey of considerable length were likely to be undertaken for merely 'problem-solving' or therapeutic purposes, and any shrine would do for pilgrims of limited means and stamina who simply wanted to 'pray', or to establish close contact with the holy embodied in the relics of a saint.

If one were to seek one word to describe the objectives of voluntary pilgrimage and to link the aspirations of the early pioneers, whether in the Atlantic or the Mediterranean, with those of their later medieval successors both lay and clerical, it might have to be the inclusive term 'devotion', signifying the desire to give expression to religious emotion and to offer prayer in the most inspiring environment possible. Early saints' lives frequently use general formulae such as 'by reason of prayer' or 'of devotion' (*orationis causa* or *devotionis causa*) to account for pilgrimages. It has already been suggested that there may be difficulties in distinguishing motivations of this class from other plausible reasons for visiting Rome or the Holy Land. The desire to offer prayer in either setting was intimately linked to a sense of special place, the Biblical landscape or the Rome of the martyrs, and this would almost inevitably entail the belief that such prayer possessed a special value.

Willibald's observations in the Holy Land inform us that there were well-established rituals, which presumably both Christian residents and visitors performed. Bathing in the Jordan commemorated Christ's baptism and might have either generally purificatory or specifically therapeutic properties. Squeezing between the pillars and the wall of the church on the Mount of Olives brought forgiveness of sins, an objective of almost all pilgrimage, whether it was conceived in terms of the individual's general sinfulness or of particular sins. In later centuries this 'pardon' would be increasingly quantified by the award of indulgences. Willibald's account shows that the original motivation of 'biblical tourism', although still not merely present but of prime importance, had been supplemented by devotional practices which addressed specific purposes. The desire to study the Scriptures in the privileged setting of the Holy Land, as St Jerome and his followers did in the fourth century, cannot be sensibly separated from the belief that, in principle, a better quality of Christian life and understanding was also attainable there. Eleven hundred years later, the young Dominican friar Felix Fabri, who went to the Holy Land in 1480 and again in 1483, claimed to believe that seeing the Bible lands with his own eyes would make him a better preacher. What is sometimes lacking in the early period is any explicit statement of what pilgrims thought the spiritual value of their experience was.

The Holy Land was and remained the supreme focus of devotional pilgrimage. Other shrines ministered much more conveniently to the needs of the sick, the blind or the crippled. It was hardly likely that the generality of pregnant women would betake themselves from western Europe to the Jordan in quest of a safe delivery, but there could be no better place to pray and receive spiritual enlightenment. Santiago de Compostela also became above all a goal of the devout and the voluntarily and involuntarily penitent rather than a healing shrine. Rome was obviously another shrine in this category, but it had a distinct significance for western Christians. When Willibald came to Rome for a second time, in company with the Spanish priest, they went into St Peter's and specifically commended themselves to the protection of the 'key-bearer'. When St Boniface first visited Rome, he and his companions sought absolution of their sins from the prince of the apostles. The role of Peter and his successors, the popes, as holders of the keys of heaven and possessors of the binding and loosing power, gave Rome a special meaning as the goal of the penitent, which was underlined by the reservation of the power of absolution from certain offences to the pope himself.

The popes themselves advertised their special powers to grant absolution for serious sins as a means of binding the peoples of Christendom, not least newly converted peoples, to Rome. The author of *Njal's Saga*, telling in the late thirteenth century the corpse-littered story of a remorseless feud which had taken place in Iceland between about 960 and 1016, imagined one of the principal protagonists walking from the English Channel to Rome to receive the honour of absolution from the pope himself, for which, it is remarked, he paid a great deal of money.[3] Another character in this saga, Hrafn the Red, driven into a river during the Battle of Clontarf in Ireland in 1014, was released by the devils who tried to drag him down into hell when he reminded St Peter aloud that he had twice been on pilgrimage to him and would do so again if he could. Alexander III, in 1171, advised the archbishop of Uppsala and his suffragans to send persons guilty of parricide, infanticide, incest and bestiality 'to vist the shrines of the apostles Peter and Paul, that in the sweat of their brow and the labour of the road they may avoid the wrath of the heavenly judge and earn His mercy'. Later popes, however, discovered that there was a certain disinclination among stiff-necked Scandinavians to perform penitential pilgrimages, and they prescribed alternative remedies such as crusades against the Lithuanians.

Some sources imply that pilgrims sought subtly different things when they went to Rome and the Holy Land respectively. Ulrich, later prior of Celle, went to Jerusalem in 1062, seeking to unburden himself from routine cares and seek Christ. While there he experienced the powerful emotions that are described in many eleventh-century accounts: 'it is impossible to tell with what emotions he beheld the monuments of the nativity, passion, resurrection and ascension of the Lord, with what genuflections he adored them and with what rivers of tears he flooded them. . . .' At Bethlehem he identified himself with the Magi, opening the treasures of his breast and offering their three gifts, 'symbolically though not in reality'. He bathed in the Jordan, recalling that in its waters the Saviour had 'washed away the guilt of our sins'. When on his return he went with a companion to Rome, 'they first went to the shrines of the holy apostles Peter and Paul, for the clemency of our Redeemer has conferred on them the power of binding and loosing, and by their merits and intercession they hoped to be granted absolution of their sins by the Lord. Most earnestly they commended their intention to them, praying that they might be enabled to complete the arduous course of their regular life, by which they longed to attain the celestial fatherland'. Jerusalem and Rome, for Ulrich, marked linked phases in his entry into a new life.

Vows and Miracles

Many voluntary pilgrimages, throughout the medieval period, were preceded by the making of a vow. In the 1530s an enemy of pilgrimage, the reforming bishop of Worcester, Hugh Latimer, argued that women especially should be prevented from making such vows without the authority of their husbands and their priests; to do this would, in his

view, effectively bring pilgrimage to an end. Was a vow in itself a motive
for pilgrimage, or rather the mechanism by which a pilgrimage was initiated? For the motive proper one may have to seek the reason for making
the vow, although, as Latimer implied, indiscriminate vow-making
could become a habit, almost a fashion.

This mattered principally because a vow transformed a voluntary
undertaking into an obligatory one. Although not infrequently made in
the same spirit and with the same degree of conviction as a New Year's
resolution, vows resembled oaths and possessed a solemn binding force
from which absolution would have to be sought if the thing vowed
proved to be impossible, insuperably difficult or simply, in the cold light
of day, less of a good idea than it had seemed at the time. Much, in practice, undoubtedly depended on whether the vow had been made aloud
in the presence of witnesses, or even put down in writing. If it were silent
and secret, it was up to the individual to decide whether it was binding in
conscience and to admit to it in public. A vow was not, however, necessarily burdensome. As Latimer probably suspected, women (or men)
who wanted a day out, a break in the routine, could claim to have made a
vow of pilgrimage which had now to be fulfilled.

Individuals undoubtedly made vows of pilgrimage which they did not
subsequently keep, frivolously, at moments of stress or out of pure
'devotion'. Sometimes this was mentioned (and punished) in miracle
stories, but it emerges also from other types of evidence. Failure to keep
vows of pilgrimage to Rome, Jerusalem or Compostela meant applica-
tion to the pope himself for dispensation or commutation, and his
responses, when preserved in the papal registers, shed some light on the
reasons individuals put forward both for vowing a pilgrimage in the first
place and then for not performing it. Age, sickness, repeated pregnancies,
preoccupation with royal service, were all adduced on the latter account.
Vows of pilgrimage to lesser destinations did not concern the pope and
we have little information about them. Wills occasionally include
references to pilgrimages not fulfilled in the testator's lifetime and now
compensated for by a pious bequest.

Women were not the only ones who made ill-considered vows. In
1458, John Chiellod, a priest of the diocese of Exeter, applied to Pope
Pius II for help. He had vowed that if he caught himself either gabbling
when he said the divine office or committing another (unnamed) sin,
'he would within a month visit the Holy Land and the shrines of the
apostles and perhaps that of St James of Compostela'. Naturally he had
defaulted, and he then made matters worse by further vowing that if he

sinned again he would give all his goods to the poor and become a Carthusian monk, and that he would never seek dispensation from any of these vows. We may wonder how it was possible to vow 'perhaps' to perform a pilgrimage; perhaps John simply could not remember what he had said.

Vows were implicated in what appears to be a later medieval change in pilgrimage patterns, which is revealed by analysis of miracle stories. Early medieval miracles are typically described as taking place at or near the shrine itself. This was consistent with the importance attached to the physical possession and location of the saint's remains within a particular ecclesiastical community. In an examination of over 5000 eleventh- and twelfth-century miracles reported at French shrines, Pierre-André Sigal found that a considerable majority were performed at or near the shrine, that is in the vicinity of the saint's relics, for suppliants who had had to drag themselves or be conveyed there. There was also what might be regarded as an intermediate category: the miracle was performed at some distance from the burial place by means of a portable relic, and was therefore dependent on the saint's presence as mediated through that relic. The process would be completed by a thanksgiving pilgrimage, or by the completion of the pilgrimage, for miracles sometimes occurred on the way to (or even from) the shrine.

Fourteenth- and fifteenth-century miracle collections present a different picture. The majority, sometimes a large majority, of the miracles described took place at long range, at least in the sense that the beneficiary was not at the shrine and was often not even in contact with a relic, but reported the miracle when making a subsequent pilgrimage to give thanks and bring an offering. The miracle itself was normally preceded, if not actually triggered, by a vow to make the pilgrimage. The vow, which was very often conditional on a successful outcome, could be made by the sufferer or on his or her behalf, especially if a child was involved; the pilgrimage might be performed either by the sufferer when restored to health, by the person or persons who had made the vow, or both. By means of the distant or intermediate miracle, the saint could deal with a wide range of troubles and afflictions, including some that required fast action. Many concerned babies and children, from stillbirth, through sudden infantile illnesses, to the accidents which children all too often suffered: drowning, falling from windows, getting crushed under wagons. Delivery from shipwreck or a burning house, or indeed the resurrection of the (apparently) dead, could scarcely wait upon a prior pilgrimage to the shrine.

It must be emphasised that, just as some miracles continued to be reported at or near shrines in the later middle ages, so saints performed some 'distance miracles' from the earliest times. As Sigal remarks, these seem to have been regarded as especially impressive displays both of the saint's spiritual power and of the suppliant's faith. The more independent of the relics miracles were seen to be, the more clearly they demonstrated that there was no magic or deception involved. There were always, therefore, some deliverances from shipwreck, difficult childbirth or even death itself. A characteristic early medieval distance miracle, which has been seen as reflecting one of the harsh realities of seigneurial society, was delivery from unjust imprisonment or even threat of execution. The lucky escapee would come to the shrine and hang up his fetters there (this was, of course, a typically male problem), as others hung up their crutches or models of afflicted body parts. St Leonard of Noblat was a specialist in this line, but most saints rescued at least one or two captives.

Potentially, at least, the saint who operated at a distance could both help people in a wider range of afflictions and intervene more rapidly over a wider geographical area. Conversely, if he or she failed to render the desired assistance, the fact would usually remain unchronicled and invisible. Disappointed long-distance customers were not in the habit of writing letters of complaint; their appeal and their vows dropped into a void, unheard unless by a few witnesses who had been near at hand. Disappointed customers at a shrine were, by contrast, visible, and many miracle stories tried to account for their disappointment by explaining that their sins rendered them unworthy. Sometimes they were successful on another occasion when they had mended their ways. The efficacy of an appeal to the saint at long range still normally depended on the good disposition of the petitioner, but, in effect, payment was made only by results. This looks like a mode of proceeding appropriate to a more commercialised society, but it is doubtful whether that by itself is an adequate explanation for the apparent change. Another possibility is a broadening social base for pilgrimage. Analysis of the 273 eleventh- and twelfth-century distance miracles identified in Sigal's study shows that 64.8 per cent of the persons cured belonged to what he calls the 'popular classes', that is, people who were not identifiably nobles, clergy, monks, merchants or bourgeois. It is possible that members of the lower orders of society were less able, or inclined, to spare the time and money needed for a speculative pilgrimage.

The Scandinavian miracle collections which have been analysed by Christian Krötzl illustrate this chronological transition and its nuances.

These collections, which range in date from the late twelfth to the
fifteenth centuries, are comparatively few in number and originate from
a rather distinctive and restricted geographical environment. Several of
the cults had a catchment area which was confined to only one of the
three northern kingdoms. At the beginning of the period covered by
these collections, in obedience to the general model, 'distance miracles'
were growing in number; by the end they were predominant. Krötzl's
analyses show, however, that the development was somewhat uneven.

Of the two collections that date from the twelfth century, that of Kjeld
of Viborg is impeccably 'early medieval' in character, for only one of his
miracles took place elsewhere than at the tomb. Olaf of Norway, the
royal saint of Trondheim, both in the twelfth century and later drew his
pilgrims from all over Scandinavia, and by contrast with Kjeld of Viborg
he performed a relatively high proportion of his miracles at long range
(37 per cent, 17 out of a total of 46). In the thirteenth century the pro-
portions were rather variable. The Danish saint William of Aebelholt,
who died in 1203 and was canonised in 1244, conformed to the earlier
medieval pattern by performing only 6 of his 31 recorded miracles at
long range; 25 therefore took place in contact with his relics, 7 of them,
which can be classified in the 'intermediate' category, with water in
which one of his teeth had been dipped. All of his clients were Danish.

Another Danish saint, Niels of Aarhus (d. 1180), ministered to an even
more localised clientele, in the eastern part of Jutland, but he was more
flexible in his methods: of his 29 recorded miracles, 18 resulted from
a pilgrimage to his tomb. Two royal cults present a slight contrast. The
Danish king Erik Plovpennig (d. 1250), venerated at Ringsted, achieved
evenly balanced results: of 49 cures or rescues attributed to him, 26
resulted from pilgrimages to the shrine. The cult of Erik, king of Sweden
(d. 1150), who was venerated at Uppsala, produced a markedly high
proportion of distance miracles, 46 out of the 51 which were recorded in
the mid- to later thirteenth century.

There was something of a hiatus in the production of Scandinavian
miracle collections for much of the fourteenth century. Towards the end
of the century, Birgitta of Sweden conformed to the emerging European
norm. Of 138 miracles collected between 1373 and 1390 and cited in her
canonisation process, 87 per cent were performed at a distance. Not very
long afterwards, the 82 miracles effected between 1408 and 1424 by the
image of the Deposition of Christ in the Dominican church at Stockholm
were exclusively distance miracles, making the collection unique among
those surviving from medieval Scandinavia. Second only to the cult of

the Deposition in this respect was that of Nikolas, bishop of Linköping: of a total of 96 accounts collected between 1410 and 1417 only two concern a miracle obtained as a result of a prior pilgrimage. The figures for these two cults highlight the relatively high proportion of miracles (13 per cent) that Birgitta was still, slightly earlier, performing at her tomb. Birgitta's daughter Katharina was venerated with her at Vadstena, and 190 miracles were attributed to her during the fifteenth century, of which 96 per cent were performed at long range. A slight anomaly among fifteenth-century cults is presented by Brynolph of Skara. Brynolph died in 1317, but he owed his fame as a saint to Birgitta's patronage, and his earliest dated miracle was performed in 1404; 26 per cent of the total were performed either at his tomb or by such means as water in which his bones had been washed, which, Krötzl comments, gives the cult a somewhat old-fashioned look.

Although these figures show the broad chronological trend, it can be seen that there was considerable variation between cults that were more or less contemporaneous. Many of these saints, both earlier and later, operated within a restricted geographical area. Where there was a shift of *modus operandi* towards the distance miracle, it meant not that the catchment areas of the cults in question were enlarged, but that the saint's power was being invoked – or was described as being invoked – in a different, more varied manner within the area of his or her fame. Within his very limited sphere of influence, for example, Niels of Aarhus performed 18 of his 29 miracles at the shrine, 11 away from it. Greater fame, conversely, meant not necessarily that a saint was more likely to perform at long range, but that he or she had a larger clientele drawn from a wider area. The peculiarities of the Scandinavian environment restricted the pulling power even of the most famous saints of the region, Olaf and Birgitta. Both drew pilgrims from all over Scandinavia, but although they were undoubtedly more widely known in Europe, there is little evidence, at least from their miracle collections, that they attracted non-Scandinavian pilgrims to their shrines.

Birgitta's celebrity meant that she operated on three levels. Still able to attract a significant number of suppliants to Vadstena, she none the less did the majority of her miracles for Scandinavian petitioners at long range, while her wider reputation, assisted by the spread of the Bridgettine Order, prompted the establishment of subsidiary shrines in many parts of Europe. In this she resembled other saints who can be described as genuinely famous Europe-wide: rarely was there only one shrine where such a saint could be invoked. Thomas Becket, of whose celebrity there can be no doubt, furnishes a comparable example. His clientele in the 1170s covered an impressively wide area, even though over half of those whose places of origin can be identified came from southern England. He operated quite frequently at long distance, even beyond the confines of the Angevin realms, sometimes through the medium of easily transported phials of his blood diluted in water, or through other relics, sometimes by means of visions, and sometimes without any visible manifestation of his presence. He also had numerous subsidiary shrines, including wayside crosses where miracles took place, but we know about these usually only if they led to a thanksgiving pilgrimage to Canterbury.

Sigal has remarked of the distance miracles in his eleventh- and twelfth-century sample that they usually became more numerous with the passage of some time after the launch of a cult. For example, of the 100 miracles performed by St Trudo in 1050–1, the first to be performed away from the relics was the twenty-sixth; sixteen of the last forty then took place at long range. Similar results can be deduced from other cults. Common sense would suggest that a saint was unlikely to be invoked from afar until news that he or she was doing miracles had had a chance to spread beyond the shrine. Fame in itself cannot, however, have been the sole factor in the long-term change. Whether pilgrimages took place in hopes of a miracle or in thanksgiving for one, the suppliant had to know about the saint beforehand, to know where to go or whom to invoke. Before the thirteenth century, the effect of fame, on the evidence of miracle stories, was to bring large numbers of hopeful suppliants to the shrine.

The most consistently powerful medium of publicity over the centuries must have been word of mouth, and one form of oral communication which was undoubtedly more widely employed after 1200, thanks to the spread of the orders of friars, was preaching. Might the trend to the distance miracle be partly explained by the increased penetration of Christian society by preaching? Preaching was certainly nourished by miracle stories, among other sources, and far more pilgrims must have been told about miracles by preachers or guides than ever experienced or even witnessed one, whether at the shrine or away from it. This line of inquiry might lead us to look more closely at the relationship between miracle stories and the experiences they purport to describe.

Few if any miracle collections constitute a complete record of a particular pilgrimage. They were not compiled throughout the lean and fat years of a shrine's existence, but at particular moments and with specific purposes, for example, when the cult was newly established or when the saint was a candidate for canonisation, or both. We are dealing here not with simple, direct reflections of actual pilgrim experience but with choices made by the authors. We know that 87 per cent of Birgitta's recorded miracles resulted in thanksgiving pilgrimages, while 13 per cent took place at Vadstena, but that does not tell us how many pilgrims in total came to the shrine, and we can therefore have only a partial view of their reasons for coming. We do not know how many people continued to come to late medieval shrines in the hope of a miracle but without result. Nor do we know whether more or fewer people came to shrines in the later middle ages not in consequence of a miracle, but simply having made a vow out of pure penitence or devotion, or in order to obtain an indulgence. It is an interesting fact that although Chaucer implies that people went to Canterbury to give thanks for 'help' previously received, the only two late medieval Becket miracles of which we have any record both took place at the shrine: the cure of an unnamed 'foreigner' was reported to Richard II in 1394, and in 1445 Alexander Stephenson of Aberdeen recovered the use of his feet at Canterbury and went on to fulfil his vow of pilgrimage to Wilsnack.

The shift of emphasis from 'shrine' or 'relic' miracle to 'distance' miracle might conceivably therefore be seen as a shift in the way the compilers of miracle collections represented the saint's activities. Whether or not miracle collections were compiled in the hope of forwarding canonisation, it is to be assumed that they were cast in a form which their authors believed to be approved and expected. The power of the saints, properly understood, was derived solely from the favour they enjoyed with Christ, and therefore partook of the universality of His own power, which was not confined in time or space. Perhaps this point was better understood by ordinary Christians in the late medieval centuries; but because we are talking about a literature produced by interested clergy, not about raw reportage of pilgrim experience, the shift of emphasis under discussion may itself constitute part of the effort to communicate it.

Undoubtedly a prime objective was to implant in the minds of as wide a public as the stories could reach an awareness of the saint's constant power and availability. From the point of view of shrine-custodians, it was desirable both to encourage visits to shrines on high days and holidays (often assisted by the availability of indulgences) and to inculcate a regular habit of remembering the saint and the church. Potential suppliants might come more readily to interpret their experiences – recovery from coma or concussion, from a severe headache, fever or food poisoning, escape from fire, fall or drowning – as miraculous or at least as having been achieved with the saint's 'help', to use Chaucer's word. The all-important climate of belief was extended beyond the vicinity of the shrine, to the benefit of church and believer alike.

These stories depict a functioning Christian community. Family, friends and neighbours witnessed miracles in the domestic setting and themselves joined in petition, vow-making and thanksgiving. Sometimes neighbours or family members who had themselves visited a shrine out of 'devotion', perhaps in the very early days of a cult, urged that a vow should be made to the saint when a child fell sick or experienced an accident. Pilgrims thus publicised the shrine and pilgrimage generated further pilgrimage. The saints belonged to this Christian community, which embraced the living and the dead, and they operated within it as channels of God's ever-present power. Brigands, unjust judges, cheating merchants or grasping landlords all came within the scope of divine justice as mediated through miracles. It remains difficult to know whether later medieval miracle stories reflect an actual change in behaviour, in that Christians to a greater extent than before invoked (and received) divine assistance in the domestic environment, in the fields or the workshop, or whether they signify a different way of depicting the relationship between the shrine and its public.

It may be pertinent to remember here that the later medieval centuries witnessed an ever-increasing number of new devotions centred on Christ Himself and on the Virgin. Such cults had their physical locations – a crucifix or other image, a relic of the True Cross or the Holy Blood, a miraculous host, sometimes garments such as those preserved at Aachen or the numerous 'girdles of the Virgin' which assisted women in childbirth – but there could be no doubt in the believer's mind that these supreme spiritual beings were unlimited in the physical and geographical scope of their actions. Viewed logically, in fact, the underlying universalism of Christ-centred devotions implied a threat to pilgrimage, although few perhaps so perceived it. If Christ Himself was fully present in every church in the sacrament of the altar, what need was there to make a long journey to see a relic which could not be half as precious? The point was already being made in the thirteenth century by the German Franciscan preacher Berthold of Regensburg, but it was neatly countered by the devotion paid to particular miraculous hosts, such as those discovered to have survived a fire at Wilsnack in Prussia in 1383. The experience of seeing relics and images did not lose its appeal in a hurry. Crucifixes and images of the Virgin were so widely distributed that physical recourse to them, whether in petition or thanksgiving, was not difficult, and many of them were reputed miraculous, at least locally. Many miracles, not usually curative but none the less widely reported, were essentially visual in character: images of the Crucified Christ or the Virgin wept, sweated, bled, moved their eyes or bowed their head. Miracles of this stamp remain popular today and are much more frequent than authenticated cures.

Seeing and even touching, being in the presence of particles of divine power made manifest, remained important objectives of the medieval pilgrim; merely seeing the sacrament was believed to be of value. It was commonplace for the proprietors of late medieval crucifixes or images of the Virgin to claim, for example when petitioning the pope for the grant of an indulgence, that the image in question had done many miracles, but we rarely have any record of what they were. There is no medieval miracle collection associated with Our Lady of Walsingham, with the Holy Blood of Hailes or with the Holy Rood of Boxley Abbey, but these were foremost among the great pilgrimage attractions of late medieval England. Lollards and early English Protestants persistently associated pilgrimage with idolatry; they had no doubt that images, including allegedly miraculous images, exerted a considerable magnetism on the gullible and ignorant. Their stress on the point that images were inanimate, unseeing and unhearing, makes sense best as a reaction to the prevalence of opposed popular beliefs.

The importance of images not only as focuses of devotion in their own right but as a means of publicising cults beyond the immediate vicinity of a shrine must of course not be overlooked. The transition to a preponderance of long-distance miracles antedated the appearance of the printing media which made possible the wide dissemination of graphic images, but it is plausible that pilgrim badges, cheap and highly portable, which began to be sold in the west in the twelfth century, may have exerted some influence. Carved or painted images in churches far distant from a saint's burial place also helped to create a wider public for him or her (as of course the distribution of relics had long done), but the effect was often to establish subsidiary focuses of devotion, rather than to direct the attention of potential suppliants to the principal, original shrine. The miracles of King Henry VI, which were reported at Windsor late in the fifteenth century, were almost all done at long range, in obedience to the contemporary norm. Some at least of the men and women involved may have been put in mind of the king by seeing an image (perhaps a pilgrim badge, for these were numerous), although there is no explicit evidence of this. Yorkshire was among the regions from

which few miracles were reported. This was not because Henry's sanctity
was unknown there, but rather, it seems, because an image of him which
had been set up in York Minster served as the cynosure of local attention, and it is possible that the small numbers of pilgrims to Windsor
from certain other parts of the kingdom had a similar explanation.

Indulgences

A different approach to the motivations for later medieval pilgrimage
lays stress on indulgences. Like miracles, or stories of miracles, indulgences
can be regarded as incentives to pilgrimage from the standpoint of both
the prospective pilgrim and the custodians of shrines, who eagerly
sought permission to advertise them. Unlike miracles, indulgences
could be offered by the church on defined terms, although they were
efficacious only if the suppliant was truly repentant. Did the quest for
indulgences become, as some have thought, the dominant motivation of
later medieval pilgrims?

A brief outline of the medieval development of indulgences was given
in the preceding chapter, where it was pointed out that by the fifteenth
century or earlier there were numerous ways of obtaining them and that
even those that were ostensibly associated with a specific pilgrimage
might be obtainable by other means. There is evidence for the development of a variety of beliefs and practices concerning the possibility of
sharing indulgences or assigning their benefits to third parties. An
appropriately businesslike exchange took place between the members of
a small Florentine party who intended to set out for the Holy Land in
1384. One of their number was prevented by civic and family business
from departing, and he asked his friends to make the third part of their
indulgences available to him notwithstanding, to which they willingly
agreed. Leonardo Frescobaldi, who narrates this transaction, observes
sagely, 'May it please God to make [these indulgences] valid for him and
for us'. Indulgences could very easily be interpreted as credits and, to
people who were familiar with that concept in their business dealings,
the idea of a market in such credits may not have seemed too far-fetched.
Testamentary bequests for pilgrimages to be performed on behalf of the
defunct expressed a similar faith that merit could be vicariously credited
to an individual's account, and there were numerous other ways, most
obviously the saying of masses, by which this could be achieved, just as
there were numerous ways other than pilgrimage of earning indulgences.

In principle, this might have made the physical performance of pilgrimage seem less essential, and the wide availability even of plenary indulgences in churches the length and breadth of Christendom may have suggested to some that it was not necessary to put oneself out unduly in order to obtain them. The author of the late fourteenth-century English guidebook *The Stacions of Rome* was insistent that so abundant were the indulgences to be had at Rome that there was no need to go to Compostela or 'over the sea' to Jerusalem. In the mid-fifteenth century the so-called *bourgeois de Paris* (in fact a member of the upper clergy) remarked that the indulgences to be had at Notre Dame de Pontoise, recently badly damaged in the Anglo-French wars, were the same as could be obtained at Rome but were easier to get.

The fact was, however, that pilgrims continued to go long distances to Rome, the Holy Land and Santiago, even if we cannot know for certain whether there were more or fewer of them than in earlier centuries. There was no road or transport revolution in the later middle ages that made these journeys substantially more comfortable than they had earlier been, although the organisation of the traffic and the provision of amenities had in some respects become more sophisticated. Written accounts and guidebooks multiply in the fourteenth and fifteenth centuries and we might, as a result, hope for a better insight into the motivations of pilgrims or at least into their reactions to their experiences. What sort of understanding of the place of indulgences, or indeed of other motives, in their thinking can be gleaned from these sources?

Already in the fourteenth century travellers to the Holy Land frequently itemised the amounts of indulgence to be obtained at the various Holy Places. They probably obtained the information from their guidebooks, for numerous manuscript and later printed specimens of this genre include it, and these broadly provided the model for the personalised narratives that some pilgrims produced on their return. Two of Leonardo Frescobaldi's companions in the Holy Land in 1384–5, Simone Sigoli and Giorgio Gucci, recorded the available indulgences, although Leonardo himself did not. The routine notation of seven years here and seven years there may seem banal, or even offensive, to a modern sensibility, but its meaning for a fourteenth- or fifteenth-century pilgrim has to be interpreted in a different context. Having made the effort to get so far, the pilgrim would certainly expect some spiritual recompense for his or her pains and doubtless took it for granted that indulgences were there for the taking on the usual conditions; but precisely because they were easily obtainable elsewhere it seems unlikely that they represented the sole measure of the benefits derived from a long, hazardous and expensive journey.

Fra Niccolo da Poggibonsi, who performed his pilgrimage in 1345, records the emotional reactions of his party on their arrival at the monastery of St Katherine at Sinai: 'We all began to weep, like people who have found what they were longing for.' Part of this reaction was sheer relief, because the crossing of the desert had been arduous and dangerous, but it would be rash to surmise that that was the whole of it. Fra Niccolo stayed on Sinai for a week, so as to see everything, although it was not usual, he said. to stay more than three days. From the summit of Mount Sinai, 'one can see the whole of Mount Sinai, and also the Red Sea and the place where the people of Israel passed and Pharaoh and his army were drowned in that sea, and one can also see all Arabia and Egypt. And on this summit we sang aloud *Salve Regina*, and prayed, and then returned to the monastery feeling very weak, for the hour was late and it was extremely cold'. There was indulgence there of *colpa e pena*, but that clearly was not all that Fra Niccolo brought back in his luggage.

The Florentines who recorded their experiences thirty years later were literate, but theirs was basically what has been termed 'pragmatic' literacy. It was relatively easy simply to describe the Holy Places, recall the associated biblical incidents and list the indulgences. If you were Giorgio Gucci it was probably second nature also to itemise your daily expenditure, and he may well have thought that this practical information would be of interest to his circle.[4] The merchant-pilgrim might also comment on the nature of the country and on the quality of inns, roads and other amenities. Even if individuals were professionally literate, as priests or as merchants, they might be unaccustomed to baring their souls in prose; if they fail to convey the inwardness of their experience we should not simply presume that there was no such dimension. Fra Niccolo was a religious professional, but that did not of itself guarantee that he would be adept at recording spiritual experience in writing; his narrative clearly reflects religious emotion, but there is no great finesse in its expression. The layman Leonardo Frescobaldi, however, strongly conveys his sheer determination to be a pilgrim. He fell ill at Venice on the outward journey, but refused to be put off by the physicians; he would willingly die, if that was God's will, rather than see Florence again before he had seen the Holy Sepulchre, and he was also determined to make the complete circuit, heading first for Alexandria and thence to Sinai. As his ship sailed down the Adriatic, an unseaworthy vessel, laden with poor pilgrims returning from the Holy Land, broke up and foundered before his eyes; Leonardo commiserated but reflected that their lot was enviable, for they were now at the feet of God.

Saints cannot be used as a measuring rod for the average pilgrim, but accounts of their devotional journeys should not be ignored, for, like miracle stories, they give us insights unobtainable elsewhere. It is clear that a number of saints, whose pilgrimages were certainly undertaken out of the most profound devotional motives and sometimes resulted in visionary experience, none the less assiduously sought indulgences. The Umbrian mystic Angela of Foligno (d. 1309) went to Rome in 1291 to pray for the gift of absolute poverty, and then to Assisi (only a few miles from her native place) to ask for Francis's own blessing on her entry into his Third Order. On the way to Assisi she experienced a vision of the Trinity, followed by further visions at Assisi itself. In August 1300 she went to Assisi for the indulgence of the Portiuncula, joining in the procession, which went from the upper church of San Francesco in the town down to the Portiuncula, culminating in the award of the indulgence. The whole process, as narrated by Brother Arnaldo, Angela's kinsman, confessor and scribe, was interpenetrated by ecstatic visions. Angela's sense of closeness to Christ was nourished by her awareness that Francis's own closeness to Him had been sealed by the reception of the Stigmata, the wounds of the Passion, on his own person. Undoubtedly she went to Assisi to obtain the indulgence, but as a separate event that was swallowed up in a greater whole.

Birgitta of Sweden also went to Assisi, and on one occasion expressed anxiety to Christ about rumours that the indulgence was invalid.[5] Christ reassured her: Francis had observed the lukewarmness of mankind towards God and their love of the world, and had sought from Christ 'a sign of love' (*signum charitatis*) by which men should be inflamed. This sign was the indulgence. At Rome, a woman who had lain sick there for a long time heard Birgitta say that there was absolution from both punishment and guilt to be had there; she repeated this 'as if in scorn'. Christ told Birgitta to reassure her. The indulgences of Rome amounted to more than they sounded; they promised, to those who came with 'a perfect heart', not only forgiveness of sin but bliss everlasting. Let a man have committed so many sins that punishment without end was due to them and he could not live enough years to perform the penance, the indulgences provided alleviation; the sick woman therefore was to have 'patience in her sickness and stability in her faith, and I shall do for her what is for her soul's health'. Here, too, indulgences were understood as a sign of love and hope. At Jerusalem, also, Birgitta received Christ's explicit assurance of the benefits pilgrims themselves and the souls of their loved ones in Purgatory received from the pious performance of their pilgrimage; but the proviso remained that they must be determined to amend their lives for the future.

The rapid translation of Birgitta's *Revelations* into English doubtless helped to promote a positive evaluation in devout English circles of the 'pardon' to be had at Rome and elsewhere. Margery Kempe knew all about Birgitta and visited her house at Rome. Although perfectly convinced of her own salvation, Margery 'purchased' indulgences, at Jerusalem, Rome, Assisi, Syon Abbey and elsewhere. Indeed, she made a second visit to Jerusalem 'to purchase her more pardon', and at Assisi she hoped to 'purchase grace, mercy and remission for herself, for all her friends, for all her enemies and for all the souls in Purgatory'. Margery took it as a sign of her son's conversion when after a sinful life he followed her example and sought out holy places and indulgences.

The understanding of indulgences which is conveyed in the lives and visions of this spiritual elite may shed some light on the ways in which ordinary pilgrims were encouraged, or were supposed, to understand them. There are likely to have been a number of intermediate levels between Birgitta's exalted understanding of the indulgence as an instrument of hope and charity and the crudely quantitative conceptions that we are perhaps too easily inclined to think must have been universal. Some pilgrims, admittedly, must have been influenced by the belief that indulgence of both *culpa* and *poena* was available at a certain place, which was all too often expressed even by people who should have understood the rationale of the device rather better.[6]

Some pilgrimages were doubtless made for single, simple reasons, whether this was to achieve a cure or to receive an indulgence. The latter were inseparable concomitants of later medieval pilgrimage, but were also often part of a more complex experience in which there could be many other ingredients, even if the protagonists did not trouble to analyse their own motives. Different destinations too had different associations, some of course much richer and more resonant than others. There were many shrines which were unlikely to attract the attention of anyone outside the locality were it not that an indulgence was on offer there, and perhaps not even then. It is hard to believe that identical motives impelled pilgrims, male or female, to go from London to Jerusalem, Our Lady of Willesden, St Alban or St Edmund, Cologne or Santiago. For some of its practitioners, too, pilgrimage provided scope for adventure, for indulging curiosity, or simply a means of escape. It is to be remembered also that motivation was not simply a matter for the isolated individual; pilgrimage was also a social experience in which people joined together. More will be said on these matters in the following chapter.

Critics

A distorted mirror-image of the motives of pilgrims can be seen in the criticisms which were made of them throughout the medieval period. In the early fifth century Rutilius Claudius Namatianus wrote a long poem recording his return journey from a Rome already threatened by the Goths, to his native Gaul. At several points along the way he noticed, with intense disapproval, the existence of Christian hermits, men who lived more like beasts than civilised Romans, young men who had gone mad and abandoned promising careers and marriage prospects. The quest for solitude and the abandonment of family responsibilities and urban life looked like barbarism to this observer. For a while, Christianity, aided by the partial destruction of the infrastructure of Roman urban civilisation, succeeded in imposing a contrary view, in which answering the gospel call and making oneself a stranger to the world, a *peregrinus* as Christ Himself had been, represented the supreme ideal, even if only a spiritual elite could fulfil it. The seven centuries that separated Charlemagne from the Reformation, however, saw the redevelopment and repopulation of an elaborate, settled and institutionalised society, on which rulers sought to impose order and discipline. In these circumstances there was always a certain tension between the call to pilgrimage and the call to stability.

In the fifteenth century the humanist Sicco Polenton wrote a life of a thirteenth-century Paduan holy man, Antony, surnamed 'the Pilgrim', presumably drawing on earlier materials which do not survive. Sicco commented that although there had been many preachers, martyrs and hermits, to live voluntarily as a beggar dedicated to perpetual pilgrimage was almost unheard of. 'In my view', he wrote, 'the labour of pilgrimage is great and there is no little shame involved in begging, especially for someone, like our Antony, who as a young man lacked for nothing, but was accustomed in his own home to be rich and to live with honour and refinement'. Having made his choice, Antony set out for Rome and then toured the shrines of Italy; he proceeded to visit St Antony in the Dauphiné and went on to Compostela. After this he saw whatever there was to be seen in France and made the long journey to Germany to venerate the Three Magi and St Ursula and her eleven thousand virgins at Cologne. He next went to the Holy Land for a period of five years. On his return to Padua, Antony was no more popular than he had been before his departure. His attempts to collect alms were derided and the fact that he had given his own wealth away to the poor was remembered with contempt. He took refuge in a church portico where he soon fell ill and died. Although Antony did miracles, the pope refused canonisation, on the grounds that it was enough for the Paduans to have one saint called Antony. The reference was to the illustrious Portuguese-born Franciscan preacher who had made Padua his major theatre of operations and was rapidly canonised after his death in 1231. The thirteenth-century Franciscan chronicler Salimbene made a glancing and contemptuous reference to the lesser Antony, predictably suggesting that the Paduans should rest content with the greater one. The mendicancy of the Franciscans (as radical rigorists within the Order indeed complained) was carefully controlled and institutionalised and served the larger purposes of the church.

Anxiety that pilgrimage might be undertaken by the wrong people and for the wrong reasons was felt, we have seen, from early times. Curiosity, frivolity, mere vagrancy were all to be avoided. The doctrine that individuals should stay at home to carry out their responsibilities was applied to many types of people. If the monk (and still more the nun) should anyway stay within his or her cloister and seek the heavenly rather than the earthly Jerusalem, how much more was the abbot or the abbess bound to stay and attend to the needs of the flock? Rulers, secular and ecclesiastical, had a prior obligation to look after their subjects; fathers and mothers should think first of their families; labourers were bound to the service of their masters. Erasmus envisaged the devout *paterfamilias* performing his pilgrimage by going from room to room of his house, seeing to the welfare of the members of his household. This belief that religion began at home was, of course, consonant with the fundamental Christian tenet which from the very beginning had put the validity of Christian pilgrimage in doubt: 'God is spirit, and those who worship him must worship in spirit and in truth'. The universal availability of Christ in the sacrament, commented on earlier, strengthened the case.

On a less exalted level, fears of vagrancy always qualified the willingness of respectable people to give unequivocal support to pilgrims. A Becket miracle story depicts the wife of a knight refusing a drink to a group of pilgrims with the words, 'Be off, *trutanni* (good-for-nothings)!' In 1384, an official of the Opera di San Jacopo in the cathedral of Pistoia, in Tuscany, recorded giving a paltry sum in alms to a group of what he called *galioffi* who had said that they were going to Compostela, but evidently did not convince him.

Fears of domestic disorder increased the perturbation of the authorities: for example, in England after the Peasants' Revolt in 1381 it was enacted by statute that pilgrims who were begging, as distinct from paying, their way, must carry a letter attesting their *bona fides* and stipulating the date that they were expected to return home. Apparent pilgrims might not be pilgrims at all: it was easy enough to assume the appearance of one and to obtain the authenticating marks, such as pilgrim badges, by gift, theft or sale. In an anonymous sequel to *The Canterbury Tales*, the Miller is depicted stuffing his shirt with looted Canterbury badges: who knows to whom he intended to dispose of them?

Alternatively, pilgrims might be deemed bogus because they had no spiritual understanding of what they were about: for example, they might indeed believe that it was sufficient to behold a relic or a shrine in order to obtain forgiveness of sin, as Hugh Latimer was by no means the first to complain. In a well-known passage of *The Vision of Piers Plowman*, the fourteenth-century English poet William Langland depicted a pilgrim who was festooned with badges, which proclaimed all the far-flung shrines he had visited, but who had never heard of a saint called Truth. It is difficult for the modern observer to know for certain whether the criticisms articulated in the late medieval period justify the judgement that there were more ill-informed and ill-intentioned pilgrims, or more as a proportion of the total, than in earlier centuries. It would seem absurd, on the face of it, to argue that fifteenth-century peasants or town-dwellers were worse-informed about their religion than their eleventh- or twelfth-century forebears, and it is important to avoid value judgements based, consciously or unconsciously, on a romantic belief in a medieval 'peak period', with its epicentre in the twelfth century, followed by a period of decline.

Criticism directed as much at the motives of those who promoted pilgrimage as at those of the pilgrims was certainly not new. Bernard of Clairvaux, in the twelfth century, questioned the investment of large sums of money in the building and decoration of churches. As he clearly perceived, this was 'bread on the water' investment; money thus laid out attracted more in gifts and offerings. The theme that God's poor lost on this deal, for money that should have gone in alms to them went instead to the proprietors of shrines, was noisily endorsed by such later dissidents as the Lollards. Lollard criticism of the rowdy and immoral behaviour of pilgrims, and their anxieties about idolatry, also had abundant precedent. If, as a Lollard, or indeed as a Cathar, a Waldensian or a Hussite, one had reached the point of rejecting the authority of the Catholic church altogether, its saints, its relics and its indulgences also forfeited their power.

Yet pilgrimage had never been entirely the creature of the official church. Officially canonised saints were few, but thousands more holy men and women were locally venerated and became objects at least of small-scale pilgrimage. Bishops were supposed to keep a check on the devotions that were practised in their dioceses, and there are well documented instances of episcopal intervention to suppress unlicensed cults, but they were not always entirely successful. Early in the fourteenth century, Archbishop Greenfield of York struggled to suppress a pilgrimage to an image of the Virgin, which had suddenly started attracting offerings to the parish church of Fraisthorpe in the East Riding. He was worried about idolatry; he wanted to know what distinguished this image from any other. The image came into the possession of Bridlington Priory, and it is clear that the canons did not share the archbishop's reservations; when Greenfield died at the end of 1315 they petitioned for his ban on the pilgrimage to be lifted.

A much more conspicuous example of local and popular resistance to official attempts at suppression concerned the cult of the Holy Blood of Wilsnack; unlike the Virgin of Fraisthorpe this became the focus of a pilgrimage that was well-known and popular over a wide area of northern Europe. In 1520 Luther included it in a list of 'extra-parochial' shrines which were the products of avarice and episcopal negligence and should be suppressed. Canonisation itself, he argued, was not actually necessary to establish a man as a saint before God; its sole use was to set up a public cult and thus reap a profit. According to such a view, shared or followed by other 'heretics', there had been, for centuries, collusion between clerical greed and pilgrim credulity.

The collusion, arguably, went deeper than that. One observer reported that the impulse for the great German Holy Land pilgrimage of 1064–5 came from the mistaken belief that the Last Judgement would occur in 1065 because Easter fell on 27 March, the actual day, as it was believed, of Christ's Resurrection. Many nobles set out for Jerusalem 'deceived' by this 'common opinion (*vulgari opinione*)'. The focus of the narrative rapidly shifts, however, to the rank and nobility of the participants, who included both lay nobles and bishops, although many common people were also moved to go. This account hints at a community of belief between high and low, priest and layman, which may in fact have favoured the maintenance of clerical authority, prestige and income but could hardly have been simply manufactured for that purpose.

There is, however, a fault-line running through the reportage of medieval pilgrimage. Pilgrimage, ideally and in principle, was meritorious; but the comments of contemporaries on popular enthusiasm for pilgrimage often revealed misgivings. If it were the case that a cult or a pilgrimage seemed to attract a mostly plebeian following, the note of censure was often strongly sounded. The same ambiguity occurs in reports of miracles. Exactly similar marvels might be the work of God through His saints, or deceptions of the devil; this was well known. To believe in the one was devotion, to believe in the other, ignorant credulity or stubborn insubordination. 'The church' was of course the adjudicating authority, but 'the church' did not always speak with one voice, and on what basis, anyway, were its judgements made? Inevitably, careful attention was paid to the fruits, or what were thought likely to be the fruits, of plebeian enthusiasms.

The point can be illustrated with reference to two late medieval episodes which turned on alleged visions of the Virgin Mary vouchsafed to humble people. In the summer of 1399 it was reported in Italy that the Virgin had appeared to a peasant – some said in England, some said in the Dauphiné – to announce that her Son intended to destroy the world and that his wrath could be staved off only if everyone went in procession, clad in white and calling for peace and mercy. A wave of popular enthusiasm swept over much of Italy and generated an intricate web of local penitential processions and pilgrimages. Hordes converged on Rome as the year 1400 approached and although this was not officially a Jubilee year it rapidly became one: Boniface IX granted indulgences and ordered exhibitions of the Veronica and other relics. Some also set off for Compostela; as it happened, 1400 was a Santiago Holy Year.

For the most part, the surviving accounts of these events seek to show a broad social consensus at work. With only occasional signs of misgiving, secular and ecclesiastical authorities embraced and appropriated the devotion, shared in it and organised it, marshalling and parading a few lower-class enthusiasts who produced supplementary visions. The original and enduring message was, after all, simply a call to repentance, and no one could object to that: the Great Schism was twenty-one years old and a source of anxiety to all right-thinking people. The famous 'merchant of Prato', Francesco di Marco Datini, a worldly enough man in all conscience, was among those who joined in these pious demonstrations.

Just over three-quarters of a century later in Franconia, there occurred the very different episode of the Drummer of Niklashausen. After a run of bad years and appallingly harsh winter weather which extended into early May 1476, a herdsman called Hans Behem, known previously only as a simple fellow who played the drum at local festivities, launched himself on a brief and explosive career as a preacher. He said that the Virgin Mary had appeared to him and given her instructions for righting the ills of the world, which were rather different from those she had given in Italy in 1399. The call was not merely for penitence but for a violent purge of the rich and powerful and the priests. For a short period pilgrims flocked from a wide area of central and southern Germany to the church of Niklashausen where, Hans allegedly said, total forgiveness of sin could be obtained without the need for the church's indulgences or mediation. Hans Behem rapidly ended his career at the stake. His appeal is represented as being solely to the lower orders of society, although some, perhaps unable to believe that such an abjectly humble person could have devised his own programme, believed that a mysterious friar was behind it.

Some bystanders, however, took it all in their stride, at least until they were authoritatively informed that the pilgrimage was illicit. Johann, count of Wertheim, did not at first know what was going on and would take repressive action, he said, if there was imposture, but for the time being his people were doing well out of supplying the wants of passing pilgrims. One hapless witness, interrogated at Würzburg, said that his wife was a candlemaker and had received orders for two candles from female pilgrims who had also bought a banner and hired a painter to decorate it. Such people, even if not personally caught up in the devotion, had no initial reason to query it. That dissident clergy and perhaps some members of the knightly class were involved cannot be excluded, but the picture given by hostile observers is of a popular insurrection against the established order of society. Hussite Bohemia was not so far to the east, and times were bad; only the previous year there had been a mass pilgrimage to Wilsnack in which many young people joined, motivated above all, it was said, by hunger.

English governments in the later middle ages were repeatedly confronted by popular enthusiasm for dead rebels against the Crown, who were hailed as saints and martyrs: Simon de Montfort in 1265, Thomas of Lancaster in 1322, Archbishop Scrope of York in 1405 and other lesser figures besides. A change of regime or simply the passage of time could change the climate and assuage anxieties. With the deposition of Edward II and the accession of Edward III, Thomas of Lancaster ceased to be a bogeyman and became a candidate for canonisation; with the death of Richard III and the accession of Henry Tudor, pilgrimage to the Lancastrian 'martyr' Henry VI ceased to be alarming. Until this happened, the government, leaning on the Church if need be, was bound to denounce such pilgrimages as not only treasonable but impious and deluded. The rapid and spontaneous assembly of large numbers of people, sometimes in confined spaces, could create legitimate alarm in the minds of public authorities, even when there was no reason to fear subversion. It was pure accident, some said caused by a panicking mule, that resulted in the deaths of over two hundred people in the crush on the Ponte Sant' Angelo during the Roman Jubilee of 1450.

Critics of pilgrimage were not inventing their grounds for criticism, but they may well have simplified the motives of both (or all) sides in the exchange mechanisms that were involved. It was inevitable that a phenomenon that involved so many people of varied rank, wealth and education would be very variously viewed. Where the evidence survives, as in the Florentine Holy Land pilgrimage of 1384 mentioned above, individual differences can be observed between the members of a group who may be presumed to have been fairly homogeneous in terms of social and economic standing and education. Many years ago R. J. Mitchell compiled an account of a Jerusalem pilgrimage that took place in 1458 and of which an unusually large number of memoirs survive. In her view the various protagonists had their experiences in common, but reacted to them according to their individual dispositions and qualities of mind.

One broad and simple distinction between categories of pilgrim motivation suggests itself. On the one hand, there were physical and practical problems from which the suppliant sought relief; on the other there were spiritual objectives, including the forgiveness of sin. Long-distance pilgrimage was more likely to be instigated from 'spiritual' motives, but there was a lot of common ground between pilgrimages of different types, including the all-pervasive conviction of the need to make reparation for the basic sinfulness and imperfection of man. The same sinfulness and imperfection ensured that not all pilgrims or pilgrimage would meet the highest standards of spiritual authenticity.

3

VARIETIES OF PILGRIM

No class of medieval society was entirely excluded from the practice of pilgrimage. Although it is obvious that wealth and high status facilitated the making of long journeys, it is also possible to glimpse people who spent much of their lives in what was effectively a condition of vagrancy lightly coloured as pilgrimage, but who were of such lowly standing that their existence attracted little attention from the authorities. Some scraped a living going on pilgrimages on behalf of others both alive and dead; humble people sought refuge from their troubles in real or alleged pilgrimage. Even the unfree were not totally debarred from access to pilgrimage, and they were not alone in having to seek permission from higher authority to go; almost all pilgrims, of whatever social rank, lay or clerical, were theoretically supposed to do that.

Pilgrimage was by no means just the concern of isolated individuals; it was often a shared experience, both in its inspiration and in its performance. Pilgrims travelled in groups for reasons of security but also out of a desire for conviviality. Sometimes groups came together by chance and decided to travel together (as Chaucer's pilgrims did), sometimes a party of family, friends and neighbours planned the trip and set out together. Reminiscences of such joint enterprises survive in a variety of sources, from the memoirs of Holy Land pilgrims, to the recollection of witnesses at an English inquisition *post mortem* that in 1335 they had joined in fulfilling a vow of pilgrimage to Canterbury made when threatened by a storm on their way home from the Lincoln assizes.

There is ample evidence also not only that pilgrims travelled in family parties but that pilgrimage, over both long and short distances, could be something of a family tradition. Early monastic pilgrims such as Willibald claimed to be seeking detachment from domestic ties as the means to a greater perfection, but he set off from England with his brother and father, asked permission of his friends and kin at Rome before he went to the Holy Land, and later rejoined Winnebald in Bavaria, where their sister Walburga also joined them; his biographer too was his kinswoman. Columba received numerous kinsmen among his visitors on Iona. In an age when monastic foundations and recruitment were often family affairs this was perhaps not surprising.

Much later, the biographer of Birgitta of Sweden (d. 1373) saw a strong hereditary element in both her holiness and her pilgrimages, for not only her father, Birger, but four generations of his family before him had been Jerusalem pilgrims. There can be few more remarkable illustrations of this propensity than the patrician Rieter family of Nuremberg. Successive generations went to Jerusalem. Hans Rieter in 1384 is the first known to have done so. Peter Rieter in 1428 went to Santiago and Finisterre and also to Rome, where he saw the Veronica and kissed the feet of Martin V. In 1432 he combined pilgrimages to Milan and to St Augustine at Pavia with a visit to the Council of Basel, and in 1436 he went with several companions to the Holy Land. His last recorded pilgrimage was to Rome for the 1450 Jubilee, and on this occasion he and his wife were accompanied by their son Sebald (who bore the name of the pilgrim-saint of Nuremberg). Sebald went to Santiago and Finisterre in 1462, incorporating other shrines, including Our Lady of Einsiedeln, into a lengthy itinerary. He undertook his Jerusalem pilgrimage two years later, and like his son Sebald the younger, who went in 1479, he left a written account of his travels. Eustachius Rieter performed his pilgrimage in 1498 and, later still, Hannibal Rieter went to the Holy Land in 1563 and Joachim Rieter in 1608 or 1609. Was so powerful a family tradition felt by succeeding generations as inspiration or as obligation?

Collective identities affected the practice of pilgrimage in other ways. Members of different social and occupational groupings enjoyed different degrees of freedom and opportunity to travel. There is much to be learned about the place pilgrimage occupied in the life of medieval society by looking at the involvement in it of different groups, and there are a number of polarities which it is instructive to examine: clergy/laity and men/women are among the most obvious.

Monks, Clergy and Holy Men

All students of medieval history are familiar with the broad division of the clergy into two segments: the seculars (those dwelling 'in the world', like parish priests and cathedral canons, who were in different ways dedicated to the public service of the church) and the regulars (monks, friars, and all those living under a religious rule, including nuns). The 'clergy' did not constitute a single homogeneous grouping. In terms of status and wealth the priest who served a poor rural parish had little in common with the bishop of Paris or Winchester. What they did have in common was that both had received priestly orders, but, particularly in the earlier medieval centuries, this was not the defining mark of the entire body of 'clergy'. It was by no means invariable for monks to be ordained priests (a status which was, of course, reserved to men) but for a variety of reasons this increasingly became the later rule. The lay brother, whose function in several religious orders was to carry out practical tasks and conduct business in the outside world, was a lesser breed, clearly demarcated from the choir monk and occupying separate accommodation.

There is evidence that lay brothers sometimes carried out pilgrimages on behalf of the communities to which they belonged. A carved gravestone from the ruined monastery of Sorö in Sweden, datable to around 1300 but known only from an eighteenth-century drawing, commemorated Jonas, a lay brother and servant, who went twice to Jerusalem, three times to Rome and once to St James. He was shown with a sword, a shell on a large purse round his waist, and a palm. Another Swedish gravestone, from the church of Tyrsted, commemorated one Petrus Kaeller, who may be identifiable with a lay brother of the monastery of Esrom who witnessed a will in 1301. He too is shown with palm, purse and shell but also with a long pilgrim staff. Perhaps the 'Pilgrim' whose burial place was recently found in Worcester Cathedral, with a magnificent ash staff and leather boots, was a servant of the cathedral community.[1]

A neat textbook list of religious orders (Benedictines, Cistercians, Carthusians, Augustinian canons, Franciscans, Dominicans and so forth) may disguise from us the sheer variety of ways of life that at any one moment were being led by individuals who regarded themselves as vowed to religion. This motley crew of hermits, recluses and miscellaneous holy men (and women) did not always enjoy the approval either of the ecclesiastical hierarchy or of the proponents of a strictly demarcated religious profession, but they existed, and received the alms and sometimes the veneration of their neighbours. Among the secular clergy, too, there clustered a host of men in minor orders below the ranks of priest and deacon, who effectively led a secular existence and were not committed to celibacy. The term 'clerk' was widely applied to persons of a certain degree of education: the young men who frequented the schools of Paris and elsewhere were commonly denoted 'clerks' (certainly in northern Europe), but were often entirely secular in both sacramental status and behaviour. Hermits too were hard to classify exactly. Large numbers of unbeneficed clergy, who were a source of anxiety to the authorities when they turned to vagabondage and even crime, scraped a living however they could; performing pilgrimages on behalf of others was one way of earning a crust.

On one level, all this suggests how difficult it can sometimes be to distinguish clergy from laity, but equally pertinent is the fact that what may be called a professional commitment to religion was too diffuse and widespread to be neatly confined within the bounds of a 'system' of approved religious orders. At all times, men (and women) who believed that they possessed this commitment were prominent among the ranks of Christian pilgrims. Indeed the quasi-permanent practice of pilgrimage could come close to being regarded as itself a form of the religious life. Abbot William of Hirsau (d. 1091) was said by his biographer to have revitalised the practice of religion in Germany by instructing 'all the grades of the ecclesiastical order' in their duties. These 'grades' were, in order: monks; bishops, priests and other clergy; laymen; virgins, widows and wives; and last of all, 'the poor of Christ and pilgrims', who were taught 'to be content with little, to tread the world and all its glory beneath their feet'. In 1335 Edward III extended his protection to William de Nesham, who had just arrived in England from the Holy Land and was dependent on the alms of the faithful; a few months later William was on his way back there. William's religious status is unspecified; he may have been a layman who had committed himself to a life of perpetual holy vagabondage or he may have belonged to what was undoubtedly a vague and extensive clerical penumbra.

To be a monk in the earlier medieval centuries, as we have already seen, did not invariably mean settling permanently within a stable community, although this option, with its promise of discipline, comradeship and collective security, more and more commended itself. Celtic or Anglo-Saxon monks often lived according to a more flexible pattern, at least for part of their lives, in which open-ended *peregrinatio* played a prominent part. An important shift took place in official attitudes to the practice of pilgrimage by monks as the monastic life itself took on a greater degree of definition and the authority of monastic 'rules' (in the west, chiefly the Rule of St Benedict) received the support and approval of both ecclesiastical and secular rulers. St Benedict, in sixth-century Italy, had strong views about the need for monastic stability and for settled obedience to an abbot within a community context, and he denounced the impropriety of rudderless wandering by monks. These views were current, although not universally endorsed, in the eighth century. At some time around the year 720, the English abbess Eangyth consulted Boniface about the advisability of the pilgrimage to Rome, which she and her daughter wanted to make for the forgiveness of their sins, as many of their kin and acquaintance had already done. She was not speaking just for nuns when she quoted the discouraging rulings of councils which had laid it down that everyone should remain in his or her appointed place, fulfilling their vows in stability. The letter clearly reveals the tension between conflicting ideals, to which the professed religious were at this period particularly liable.

Patterns of life in which pilgrimage formed one strand in a long-term professional commitment to religion can be observed in later centuries. The Armenian hermit Simeon, already mentioned as the first pilgrim known to have gone from Italy to Compostela, around 980, spent some time in the Holy Land before coming west to Rome. From there he set out for Tuscany and then took the road across the Alps, venerating the relics at Piacenza and Pavia before visiting Santiago and St Martin of Tours. On his return to Italy he settled to the religious life at the monastery of San Benedetto Po near Mantua, where he died around 1016. In the mid-twelfth century, Godric of Finchale near Durham and Raniero of Pisa were merchants-cum-pilgrims during the earlier phases of their careers. Godric went to Jerusalem and also to Rome and Compostela, and nearer home he was a devotee of St Cuthbert and other regional saints. Raniero in his early years was influenced by a Corsican holy man called Albert who toured the shrines of the far west barefoot, going to Compostela, Finisterre and Tours, spending three years at Paris (where he tried to dissuade Louis VII from going on crusade), and dying eventually at the great Cistercian monastery of Clairvaux. Raniero's own pilgrimage path took him in a different direction. Still not quite resolved on a holy life, he went to Jerusalem with a load of cheeses, which he hoped to sell during the Lenten fast; when he noticed a foul stench arising from them he took the hint, gave away all his property and adopted the life of a hermit.

The description of Raniero's years in the east introduces us to the solitaries who lived on the walls of Jerusalem, who were his dining companions. One of them fell out with Raniero when the latter received notice from God that he was henceforth only to drink water. On another occasion he was bitten by 'some beast' while eating with a solitary, and undertook a pilgrimage to 'St Abrahaminus' (presumably the tomb of Abraham) to seek a cure. On this trip he was accompanied by a 'religious man' from 'our part of the world' called Homodei ('man of God') who was so badly lacerated as a result of the journey that he died on return to Jerusalem; the road was so rough that horses came unshod, and shoes unsoled on it. Raniero then took lodgings with a 'religious matron' and organised a boy to collect alms for him. The emphasis now shifts to his visits to the Holy Sepulchre, his visions, his reading of the Psalter and his prayers for his kin and friends. He came to believe, layman though he was, that he had received a call to do penance on behalf of God's people. His long-term Holy Land residence encapsulated particular pilgrimages, to the site of Christ's transfiguration on Mount Tabor, and to Bethlehem (to which he was miraculously transported from Jerusalem in time for the vigil of the Nativity). He was intermittently in contact with other Pisans who came to Jerusalem to pray while on business to the Holy Land, and he eventually returned to his native city in the company of one of them.

Both Godric and Raniero exemplified the fluidity of the options open to religious enthusiasts. So too did Raimondo Palmario of Piacenza (d. 1200), who derived his nickname from his pilgrimage to Jerusalem as a very young man. His early aspirations to a life of holiness were frustrated by marriage and family cares; after the death of his wife and all but one of his children he dreamed of becoming a perpetual pilgrim and of returning to Jerusalem to die. He had already been to Compostela and the shrines of Provence when Christ revealed to him at Rome that he must return to Piacenza and devote himself to works of charity. He then spent twenty-two years labouring in the hospital he himself founded in his native city. For all these men, pilgrimage was, at least in the earlier part of their lives, a pious and ascetic exercise which served as a staging post on the way to a greater perfection; by somewhat different routes all of them moved on, although Raimondo had to have the path pointed out to him. His story even suggests that, if persisted in beyond a certain stage, pilgrimage constituted an abnegation of responsibility. Raniero too returned to his native city and took on the role of counsellor to his fellow-citizens.

The steps which carried the holy man towards perfection led to a life of either charity or contemplation and away from a type of pious exercise which, however meritorious, required bodily strength rather than mature wisdom. Antony the Pilgrim of Padua, mentioned in the previous chapter, seems not to have convinced his fellow-citizens of the validity of a life of perpetual mendicancy and pilgrimage. Another thirteenth-century north Italian holy man, the goldsmith Fazio of Cremona, is supposed to have gone eighteen times to Compostela and as many times to Rome, but he struck a very different balance; he continued to ply his trade, making liturgical vessels for preference, and he was also active in charitable work on behalf of others.

In the ideal structure of the medieval church, the monk was bound to the cloister by a vow of stability and forfeited freedom of movement. As the monastic 'order' became more narrowly defined, monks took on roles which were essentially discharged within the cloister and, more specifically still, within the choir, primarily as exponents of liturgy and intercessory prayer, secondarily of biblical scholarship, historiography or the literature of contemplation. Monastic writers in the eleventh and twelfth centuries insisted on this prior commitment to obedience, stability and contemplation. The spiritual man was to be alienated from the world, a *peregrinus*, a stranger in relation to it, but not a vagrant. It was not merely possible, but tempting, to interpret life itself, that ineluctable progress from the cradle to the grave, as a pilgrimage from an earthly to a heavenly birth. The monk had chosen the perfect environment in which to enact this pilgrimage.

It is none the less apparent that the longing to give a more physical expression to the alienation of the self from the world, as well as to visit shrines and holy places as other Christians did, remained very much alive among the cloistered religious, and as new peoples entered into the circle of Roman Christianity, so the monks among them (like the Icelander Niklas of Munkathvera who went to Rome and the Holy Land *c*.1150) felt the same attractions. The obvious danger, to which religious superiors had to be alive, was that mere boredom, restlessness and curiosity could easily be dressed up as something more exalted. In principle, restrictions applied to domestic as well as to foreign pilgrimage by monks. At the end of the twelfth century, a papal legate endeavoured to prevent English monks from going on pilgrimage to St Thomas (at Canterbury) or St Edmund (at Bury). It was significant here that Abbot Samson of Bury objected to what he interpreted as an infringement on his authority over his monks: the power to forbid or to permit was, on this view, vested in the abbot. A century later Archbishop Winchelsey of Canterbury was complaining that the monks of Christ Church were gadding about after the new St Thomas (Thomas Cantilupe of Hereford) and the new St Edmund (Edmund of Abingdon, archbishop of Canterbury, enshrined at the Cistercian abbey of Pontigny in Burgundy). Chaucer's Monk, we are explicitly told, cared not a straw for any rule that would confine him to his cloister.

As Samson's objections suggested, abbots enjoyed both special freedoms and special responsibilities. Early in the twelfth century, Geoffrey of Vendôme argued strongly that an abbot's duty to the monks in his care should deter him from pilgrimage. The particular case that prompted his letter admittedly involved a pilgrimage to Jerusalem, which would mean the maximum length of absence (and risk of not returning at all), although the argument could be applied to journeys of any length. The letter belonged to a period – just after the Christian conquest of Jerusalem – when the lure of the Holy Places was perhaps at its strongest; abbots as well as bishops had been among those who sucumbed to it during that earlier phase of increasing pilgrimage from the west which preceded, and helped to prepare for, the First Crusade.

One of them was Richard, abbot of La Chaise-Dieu in Normandy, who in 1026–8 led a mass pilgrimage to the east sponsored by the duke of Normandy. For Richard the journey was felt as spiritual obligation rather than dereliction of duty. The same fervour which had ended by making him the head of a religious community meant that he became restive after a period of monastic stability and, like Willibald four hundred years previously, felt the compulsion to expose himself to privation and peril for the sake of the Lord. Richard's pilgrimage was ultimately beneficial to those he left at home. Like Wilfrid or Benedict Biscop returning from Rome over four hundred years earlier, he came back not only spiritually strengthened but armed with relics with which he enriched friends and other communities. Bede had explicitly reasoned that Benedict's journeys, apart from being instructive to himself, were profitable to his monks, not only because of what he brought back but because by undertaking the burdens of travel himself he freed the rest of them to remain in their peaceful seclusion.

After c.1100 new religious orders appeared upon the western European scene, which combined features of monasticism with the pastoral responsibilities of priests. First came the varieties of regular canons who lived under the so-called Rule of St Augustine, adapted to the purposes of particular congregations. These communities varied greatly in character, some of them in fact strongly resembling groups of monks and placing their chief emphasis on scholarship and contemplation, others becoming more involved in charitable activity or in missionary and colonising enterprise, as the Premonstratensians did in central Europe. The military religious orders, Templars, Hospitallers and the rest, represented specialised offshoots of this tendency, as also did the Order of Preachers, whose founding father St Dominic was himself an Augustinian canon, in the early thirteenth century.

The Templars and Hospitallers were to a peculiar degree involved with pilgrimage because of their special responsibilities for the welfare of travellers to the Holy Land. These were all priestly orders, and so the Friars Minor also rapidly became, although their founder St Francis was himself never ordained priest. Albeit they all lived under obedience and were therefore obliged to seek permission for pilgrimage as for other journeys, members of these orders were not subject to precisely the same constraints that were supposed to apply to cloistered monks. Friars, like monks, might and did become bishops (although not everyone approved), but the burdens of routine pastoral care fell on the clerical order, and the members of that order, serving the world, were at liberty to travel around it on pilgrimage as for other purposes. Pastoral responsibility of course imposed its own contraints: a priest was supposed to seek leave of absence from his diocesan bishop and to make arrangements for the care of his parish before embarking on a long-distance pilgrimage.

Throughout the centuries Rome, the seat of the chief bishop of Christendom, attracted especially large numbers of clergy, who were pilgrims at the same time as they pursued other business. The supreme power of absolution possessed by the successor of St Peter was but one facet, albeit a very important one, of an authority which commanded the loyalty of men who were engaged in building up the church in their native lands and strengthening its hold over a still barbarian society, or who were engaged in missionary work. Rome was both the fount of this authority and also an inexhaustible source of the visible emblems of spiritual power – relics, books, images. As the papacy established itself at the head of an ever more elaborate and bureaucratised governmental structure, the inducements to take the road to Rome increased for both regular and secular clergy. Archbishops went to Rome to receive the *pallium*, which was the symbol of their office, and in the later middle ages bishops made, or were supposed to make, regular duty calls on the pope; lesser clergy went in quest of benefices and there was a stream of envoys and proctors pursuing lawsuits and other ecclesiastical business at the curia.

Already in the late seventh century St Wilfrid went to Rome as both litigant and pilgrim, and we know what urban churches Archbishop Sigeric of Canterbury visited, and in what order, when he went to Rome in 993 to receive his *pallium*. The term applied to an official episcopal visit to the pope, *ad limina*, implicitly identified it as a pilgrimage to the 'thresholds' or shrines of the apostles (*ad limina apostolorum*), and also referred unmistakably to the identification of the pope with St Peter. For much of the fourteenth century, however, this traffic went to Avignon rather than to Rome; the displacement of the Vicar of Christ and successor of the apostles from the shrines and relics which it was his responsibility to guard was a source of increasing discomfort to many observers.

Measures taken by the popes to promote pilgrimage to Rome aroused a response as much from the clergy, secular and regular, as from the laity. We know that Willam of Derby, monk and previously prior of St Mary's Abbey at York, went to the Jubilee of 1300, because he died of injuries received in a crowd of people who pressed forward to see the exhibition of the Veronica at St Peter's. Subsequent Jubilees continued to attract monks and it did not escape notice that this raised an issue of principle. Should the Vicar of Christ be encouraging monks to evade their confines and even disobey their superiors? A falsified version of the bull (*Unigenitus*) by which Clement VI in 1343 proclaimed the Jubilee that was to be held in 1350, declared that monks were authorised to go to Rome to receive the Jubilee indulgence even if they could not obtain the permission of their superiors. The pope had not in fact said any such thing, but he was called upon subsequently to deal with several cases of monks who had acted on his presumed permission and were now seeking re-admission to their communities (sometimes they had committed the additional impropriety of dressing as laymen for greater security). So deep an impression did the forged version of *Unigenitus* make in England, that, when preparations for the 1450 Jubilee were afoot, Henry VI's proctor at the curia (an abbot) sought to impress on Nicholas V the evil consequences of 'Clement VI's statute' and to urge that the benefits of the indulgence should be made available to English monks on easier terms.

It is apparent from the permissions to travel that were quite frequently granted by the kings of England that abbots, who occupied a uniquely privileged position within their communities, made pilgrimages not only to Rome but to other shrines. These journeys, like those of archbishops and other senior clergy, whether or not they were designated pilgrimages, were of interest to the kings, as indeed were those of all their more powerful and influential subjects both lay and ecclesiastical. This was particularly so in the fourteenth century, when efforts were being made not only to limit the flow of men, money and horses abroad at a time of nearly perpetual warfare, but to stem the influence of a papacy which was suspected of bias towards the French. An ostensible pilgrim to Compostela, once across the channel, might easily decide to call in at Avignon. The movements of lowlier secular clergy were less controversial, although after the middle of the fourteenth century the English government made intermittent efforts to block the flow of bene-fice-seekers to Rome as part of its policy of diminishing papal influence over the English church. When the kings of England granted licences to shipmasters to convey a stated number of pilgrims to Compostela, it was not infrequently stipulated that there should be no clergy among the passengers. In 1390, however, Richard II authorised several English clerks to go to Rome for the Jubilee indulgence of that year and one of them was explicitly permitted to seek a benefice.

There was another reason for clerical pilgrimage. Laymen (as of course also ecclesiastics) of rank travelled with an entourage that included household clerks, who ministered to their spiritual needs en route. They naturally accompanied their lords on pilgrimage and may often have acted as interpreters, in so far as they were masters of the international language of the educated. Earl Rognvald of the Orkneys, embarking on his Holy Land pilgrimage in the 1150s, requested his bishop, William, to accompany him for this very purpose, and a similar role was played by a monk who accompanied Cocubur, a kinsman of the king of Connaught, to Canterbury in the early 1170s. Communication with noble pilgrims who came from Poland to St Gilles de Provence in the early twelfth century may well have been effected by the same means.

The records of the almsgiving of the Opera di San Jacopo of Pistoia in the late fourteenth and fifteenth centuries occasionally mention a 'poor priest' who had passed through the city on his way to Rome. Sometimes foreign priests sang in the cathedral and were paid for their trouble. Such people probably belonged to the unknowable number of unbene-ficed priests who existed all over Europe. They may have lived in hopes of obtaining a benefice at Rome or, resigned to a life of more or less holy vagabondage, picked up scraps of sacerdotal (and musical) employment where they could, perhaps performing pilgrimages on behalf of deceased persons who had stipulated in their wills that an 'honest priest' should carry out one or more pilgrimages on their behalf. English testators in the fifteenth and early sixteenth centuries sometimes requested that masses should be said at 'Scala Celi', a chapel at the church of Sant' Anastasio just outside Rome, where, it was believed, St Bernard of Clairvaux had experienced a vision of the release of a soul from Purgatory. Masses said there were consequently believed to be particularly efficacious for that purpose. For all these reasons we can imagine that there was at most times a goodly number of the 'clerical proletariat' on the road to Rome and elsewhere. Margery Kempe's encounters on her last overseas pilgrimage in the 1430s indicate that it was not uncommon to find religious people of different kinds on the road. At Aachen she met an English monk who was on his way to Rome, and she had reason to be glad of the company of a 'poor friar' on the long road back to Calais.

There were no women priests, but in essentials the same restrictions applied to pilgrimage by both male and female religious. They had embarked on an interior quest for the heavenly Jerusalem and should not be distracted from it by the yearning to set eyes on the mere earthly city. Anxiety about pilgrimage by nuns had a particularly sharp edge, however, for here concerns about the propriety of travel by cloistered religious and about the frailty of women came together.

Women

There is no room here to rehearse in detail the mixed and debatable effects which the coming of Christianity had on the status of women and the attitudes of men to them. Their social and legal status had not remained unchanging during the long development of the Mediterranean civilisation into which Christianity was born, nor was it uniform in every geographical area of that civilisation. In broad terms it can be said that while in principle Christianity inculcated a belief in the spiritual equality of the sexes which could never be totally denied, it failed to overcome social prejudices and deeply ingrained beliefs in the intellectual inferiority and moral as well as physical frailty of women. In medieval Christendom therefore they remained largely confined to the domestic roles which were deemed to serve the purposes of the family and thereby of the larger society.

There was, as a result, a distinct unease in face of some of the claims that were made by women who enthusiastically embraced the new faith, among them the right to express their spiritual liberty by breaking out of the seclusion that was deemed appropriate to respectable women and joining their male counterparts in pilgrimage. This unease was vigorously expressed by a Roman aristocrat turned eastern hermit, Abba Arsenius, who, at some time in the early years of the fifth century, was visited, against his will, by a 'pious Roman virgin' who had refused to heed advice that he would not want to see her. His reception of her must have been disconcerting: 'Do you not know you are a woman and cannot just go anywhere you like?'

As the documented history of medieval pilgrimage and the evidence of hundreds of miracle stories make perfectly plain, ordinary Christian women did in fact enjoy a large measure of freedom to go on pilgrimage throughout the medieval centuries. The difficulties and restrictions they laboured under applied, for the most part, to their participation in travel of any kind rather than to pilgrimage in particular, and some of them still hamper female travellers today. The unluckiest ones were, perhaps paradoxically, the most pious, the spiritual descendants of Egeria and the Roman virgin who was so brusquely rebuffed by Abba Arsenius. As the status of the 'nun', the woman vowed to the lifelong profession of religion, gradually took on sharper definition, so the conviction that this profession implied strict enclosure gained ground. To an extent this development paralleled that of the view, already noted, that the monk too should preserve *stabilitas* within his cloister, but the deep-seated belief that women, as daughters of Eve, were innately sensual and fragile beings intensified these fears.

We have Bede's authority for the growing popularity of Rome with Englishmen and women alike by 700. In a well-known letter written about 750, Boniface of Wessex urged Archbishop Cuthbert of Canterbury and the other English bishops to prevent the pilgrimages of 'matrons and veiled women' to Rome; if Boniface was to be believed, they fell by the wayside with alarming frequency, so that there was scarcely a town between England and Rome which did not boast a harlot of English stock. Only a few years before he wrote to Archbishop Cuthbert, however, Boniface had met at Rome the saintly abbess of Minster in Thanet, Eadburga. Earlier still, like the abbess Eangyth already mentioned, she had consulted him about her prospective pilgrimage; they were old friends and correspondents and a great mutual respect clearly existed between them. He had replied that he would not presume to advise her for or against going to Rome, but he would admit that another holy woman, 'our sister Wiethburga', said that she had found great peace of mind at the shrines of the apostles. Boniface then struck a practical note: he would advise Eadburga not to travel until she received word that the depredations of the Saracens in the vicinity of Rome had abated. Perhaps he later changed his mind about the desirability of women going on pilgrimage at all, or perhaps his letter to Cuthbert simply stated a prudent general rule, which need not apply to a woman or women who possessed superior qualities. Certainly he had not been consistently discouraging: a letter written to him in 745 by the Cardinal Deacon Gemmulus indicates that Boniface had provided 'handmaids of God' with introductions when they visited the *limina apostolorum*. The movements of nuns remained a matter of special concern. A synod held at Friuli in north-eastern Italy in the early 790s prohibited pilgrimage by nuns and spelled out an insuperable objection. Religious women were bound to avoid all contact with men, but all the world knew that women could not travel without a male escort. The conclusion was simple and inescapable: such women could not go on pilgrimage. A special responsibility rested on nuns who ruled over their communities. The biographer of Altmann, bishop of Passau, narrated with a sort of gloating horror the atrocious fate of the well-born and beautiful young abbess who insisted, against all advice, on joining the great German pilgrimage to the Holy Land in 1064–5; seized by the Saracens, she was raped repeatedly until she died. Not only had she exposed her sanctified person to unnecessary risk, she had ignored good advice and abandoned the nuns who were entrusted to her care.

In 1299 Pope Boniface VIII affirmed the necessity of strict enclosure of nuns, in the bull *Pericoloso*. The bull made no explicit reference to pilgrimage. Nuns left the cloister for other reasons; estate business and litigation seem to have been uppermost in the pope's mind. Some bishops, attempting to enforce the provisions of the bull, logically interpreted the prohibition as applying to pilgrimage. That there was a general acceptance of the principle is indicated by the fact that in 1350 the king of France and others requested Pope Clement VI to permit the benefits of the Jubilee indulgence to be made available to certain categories of people who were unable to make the journey to Rome, among them enclosed nuns. Among the permissions to travel to Rome which Edward III issued in the course of 1350 only one was for a nun, the abbess of Barking. She was Matilda Montague, a member of a distinguished family which was high in the royal favour, and not perhaps to be regarded as a typical nun, or even as a typical abbess. Chaucer's fictional Prioress on the road to Canterbury a few decades later has often been taken to be a gently satirical portrait precisely because she should not really have been there, but it seems clear that modest domestic pilgrimages were in fact undertaken by nuns, with or without the approval of the diocesan bishop. Matilda Montague on the road to Rome or the Prioress on the road to Canterbury had to be properly escorted. The Prioress had two other nuns with her and also her priest, who told his own Tale. We do not know what Matilda Montague's entourage was, but she must have had priests and male servants with her and may well have attached herself to a larger party for greater security. Naturally she had to take ship across the channel, thus inevitably coming into further contact with men.

Securing an appropriate escort was also a problem for women who had dedicated themselves to God without actually entering the cloister, the female equivalents of the holy men whom we have already encountered. Some particularly favoured individuals received supernatural help. Bona of Pisa (d. 1207), whose mobility and capacity for levitation were such that she has been proclaimed the patron saint of air hostesses, was a great devotee of St James and a frequent pilgrim to Compostela; sometimes she travelled with the usual sort of mixed party, but sometimes she was escorted by St James himself. Two centuries later, Ursulina of Parma set out with her mother to confront the antipope Clement VII at Avignon and decided to visit the shrine of St Mary Magdalen in Provence on the way. Her mother was exceedingly nervous about undertaking this journey unprotected, but they were accompanied, until they were close to the Magdalen's shrine, by a young man who (as Ursulina knew) was really St John the Evangelist.

Such marvellous stories dramatise very real anxieties, which were at their most acute for women whose religious aspirations imposed the absolute requirement of virginity, or at least chastity. Margery Kempe of Lynn, a generation after Ursulina, adopted the role of holy woman despite her marriage and numerous children, but she had an unequalled gift for alienating her travelling companions by her extravagantly devout behaviour. Attempting to get back across Europe from her last pilgrimage to Wilsnack in Prussia she was conscious of the physical weakness of advancing age, as she struggled to limp along fast enough to keep up with her temporary companions, and she was also horribly afraid of rape. An innkeeper's wife disapproved strongly of her travelling alone with the poor friar who had befriended her and tried to attach her to a larger party who were travelling with a cart. No disguised saint came to Margery's rescue, but Christ assured her of her safety, and somehow or other she always found someone, however reluctant, to bear her company. For women whose daily lot as wives and mothers brought them into familiar and even carnal contact with men, the necessity of male escort was less problematical, and for many who were of middling to lower social rank, and who did not traverse vast distances to contract their marriages, accompany their husbands on foreign expeditions or look after estate business, pilgrimage must have been a major pretext for travel. It is beyond dispute that thousands of medieval women did in fact make pilgrimages of varying lengths, but this does not mean that they encountered no difficulties or restrictions in doing so. The respectable woman was obliged to travel in a respectable manner, suitably escorted according to her rank and marital status. During her travels, Margery Kempe encountered Dame Margaret Florentyne, who had come from Rome to Assisi for the indulgence of the Portiuncula, accompanied by a high-class retinue; at Aachen there was a worshipful woman of London to whose party Margery tried unsuccessfully to attach herself. Wives frequently went on pilgrimage with their husbands, younger women with their parents, widows with their sons or in a larger party of widows.

Women doubtless usually set out with people who were already known to them, like Elizabeth Keynes, who went from Dorset to the Holy Land with a party of neighbours late in 1373 and died there, as the neighbours testified on their return. In September 1378 Ralph Flesshewer of Chesterfield received permission to go to Rome with his wife and son, but the party also included six other women with different surnames; this may have been a party of neighbours assembled around the nucleus of the Flesshewer family. A thirteenth-century Tuscan holy woman, Viridiana of Castelfiorentino, went both to Compostela and to Rome as companion to a group of *matronae*, but it must be supposed that there were also male servants in the party, to look after the horses and handle the baggage as well as to provide protection. Dorothea of Montau's difficult husband caused a sensation when he dismissed the *auriga* who was driving their cart on the way to Einsiedeln in 1385; he himself was ailing, and Dorothea had to take over the reins, attend to the horses and service the cart. All along the way people flocked to see this spectacle.

The permissions to travel issued to pilgrims both male and female by the English royal government sometimes but by no means invariably specify the numbers of servants and horses the named pilgrim was licensed to take with him or her. In 1403, for example, Agnes Bardolf, widow of Thomas Mortimer, knight, received licence to go to Rome, Cologne and other parts with twelve men and twelve horses. The numbers are often much smaller than this, and it is obvious that such little groups must have joined up with others for company and safety on the roads. Elizabeth Ashton, who went to the Holy Land in 1348, was licensed to travel with a chaplain and two yeomen, but this was scarcely sufficient escort for such a journey. She must have taken at least one lady's maid, and it is probable that the royal licence mentions only the clerk and the able-bodied man in whose movements the government was interested. We do not know what company Isolda Parewastel of Bridgwater in Somerset had in the Holy Land, where she spent three years in the 1360s, but it did not prevent her from being seized and tortured, so she said, by the Saracens.

If ideology did little to prevent the laywoman from setting out on pilgrimage, there were restrictions on female access to certain shrines, especially those in monastic custody. At the beginning of the ninth century the women among a mixed crowd of pilgrims demanded to be allowed to venerate some relics which had recently arrived at the abbey of Fleury; the monks contrived a solution by erecting a sort of marquee outside the church, in which they exhibited the relics at stated times. Women were barred from St Cuthbert's shrine at Durham after the installation of monks there in the late eleventh century, which helped to account for the fact that St Godric (d. 1170) did over 60 per cent of his recorded miracles at Finchale, only a few miles away, for female clients. Women required special dispensation to enter Cistercian churches as pilgrims; in the second half of the thirteenth century Englishwomen were given such dispensation so that they could venerate their fellow countryman Edmund of Abingdon at his tomb in the Burgundian abbey of Pontigny. Women were sometimes restricted to shrines in the cemeteries or gatehouses of churches of the stricter orders. There was no admission for women to the chapel of St John the Baptist in St John Lateran, but they could obtain the same indulgences by touching the door.

An abundance of anecdotal and record evidence makes it plain that some women made the long and arduous journeys from the far corners of Europe to Rome, Jerusalem or Compostela. Few can have led a more adventurous life than the tenth-century Icelander Gudrid who survived shipwreck with her first husband, went to Greenland with her second, and to 'Vinland', where she gave birth to a son, with her third. A widow yet again, she went from Iceland to Rome as a pilgrim; on her return she built a church and lived as an anchoress until her death. Hers was hardly the typical life of the medieval European woman, yet in its final stages – pilgrimage as a widow, followed by a life of pious seclusion – it exemplified a not uncommon pattern. When the chronicler Ralph Glaber early in the eleventh century remarked on the surge of pilgrimage to the Holy Land that occurred after 1000, he laid particular stress on the unprecedented participation of women. Four centuries and more later there were women among the passengers on the Venetian galleys which plied a regular trade to the Holy Land. The fictional Wife of Bath and the real Margery Kempe of Kings Lynn were both among them; both also went to Rome and to Santiago de Compostela. Birgitta of Sweden went with her husband to Santiago in 1343 and to Rome for the Jubilee of 1350, taking up permanent residence there; but in 1372, the year before her death, she was divinely instructed that the time had come for her to set out on the Jerusalem pilgrimage that Christ and the Virgin had long promised her she would one day make, and so she did, accompanied by her daughter.

Some of these female pilgrims are known to us by name, but the majority are not, nor can we know exactly how many of them there were or what proportion of long-distance pilgrims they represented. The indicators that they were in a minority, perhaps a small minority, are persuasive. The records of the Opera di San Jacopo of Pistoia list over 3000 pilgrims, mostly to Compostela, who received alms between c.1360 and c.1480. The gender of some of these pilgrims is unknowable, but of those who can be identifed, only 200 or so were women. They included some humble people as well as women of substance: there was a cook, a laundress, the wife of a porter who served the Opera. The Dominican friar of Ulm, Felix Fabri, who went twice to the Holy Land in the late fifteenth century, hints that the presence of women on both his journeys was noticeable and not altogether to the liking of their fellow-passengers. On his first trip, in 1480, there were six old ladies, presumably widows, who were so decrepit that they could hardly stand; the nobles in the company objected to them strongly, but they proved their worth when illness broke out on the ship between Cyprus and the Holy Land. Completely unscathed, they busied themselves nursing everybody else. On the second journey there was the wife of a Flemish pilgrim who irritated everyone intensely by running around poking her nose into everything. She may have been the only woman on board; rather significantly we are told that the master, Federigo Contarini, had originally intended that the couple should travel on board his own galley.

If women went to Rome, to Santiago and to Jerusalem, as to all the other major shrines of Europe, in relatively small numbers, local and regional pilgrimage was a different matter. Sigal's analyses of over 5000 miracle stories from eleventh- and twelfth-century France reveal that women constituted a higher proportion of the total of lower-class pilgrims than they did of the upper-class total (partly because the 'upper class' is taken to include clergy). Lower-class pilgrims of both sexes, unsurprisingly, usually travelled shorter distances on their pilgrimages; women, therefore, typically came from within a modest radius of the shrine. Was this the result of ideological or of practical circumscription?

Women, as we have seen, were not prevented from setting out on pilgrimage, provided certain basic conditions were met. The married woman had to obtain the permission of her husband, indeed the married person, male or female, was supposed to obtain the permision of his or her spouse before embarking on a long-distance pilgrimage. In the fifteenth century, Margery Kempe was asked to produce a letter to that effect when she went to the shrine of St Willam at York. She objected that her husband had given her his verbal permission and that the other women present were not being asked to produce such letters. Because of their well-known weakness and frivolity, women were undoubtedly regarded as more in need of their husbands' permission than their husbands were of theirs. The anonymous author of the fifteenth-century French satire *Les Quinze Joies de Mariage* draws a vivid picture of a largely female crowd at the shrine of the Virgin of Le Puy, their husbands physically propelling them through the crush and producing the money for their insatiable consumption of souvenirs and knicknacks. In the 1530s the Protestant reformer Hugh Latimer urged that the tendency of women to make irresponsible vows of pilgrimage should be subject to the veto of their husbands and their priests. The age-old belief in the moral fragility of women was grist to the mill of critics: Thomas More reported a preacher's advice to husbands that they should either accompany their wives to the shrine of Our Lady of Willesden or keep them at home. Such comments depended on the perception that, like it or not, women were in fact frequent pilgrims, at least over short distances.

Their relative physical frailty (however robust certain individuals may actually have been) was clearly one of the limiting factors which confined them principally to shorter-range pilgrimages. This frailty was aggravated during the childbearing years. Here there is an important and obvious clue to the smaller numbers of female pilgrims over longer distances.

Once past puberty, most women were either nuns or actual or potential child-bearers. If a woman proved sterile, that might itself send her to a shrine for help, but if she was fertile her time and energy would be occupied both before and after the birth of children. It is hard to suppose that many women set out on pilgrimage knowing that they were pregnant, although one such woman came to the shrine of St Foy at Conques against her husband's will and was seized by impending labour pains; the saint had to intervene to prevent delivery before she got home. A pregnant woman in the crush at the exhibition of St Martial's head at Limoges in 1388 fell as if dead, but was revived when carried before the relic. In 1370 a 'foreign pilgrim' of unspecified nationality gave birth to a male child in a hospital at Pistoia and received alms from the Opera di San Jacopo.

Pregnancy often forestalled or prevented pilgrimage: in 1331 two Parisian husbands asked the pope for dispensation from vows of pilgrimage to Compostela on behalf of their wives who were repeatedly pregnant. A Milanese widow in 1364 sought dispensation on her own account. When pregnant, in her husband's lifetime, she had vowed to go to Compostela if she should bear a living child; not only was she now a widow, but the child had died after a year, and she pleaded disinclination to face 'the dangers of the sea'. In 1391 Margaret, wife of George Frungg, knight, of London, was suffering from multiple obstructions to the fulfilment of a vow of pilgrimage which she had made during the lifetime of her first husband, Thomas de Naughton, with his encouragement and consent. To her age and the number of her children was now added the disapproval of her present husband, and she therefore asked for the pope's dispensation from her vow.

Once children were born, both mothers and fathers went on pilgrimages in quest of remedies for their illnesses and injuries, but routine maternal duties hardly made it easy for women to embark on long journeys. This meant that the segment of the female lifespan available for large-scale pilgrimage was relatively limited. If child-bearing and the care of small children were past, health and energy must still suffice. In 1343 the pious Elizabeth de Burgh, lady of Clare, sought papal dispensation from a vow of pilgrimage to Compostela because she was forty and could not hope to fulfil it. If she meant what she said, she was made of less stern stuff than Felix Fabri's doughty old widows on board ship for Jerusalem or, perhaps, than Sybil Boys of Norfolk who vowed to go to Rome in 1450 (presumably for the Jubilee) but, being eighty years old, thought better of it.

The conventional view that women's lives were largely bounded and confined by their domestic roles is not inconsistent with the evidence for their participation in pilgrimage. The health of their husbands and children and other household concerns often provided the motives for their pilgrimages. A Lollard preacher complained that women who had lost their keys would spend more on a pilgrimage to the servant-saint Zita (who had been a housekeeper in life) than the keys were worth. For the leisure, and perhaps the command of income, to go to Rome or Jerusalem a woman might have to wait for widowhood, but her ability to go then would depend on her state of fitness. Family ties continued to bind beyond the grave; it was by no means unknown for men to leave instructions in their wills for their female kin to undertake pilgrimages on their behalf. Citizens of Lübeck and Hamburg called upon wives, sisters, daughters and nieces to fulfil this pious duty. This in itself furnishes evidence that for these ordinary laymen pilgrimage by women, so far from being unseemly, might in certain circumstances represent the fulfilment of their duty to husband and family. Marital duty however prevented Dorothea of Montau from staying among the hermits at Einsiedeln as she wished and sending her husband home to Gdansk with their daughter. The parish priest to whom they applied for a testimonial letter, mindful of the law of God, refused to allow Dorothea to remain without her husband.

For the widow, pilgrimage might be a means of enjoying a new freedom of movement and change of scene in congenial company (often that of other widows), the overture to a pious old age and edifying death, or, of course, both; but the conditions of wealth and health had to be right and the opportunities were not open to all women. Men, especially of the lower orders, were also subject to some restrictions on their freedom of movement, but a man's biology as well as his social role was in several respects friendlier to his chances of undertaking lengthy journeys during a larger proportion of his lifetime.

Kings and Queens

It is apparent from the foregoing that members of the secular clergy and laymen enjoyed the greatest degree of freedom to participate in pilgrimage, above all in long-distance pilgrimage. Both groups could be described as men of the world. Unlike monks and unlike women, their basic right to be seen abroad, in the streets and on the highways, was not in question. This did not mean that they lived without any constraints on their freedom of action and movement, which varied, however, very considerably from one level of society to another. It could plausibly be maintained that the only member of a tightly integrated society such as that of post-conquest England who did not need to ask anyone's permission to undertake foreign travel, for pilgrimage or any other reason, was the king himself. His principal subjects, both laymen of standing and bishops, archbishops and abbots, would be ill-advised to leave the kingdom without his knowledge, and well-advised to seek his consent and the assurance of his protection for their property and dependants in their absence. The kingdom of England was unusually compact and highly organised, but similar principles applied everywhere: at every level of society the consent of superiors, lay and ecclesiastical, needed to be sought.

Even if kings were uniquely exempt from this requirement, they were, paradoxically, unlikely to take much advantage of it. They could not lightly abandon their kingdoms and go at will to Rome or Jerusalem. Several Anglo-Saxon monarchs of the seventh and eighth centuries, in effect, abdicated and retired prudently to Rome to die under the protection of the apostles. In 853, however, the future King Alfred successfully accomplished the return journey, followed two years later by his father Aethelwulf, who spent a year at Rome but also returned home. When Cnut the Great went to Rome in 1027 his journey combined pious purposes with the intention of conferring with the pope and the Emperor Conrad, thereby, as he proudly announced, obtaining commercial privileges for his subjects. Cnut must have been confident of the security of his northern kingdoms; he must also have calculated that the advantages, both heavenly and earthly, that his pilgrimage would gain for him outweighed any risks it might involve.

Cnut represented a race which had only recently entered respectable Christian circles, but his contemporary Robert the Pious of France was already well established in that league when in the spring of 1020 he embarked on an extensive Lenten tour of the shrines of southern France. His precise purpose is not clear and was certainly not made explicit, but here again one may suppose that it combined the desire to earn spiritual benefits with the intention of advertising the royal piety to a wide audience. It is not to accuse kings of cynicism, or to underrate the earnestness with which they viewed their own salvation and anything that would help towards it, to suppose that they performed some such mental calculus whenever they planned pilgrimages, at home or abroad.

Kings were to a greater or lesser degree itinerant throughout the medieval period and pilgrimages could sometimes be conveniently fitted into the display and advertisement of kingship. A king's progress through the streets of a city to a great church, the humility of his bearing and the opulence of his offering, all possessed a visual and symbolic value.

Differing configurations of territorial power meant that every European ruler performed against a different backdrop, but for each of them there existed both shrines in the heartlands of their power which came to be specially associated with the monarchy and many others which it was wise for them to notice and to favour with offerings and the occasional visit. It has been suggested that the kings of the Asturias in the ninth century showed favour to the nascent shrine of St James of Compostela as part of a programme of extending their influence into the province of Galicia, and that the kings of Wessex took an interest for similar reasons in northern shrines such as those of St John of Beverley and St Cuthbert, in a region which was at the time peripheral to the centre of their power and adjacent to their enemies the Scots. The mausoleum of the French kings was located at the shrine of St Denis, just to the north of the royal capital and from Merovingian times closely associated with the monarchy, while the kings received unction and coronation under the protection of another ancient saint, St Remi at Reims a little to the east. To the south-west, the important shrine of St Martin of Tours, famous throughout the west as a goal of pilgrimage, was originally peripheral to the sphere of influence of the Merovingian kings, but they were careful to show the saint marks of respect. Tours became peripheral once more with the disintegration of the Carolingian monarchy and came definitively under royal control only with Philip Augustus (1180–1223).

For the rulers of the kingdoms of the twelfth century and later, pilgrimage most often began and ended at home. The overseas pilgrimage most likely to attract them was the greatest of them all, the armed pilgrimage to the Holy Land. A succession of French kings – Louis VII, Philip II and Louis IX – answered this call, with limited military results. Philip II left the Holy Land early in 1191 and returned to France to take advantage of the continued absence of one erstwhile fellow-crusader, Richard the Lionheart, and the death of another, Philip, count of Flanders. He was able on his way home to present himself as a pilgrim at Rome and to receive a private view of the Veronica. Philip's grandson Louis IX was the last king of France to go to the Holy Land, but by no means the last to announce his intention of doing so. The enormous cost of his crusade and the disasters that attended it, including the death of the king's brother Robert of Artois and his own captivity and ransom, graphically illustrated the hazards of crusade and pilgrimage when undertaken by kings. Richard I of England, sixty years earlier, had been captured and held to ransom on his way home from the Holy Land, which showed that the infidel was not the only, or even the chief, enemy that a royal pilgrim might have to reckon with overseas.

No later king of England undertook a Holy Land pilgrimage, but Edward I went on crusade as heir to the throne (becoming king while he was away) and Henry Bolingbroke, the future Henry IV, participated in crusades to both Prussia and Palestine in the early 1390s and dreamed of dying in Jerusalem. Opportunities for continental pilgrimage by the kings of England were somewhat more abundant while they still ruled substantial tracts of French territory. Henry II, in 1163, was the earliest pilgrim to the Marian shrine of Rocamadour whose name is known to us, and he went there again in 1170, but his stated intention of going to Santiago in 1176 remained unfulfilled. With the reign of John the English kings began to lose their grip on their French lands. When Henry III went to Pontigny in 1256 to do reverence to St Edmund it was with the permission and in the company of Louis IX. Henry took the opportunity to visit other French shrines as well, and he performed another Burgundian pilgrimage in 1262, somewhat to the exasperation of one of his entourage, who wrote that the king was far from well but had insisted on going. Continental warfare in the fourteenth century created new possibilities: in 1360 Edward III went to Pontigny with the Black Prince. In 1353, the pope had absolved Edward III and several of his boon companions from their vows to go to Santiago; it was surely highly unlikely that the king would ever have been able to fulfil such a vow.

No king of England between Cnut and Edward I, and no later medieval English king, went to Rome. It seems unnecessary to suggest that the crowned heads of Europe failed to attend the Roman Jubilee in 1300 because they were reluctant to stoke Boniface VIII's already considerable self-esteem; long-distance pilgrimage was simply not on the agenda. Kings and queens fulfilled their aspirations for the most part vicariously, by sending hirelings on their behalf, by leaving bequests for pilgrimage in their wills or by obtaining the grant of indulgences on condition of pious works or benefactions. Clement VI thus made the 1350 Jubilee indulgence restrospectively available to Edward III and the English royal family, and such grants to privileged persons and corporations all over Christendom became normal. Queens and queen mothers were somewhat more at leisure to undertake pilgrimage tours, but these too were normally domestic. There were exceptions: Elizabeth, queen mother of Hungary, not only went to Rome in 1343–4 but accompanied the Emperor Charles IV to Aachen, Marburg and Cologne in 1357. English royal pilgrimage, performed in the relatively secure environment of the kingdom itself, played a not unimportant part in the practice of kingship. Four English shrines, apart from the royal foundation at Westminster where Edward the Confessor (canonised in 1163) was buried, received the kings' special attention: Thomas Becket's at Canterbury, St Alban's at the monastery which bore his name, to the north of London, St Edmund's at Bury in Suffolk, and Our Lady of Walsingham in Norfolk. The concentration of notable shrines in eastern England, which included also the Holy Rood at Bromholm in Norfolk and St Etheldreda at Ely, often resulted in the performance of veritable royal pilgrimage tours of that region, but a host of other shrines claimed their share of the royal attention from time to time: in the north, St Cuthbert at Durham, St Willam of York, St John of Beverley and later St John of Bridlington; in the west, St Wulfstan of Worcester and St Thomas Cantilupe of Hereford, and many more besides.

The Scandinavian monarchs of the later middle ages, male and female, were somewhat more mobile than most as pilgrims, as if in homage to their Viking antecedents. Erik Ejegod of Denmark had gone to Rome and Bari in 1098 and later died in Cyprus on his way (with his queen) to Jerusalem. Two and a half centuries later, in 1347, Waldemar Atterdag went to Jerusalem; his contemporary Magnus Eriksson of Sweden simultaneously made plans to do so too, but it does not seem that he fulfilled them. Erik of Pomerania, ruler at least in name of all three Scandinavian kingdoms, went to Jerusalem in 1423–5, leaving his very capable wife in charge. His nephew and successor Christopher of Bavaria was one of several Scandinavian kings and queens to go to Wilsnack in the fifteenth century, while Christian I of Denmark visited Rome in 1474 and took part in the Easter ceremonies. In 1488 the Danish Queen Dorothea went to both Rome and the Holy Land.

Royal pilgrims might have had concerns other than enemy action when they contemplated foreign pilgrimage. In 1476, James III of Scotland applied to Edward IV for a safeconduct to enable him to cross England on his way to St John at Amiens. Scots very often made the entire journey by sea, precisely to avoid traversing the neighbour kingdom; but, as Edward delicately put it, his brother of Scotland feared 'that the sea-crossing would be in no small measure damaging to his disposition and bodily health'. The unfortunate James had no alternative to braving the short crossing from Dover.

Nobles

Kings were nobles and lived surrounded by nobles. Closest of all were their blood kin and their in-laws. It would have been unwise of Edward IV to turn his back on a kingdom which he had already lost once, but his brother-in-law Anthony Woodville was able to go to Rome for the Jubilee of 1475. It was far from unknown for the king's closest associates to make vows of pilgrimage which they proved unable or unwilling subsequently to carry out or which the demands of the royal service obstructed. In 1337, Bartholomew Burghersh was absolved, at Edward III's request, from a vow he had made, before the war with France erupted, to go to the Holy Sepulchre and not to bear arms until he did so. Almost a century later, Thomas Montacute, earl of Salisbury, had to seek dispensation from a vow made when he fell ill returning from the Holy Sepulchre; he had promised to revisit the Holy Land, but in the admittedly difficult times that followed the early death of Henry V, he could not obtain permission to do so, although it was claimed that he had made three serious attempts to set out.

Even when due allowance has been made for extravagant gestures made with no real thought of fulfilment, it seems entirely plausible that pilgrimage to distant lands, with its rigours and dangers, appealed to the self-image of the noble, who from infancy was trained and conditioned for physical rather than mental exertion and for whom, therefore, it was congenial to earn spiritual merit by such means. It could and should of course be accompanied, as it was in the life of Gerald of Aurillac, by rejection of the characteristic vices of nobles, such as violence, injustice, oppression of the poor and indulgence in lust and luxury. Gerald had less illustrious members of the knightly classes of southern France as companions on his pilgrimages. In about 925 Amaury, a knight of Vergonzac, restored the church of Palazinges, dedicated of old to St Peter and richly endowed with Roman relics, which had been destroyed by the Vikings. In the deed recording his action and his other gifts to the church it was recalled that he had many times gone to Rome with his kinsman Gerald of Aurillac.

In the eyes of monastic observers, who were increasingly concerned that monks should not go a-wandering beyond the cloister, pilgrimage could be recommended to laymen precisely because they were not vowed to cloistered perfection. St Peter Damian spelled this doctrine out, in the middle of the eleventh century, for the benefit of the marquis Raniero, on whom he had imposed a penitential pilgrimage to Jerusalem but who was proving reluctant to go. A little later, the Holy Land crusade, with its built-in military component, represented the perfection of this activist pilgrimage, undertaken in reparation for all the layman's many sins. As new nations entered the fold of Roman Christianity, so their great men (and sometimes women) showed themselves responsive to its allure. The sagas preserve several stories of Viking chieftains who in the eleventh and twelfth centuries went to Rome and Jerusalem. The physical rigours of travel, by land or sea, were embraced both as an extension of their previous way of life and as a suitable means of penance for men who had come to understand that from a Christian perspective they had a great deal to repent. The curiosity, the desire to see, to explore and at least mentally to map new landscapes which is reflected in the saga accounts of expeditions to Greenland and Vinland found another outlet in the Christian East.

In the mid-twelfth century Earl Rognvald of the Orkneys was incited to undertake the Holy Land pilgrimage by another Viking who had served as a mercenary at Constantinople. He thought it odd that the earl did not want to see the Holy Places with his own eyes but relied on travellers' tales; he owed it to himself as a man of parts to go in person, and it would add to his standing if he was seen to mix with the best people (who were presumably making the pilgrimage as their remote descendants might have made the Grand Tour). Rognvald was accompanied by men who shared with him a predilection for versifying; the *Orkneyinga Saga* shows them swimming in the Jordan and composing verses. The earl himself made one, depicting himself as a bard with a cross on his breast and a palm on his back, as they approached Jerusalem.

In later centuries, a similar mixture of motives characterised prominent members of the knightly classes: pilgrimage could be seen as a chivalric exercise, in which the pilgrim put himself at risk for the Lord's sake and reaped a spiritual reward. In his treatise on chivalry Geoffroi de Charny (d. 1356) reckoned pilgrimages among the adventurous enterprises that knights might undertake in order to win a reputation. An expedition undertaken by James, Lord Douglas, in 1329 combined a number of chivalric elements. He set out to bear the heart of Robert the Bruce to the Holy Land, but died en route, fighting the Moors in Spain. The Holy Land was the supreme destination for such pilgrims, as it was for Vikings and crusaders, but Santiago was also suitable and so too was St Patrick's Purgatory, because of its geographical remoteness on the fringes of Christendom and the nature of the ordeal which the pilgrim there had to undergo.

The Purgatory was (and is) a cave on an island in Lough Derg in County Donegal, which attracted pilgrims largely thanks to the well-publicised visions of the knight Owain in the twelfth century. After suitable spiritual preparations the pilgrim was immured in the cave for twenty-four hours in a state of darkness, cold and sensory deprivation, which was calculated to inspire further visions, as indeed it sometimes did. One notable pilgrim, in 1353, was a Hungarian knight, George Grissaphan. Repenting of the cruelties he had committed in the service of King Louis of Naples he betook himself first to Compostela and lived for a while as a hermit near the church of St Mary at Finisterre; then he decided to go to the Purgatory, making his way there on foot via Gascony, France and England. The visions he experienced in the cave, which the archbishop of Armagh urged him to publicise to the pope at Avignon, crowned his quest for penance. In 1411–12 the Hungarian Laurence Pazthó followed in George's footsteps. He came to England bearing a testimonial letter from the Emperor Sigismund, according to which he also intended to go to Compostela. Wherever he went, Laurence was received as befitted a nobleman and seems to have gloried in it; he recorded his visit to the Purgatory with great satisfaction.

Another noble who was Hungarian by name although not by birth went both to St Patrick's Purgatory and to Jerusalem. Malatesta 'Ungaro', so-called because he had been knighted by King Louis, was a member of the ruling dynasty of Rimini, and in 1349 went to the Holy Land with his uncle Galeotto. Their suite included the Florentine courtier and musician Dolcibene de' Tori, who, according to the novelist Franco Sacchetti (himself a pious man), had no very good reputation, and amused his masters by attempting to reserve himself a place at the Last Judgement by defecating in the valley of Jehoshaphat. Yet, as Sacchetti observed, Dolcibene was not such a great rascal that he did not also compose a song of praise to the Virgin (which survives) in commemoration of the pilgrimage. In 1358 Malatesta Ungaro obtained a certificate from Edward III of England to the effect that he had completed the ordeal of St Patrick's Purgatory, in company with Niccolò Beccaria, a young esquire of Lombardy. It seems that Malatesta laid plans to go again to Jerusalem, for in 1364, Pope Urban V granted him permission to defer his intended pilgrimage to the Holy Land for two years.

We have detailed information about two long-distance pilgrimages undertaken by Niccolò d'Este, lord of Ferrara and also of Modena, Reggio and Parma, of which the Holy Land pilgrimage he made in 1413 seems to have been the less troublesome and certainly the more splendid. The party consisted of fifty-four people in all. Of these, ten were reckoned to be 'gentlemen', that is, nobles, and the prince's companions. They included Pietro Contarini, captain of the fully equipped galley with which the Venetians supplied the party. Of these ten individuals, Niccolò knighted six, but one of them, Alberto della Salla of Ferrara, later renounced his knighthood so that he could receive it again at the Holy Sepulchre (a prized ambition of many upper-class pilgrims). The rest of the party consisted of counsellors, chamberlains, courtiers and servants, including a barber, two trumpeters, and most intriguing, Avichino, an 'English tailor' and citizen of Ferrara.

In the following year Niccolò undertook a very different journey. In June 1414 he set off 'with staff and satchel' to St Antony of Vienne, accompanied by a rather smaller party. After paying his respects to the saint, he made his way north to Paris, where he inspected the relics and royal tombs at St Denis. He then presented himself to King Charles VI of France at Bray-sur-Somme. It has been suggested that he was carrying out a diplomatic mission, perhaps concerning the forthcoming Council of Constance, on behalf of Pope John XXIII, who had visited Ferrara earlier in the year. The French part of the journey passed without incident, except for a little unpleasantness from the bishop of Lyon, who had once been put to inconvenience by customs officials at Ferrara. Re-entering Italy by the Monte Cenis pass, however, Niccolò was seized and held to ransom by the castellan of San Michele di Ceva in Piedmont, who had thoughts of handing him over to the duke of Milan for 40,000 ducats. As it happened, the danger Niccolò incurred had nothing to do with his pilgrimage as such, but potential hazards existed on every side.

The wealth of nobles, or at least their ability to raise money, in some respects obviously facilitated pilgrimage, in that they could afford to take an adequate escort with them and to pay for their requirements in food and accommodation. They were also likely to receive splendid presents and lavish assistance (such as the galley the Venetians made available to Niccolò d'Este). Their status made them conspicuous, however, and to that extent potentially vulnerable. In the twelfth century a servant of the Polish king came to St Gilles du Provence to give thanks for delive ance from some unspecified trouble, but he travelled incognito, it was noted, 'as is the way of nobles when they travel in foreign parts'. It was not always easy to carry off convincingly. The attempt made by Gunther, bishop of Bamberg, to conceal his identity when he headed the great German pilgrimage to Jerusalem in 1064–5, had faintly comical results: so splendid was his appearance that he was believed at Constantinople to be the western Emperor in disguise. Nearly three hundred years later, in May 1350, Pope Clement VI wrote to Napoleone Orsini to thank him for the courtesy he had shown to the pope's kinsman, the bishop of Rodez, who had been travelling incognito to Rome for the Jubilee. He had come to Sant' Antimo, where all available accommodation was taken up by Napoleone's entourage, but the latter recognised him instantly and made him comfortable. It was evidently not easy for the noble medieval leopard, lay or ecclesiastical, to change his spots.

It seems that pilgrimages performed by nobles not only served the purposes of penitence and devotion that they might serve for any Christian, but were also felt to be public demonstrations of piety appropriate to their social standing. Like kings above them in the social scale and, increasingly, the wealthier bourgeoisie below them, the nobles were often associated, as benefactors and pilgrims, with one or more local churches. Richard of Clare, earl of Gloucester, had close family relations with Tewkesbury Abbey, and the abbey chronicler recorded not only that the earl went to Compostela in 1250, but that the monks had helped him raise the money for his journey. Nobles had been making similar arrangements before going on pilgrimage and crusade at least since the tenth century.

A list of medieval European pilgrims who could be classified as noble would be endless. The term was used very widely and indefinitely, often to describe people who from the point of view of a given observer looked superior or who behaved as if they so viewed themselves. To Margery Kempe, Dame Margaret Florentyne, who was kind to her both at Assisi and later at Rome, occupied a position of marked social advantage, and it is not easy to determine how 'noble' she was, or how much more noble than the London woman who unkindly left Margery in the lurch at Aachen on her later German pilgrimage. This woman was 'worshipful', from Margery's point of view, but was quite probably no more than the wife of a prosperous London citizen. Chaucer's company on the road to Canterbury, obviously designed as a gallery of social types, embraces at one extreme the Knight and his son the Squire, who exhibited chivalric attributes but were not strictly noble, and at the other, the Miller. The Franklin, who was able to offer lavish hospitality, might have been regarded, like the Knight, as 'worshipful'; the Merchant, whose mind was taken up with his profits and the keeping of the seas, perhaps hoped to achieve that standing one day.

Merchants and Other Ranks

The merchant is a figure much involved in the history of pilgrimage, simultaneously as a pilgrim himself and as a provider of services to pilgrims. The merchants-turned-pilgrims (and saints) Godric of Finchale and Raniero of Pisa have already been mentioned, and the association of pilgrims with merchants as fellow-travellers is endlessly repeated. On one of his journeys to Rome early in the thirteenth century Gerald of Wales was compelled by war in Flanders to make a long detour through the 'horrid woods' of the Ardennes. It was with relief that on leaving Champagne and entering Burgundy 'he at last reached the public road, travelling with pilgrims and merchants'. Merchants and pilgrims resembled one another in being peaceful travellers who were presumed to be unarmed or at least not professionally capable of defending themselves, and as such they were repeatedly coupled in both ecclesiastical and secular legislation, which prescribed penalties for assaults on them.

The merchant's professional mobility afforded him built-in opportunities for pilgrimage; he possessed, or was accustomed to hiring, the horses and even the ships which made it possible, and he used the roads and inns that pilgrims used. All over Europe, the churches which attracted pilgrimage also attracted fairs and markets. Some of the eleventh-century miracle stories of St Foy at Conques concern merchants who had seen business opportunities in the crowds who went to her shrine: there was, for example, the Gascon who on his way there was robbed of a piece of cloth, which he had brought with him to sell. Because he was truly devoted to the saint, he did not complain and she therefore saw that it was restored to him, but another man, who thought to make a killing in wax at the expense of the saint's pilgrims, did not fare so well. It was not uncommon for saints to intervene to restore stolen money, goods or horses to *bona fide* merchants and other pilgrims.

Knowledge of an area acquired by way of trade could lead to an interest in its shrines. There is little clear evidence of pilgrimage to Scandinavian shrines by non-Scandinavians, but what there is includes a few bequests for pilgrimage to St Olaf at Trondheim in wills made by members of the Lübeck company of Bergenfarers, specialists in the Norwegian trade.

The frequenting of the fairs of central and eastern Europe by south German merchants must have had similar effects. The evidence of miracle stories suggests that mariners had frequent occasion to call upon the saints and often followed deliverance from shipwreck with pilgrimages and offerings. St Nicholas and St Clement, as well as the Virgin, were established European specialists in the rescue of sailors, and Wulfstan of Worester and Thomas Cantilupe of Hereford both intervened to deliver seafarers between Bristol and Ireland; Thomas also rescued merchants engaged in the wine trade between Gascony and England. A will made by a Nottinghamshire man in 1400 recalled a vow of pilgrimage made when he was in danger of death between Ireland and Norway, but the nature of his business is not stated. Many saints rescued seafarers at one time or another and received ship models, in metal, wax or silver, as offerings at their shrines.

Men of standing in urban communities were frequently members of confraternities that had some connection with pilgrimage. All over Christendom there were brotherhoods which, either in origin or in actuality, were reserved for those who had made the pilgrimage to Jerusalem, Rome or the Holy Land. In Ludlow in Shropshire there was a Palmers' Gild, founded in the mid-thirteenth century, which suggests that someone locally had made the Jerusalem pilgrimage, but the gild also bore the name of the Blessed Mary and it seems unlikely that it can have been exclusively reserved to Holy Land pilgrims. At least two Ludlow men, one of them probably identifiable as a wool merchant, are known to have gone to Santiago in the fourteenth century. The gild of St James at Burgh in Lincolnshire was actually set up as the result of a Compostela pilgrimage which certain inhabitants of the place made in about 1365. In danger at sea on their return voyage, they vowed to establish an altar in the parish church in honour of the saint and to make an annual contribution of barley to the upkeep of the fabric; since then, the fraternity, men and women, had met every year for a common meal. As this example indicates, whatever the origins of these brotherhoods they served other purposes of sociability and often charity. Some of the better-endowed founded and ran hospitals, as the fraternity in honour of St James and St Antony at Assisi did in the fifteenth century. Membership was sometimes both expensive and exclusive, although not aristocratic in the strict sense; this was often the case in the cities of the Netherlands.

Gilds of course abounded in medieval society and covered quite a wide spectrum of the population. Even when they had no specific connection with pilgrimage it might be provided in the statutes that the members should contribute a small sum towards the expenses of any brother (or sister) who was proposing to undertake a lengthy pilgrimage. Sometimes too the other members were to escort their fellow on his way when he departed and if possible greet him on his return. This underlined the social and public character of the pilgrim enterprise. The departing pilgrim received a public blessing on his, or her, scrip and staff, and the event might be noted in the parish missal. Witnesses at English inquisitions *post mortem* sometimes remembered both the ceremonies that marked their departure on pilgrimage and the greetings of their neighbours on their homecoming.

It made sense for merchants and other humbler fry to travel under the wing of greater men when they could. Indeed every great man inevitably took lesser pilgrims with him, from his household clerks to his grooms. When Laurence Pazthó went to St Patrick's Purgatory in 1411 he was accompanied by Antonio Manni, a Florentine merchant who had been resident for some time in Dublin and who had long wanted to perfom the pilgrimage. Manni was a relatively fragile specimen of his breed. For health reasons he was advised against undergoing the full twenty-four-hour ordeal of the cave, and he said he had never been so cold in his life; he was also scared almost out of his wits, on the boat trip to the island, by shrieking black birds (cormorants?), which he took to be devils incarnate. In recording his reactions to his experiences, he and other late medieval pilgrims of similar origins were extending the range of the literature not merely of pilgrimage but of travel.

Among the pilgrims who enjoyed the theoretical benefits of safe-conducts and other protective measures taken by both lay and ecclesiastical authorities was a quite unknowable number of people of very lowly rank. It is safe to assume that by far the greater part of the pilgrimage undertaken by peasants and also by humbler members of the urban population took place over short distances, but statistical precision is hardly possible, not least because, as already noted, we have no idea how many people in total went on pilgrimage, whether long or short-range. Miracle collections often include particulars of the name and gender, place of origin and occupation, of pilgrims, and thus far they are invaluable, but they only permit a rough and ready sociological analysis and anyway do not exist for every shrine and pilgrimage. Such analyses as have been undertaken, for example Sigal's of eleventh- and twelfth-century French miracles, work on the not unreasonable assumption that where a pilgrim is not specifically described otherwise, he or she is a peasant (or the urban equivalent). Analysis of a smaller sample, the 333 recorded pilgrims to the tomb of Simon de Montfort at Evesham after his violent death in 1265, suggests that over 60 per cent of the total were 'peasants'. Lower-class pilgrimage over long distances is even more difficult to quantify. Many miracle collections include a story of a pilgrim from some remote region who at last finds relief for his (sometimes even her) troubles at the shrine in question, but, even leaving aside the dubious and generic character of these stories, they do not always make it clear what sort of person the supposed pilgrim is. A factual source like the Pistoiese records of almsgiving to pilgrims to Compostela is of limited usefulness, for the pilgrims are named but only rarely described; most of them would have to be traced in other records before they could be allotted a social classification. A few inhabitants of Pistoia itself and its immediate region receive an occupational label, such as Antonio the farrier (*malischalco*) and Giovanni Corsini, who came from a rural community a few miles away and for many years supplied the Opera with charcoal. These individuals look like small businessmen rather than prosperous merchants; probably many of these pilgrims were people of humble origins. Occasionally unnamed individuals of doubtful character are mentioned, like the *galioffi* ('good for nothings') who claimed in 1384 that they were going to Compostela, or the sixteen *viandanti* (wayfarers) who received alms in 1389. The Opera gave alms in 1382 to a 'poor man who says that he has escaped from prison' and who was going to Santiago. The man with his wife and five children, described as *peregrini*, who received alms in 1368, seem hardly likely to have been people of substance.

The unfree were not actually debarred from pilgrimage, but naturally had to seek leave of absence from their lords. In 1380 Agnes Snell of Knowsthorpe in Yorkshire obtained the permission of John of Gaunt to go on pilgrimage to Rome, where she promised she would pray for him and her other benefactors. A century earlier a Wiltshire serf had been granted leave to sell his possessions and depart for Jerusalem. Some people who were free, albeit of lowly rank, were simply restricted by their circumstances, perhaps also by their physical frailties. Others, by contrast, sought relief in pilgrimage from famine, plague or simple desperation, like the hungry hordes who went to Wilsnack in 1475. Yorkshire court records of the early thirteenth century preserve some touching stories of lower-class pilgrims who allegedly sought refuge in pilgrimage from troubles that threatened to overwhelm them. A woman who feared she would be held responsible for the death of her child had taken herself off to Jerusalem, or so the jury said; a carter who had killed a robber in self-defence had done likewise.

When Margery Kempe was making her painful way back to Calais from Wilsnack in 1433, she fell in with a party of poor people who were going to venerate the relics at Aachen. They were not desirable company, but given her difficulty in retaining companions they were better than nothing. She noted with a shudder that when they were about to enter a town they conscientiously sat down and deloused themselves. (Inevitably they communicated their vermin to her.) We do not know how far they had come, or whether their pilgrimage ended at Aachen, but their condition suggests that it was both charitable and prudent of Geseke, widow of Heinrich Oldekoppes of Hildesheim, to leave money in 1474 for the provision of two baths, at opposite gates of the town, for the use of Aachen pilgrims who passed through. Separate provision was made for men and women.

Margery Kempe's verminous companions were not necessarily vagrants, still less criminals, but the pilgrim population undoubtedly overlapped with a half-world of vagabonds and displaced persons. The English government in the century after the Peasants' Revolt in 1381 was recurrently inclined to fear that pilgrimage was being used as a front by peasants and artisans in flight from their lords and honest toil, who used it as an excuse for begging. Anxieties about popular unrest and labour shortages prompted a strengthening of the rules. Begging pilgrims (those who paid their way were not the problem) were required to carry with them testimonial letters declaring the purpose of their journey and the date at which they were expected back home. Anxieties about the public assembly of large numbers of humble people and also scepticism about their ability to discriminate true miracles from false helped to fuel criticism of pilgrimage.

Some have thought that pilgrimage became a more plebeian activity by the end of the middle ages. If so, it may have been due as much to the wider diffusion of a modest degree of spending power following the Black Death, or to the effects of preaching, as to an increase in vagrancy and destitution. It may have been truer of Compostela than of Holy Land pilgrimage, although we may remember how in 1384 Leonardo Frescobaldi saw an unseaworthy ship laden with poor pilgrims returning from the Holy Land founder in the Adriatic. It has been suggested that the sea route from the British Isles to Galicia was not only cheaper and quicker than the overland trip, but, by the fifteenth century, safer than it had been thanks to improvements in navigation and ship design. Royal licences to shipmasters permitting them to convey given numbers of pilgrims to Santiago usually specified that no nobles or men at arms, and sometimes no clergy, were to be carried; there was less concern about nameless individuals of little social, economic or military importance. Surviving figures suggest that take-up was high, especially in Santiago Holy Years.[2]

The first people to withdraw from participation in pilgrimage were probably a self-constituted elite who took to heart the scriptural counsel that God was to be worshipped in spirit and truth. Men and women who had access to books and, perhaps, personal spiritual advisers, had other sources of spiritual nourishment. They were perhaps also likely to be repelled by the coarser manifestations of popular enthusiasm and by plebeian behaviour on the roads and in the taverns. Erasmus evoked humanist disdain for the impostures of shrine custodians and the credulity of their customers when he described his visit to Canterbury with John Colet, dean of St Paul's, early in the sixteenth century; Colet raged against the ridiculous things they were told and shown, while Erasmus himself was more tolerant. To generalise from such an episode would, however, be rash. Lollard and Protestant radicals certainly regarded themselves as having a mission to enlighten the deluded in the matter of pilgrimage as of other mistaken practices, but it is unlikely that the available evidence suffices for a thorough social analysis of the late medieval pilgrimage public.

4

THE GEOGRAPHY OF PILGRIMAGE

Pilgrims were not the only travellers on the highways and waterways of medieval Europe and, as we have seen, they were not alone in shaping routes and the provision of services along them. As road-users merchants and pilgrims alike built on the foundations laid by innumerable generations of previous travellers. Shrines and roads existed in a complex symbiosis. The fact that a city was of major importance or enjoyed an advantageous situation did not of itself guarantee that it would be comparably important for pilgrims, except perhaps as a convenient halt. Conversely, while shrines often derived additional custom from their position on a well-frequented road, that was not normally the sole reason for the appearance of a shrine of major importance. The goals of pilgrimage were set in a variety of historical circumstances and sometimes in curious places. In their efforts to reach them, pilgrims had good practical reasons to try to make their journeys as easy and secure as it was possible for them to be in pre-modern conditions. Wherever they could, they adopted roads which were already viable and offered the best available security and amenities; at the same time, the increased traffic created by pilgrimage sharpened both commercial and charitable incentives to provide and improve support services along those roads, as well as to create, or at least promote, shrines along or within reach of them.

Rome was the most special of special cases. Roads were built to lead to it, serving the purposes of its army and its empire, long before it became a Christian holy city. Christian pilgrimage utilised and helped to preserve the importance of many of those roads, although that did not suffice to keep their surfaces in good repair after the decay of the unitary

authority of the Empire. Pilgrimage to Rome cannot be neatly separated
from the traffic of prelates, princes, diplomats and lawyers, which grew
in volume as the papacy established itself as the governmental centre of
the western Church, but its historical and spiritual pre-eminence was
revealed in its continued magnetism during the period of the popes'
residence at Avignon, between 1309 and 1377. Avignon itself was an
excellent centre for the administrative and diplomatic business of the
curia, but it was not seriously promoted as a focus of pilgrimage, still less
as a rival to Rome. Rome remained the Holy City, the apostolic capital to
which (at least in theory) the Avignon popes always aspired to return,
and especially from the moment that Clement VI announced, early in
1343, that a second Jubilee would take place in 1350 they went to some
pains to encourage pilgrimage to Rome even in their own absence. This
was a matter of considerable concern to the innkeepers and shopkeepers
of the city and in other places on the roads to Rome, and also to the
rulers of other Italian cities who tried to tax the profits of the hotel and
catering industries.

Other major pilgrimage centres had very varied relationships with
pre-existing political and economic networks. The ascendancy of Santiago de Compostela in its remote corner of Galicia is hard to account for
in simple commercial terms, but once it had become important a number
of interlocking processes came into play in shaping the approach roads
to it across southern France and northern Spain. Cologne's situation on
the Rhine undoubtedly contributed to its political, economic and ecclesiastical prominence. Lavishly endowed with saints, it became a major
pilgrimage centre, especially after the supposed acquisition of the relics
of the Three Magi in 1164. Canterbury lay on the major Roman road
from London to Dover, but it was partly accidental that it became and
remained the chief episcopal see of England, and it is not to be supposed
that the four knights who murdered Thomas Becket in his own cathedral on 29 December 1171 were being encouraged by the local chamber
of commerce to create a major pilgrimage. Political, cultural and economic
power influenced the map of pilgrimage, but did not draw or redraw it
unaided.

Capital Cities

As the dominant power in Tuscany, Florence possessed shrines of local
and regional importance, most notably, by the fifteenth century, the

Virgin of the Annunziata, which was known beyond the confines of Tuscany, but it never joined the upper ranks of pilgrimage centres. The same might be said of numerous other cities, in Italy and elsewhere, which undoubtedly witnessed a considerable passage of travellers of all kinds. Venice was an attraction for pilgrims above all because it was a major port of embarkation for the Holy Land, and its own shrines profited accordingly. Milan benefited from the development of the St Gotthard pass, and the cult of the Virgin at the cathedral (the massive rebuilding of which began at the end of the fourteenth century) exerted some attraction on pilgrims. It was on some of the lists used by Netherlandish civic courts which sentenced criminals to penitential pilgrimages; in 1443 the Milanese authorities issued a certificate for such a penitent, who had been sent there from Lier (near Antwerp), and one client of King Henry VI at Windsor, in 1492, was directed in a vision to visit Our Lady there. Visitors to Milan were doubtless also interested in St Ambrose, in the church which bore his name, and the Dominican St Peter Martyr at the church of Sant' Eustorgio, and might also (like Peter Rieter of Nuremberg in 1432) visit St Augustine at Pavia not far away.

The great university city of Bologna, strategically situated on the Via Emilia, is another interesting example. Its civic cults were of little interest beyond the immediate vicinity, but by a happy chance the Friars Preachers of Bologna possessed the body of their founder St Dominic. Like their brethren at Milan with St Peter Martyr, the Bolognese Dominicans spent money on the shrine, in a number of phases: the young Michelangelo was a late contributor to its making. To honour the founder's remains was anyway a pious necessity, but there is sufficient mention of Dominic's shrine in a variety of sources to suggest that he exerted some pull on a public beyond the confines of his order and of Italy. Bologna probably saw more pilgrimage traffic after the thirteenth century, when the major route to and from Rome was diverted from the old course of the Via Francigena to run via Florence. It was one of the destinations to which the inquisitors of southern France sent penitent heretics in the fourteenth century, fittingly in view of Dominican involvement in the inquisition. Inhabitants of Bologna were of course themselves participants in pilgrimage; large numbers went to Compostela and to St Antony of Vienne in the fourteenth century, receiving alms to help them on their way.

What could be said of Milan, Bologna or Florence might, with the appropriate adjustments, be said also of Paris or London. Royal capitals and other important political or commercial centres everywhere nourished cults, even if only for local consumption, because large numbers of people had other reasons to be there. The establishment of shrines served, like other features of the urban environment such as markets, to attract people from the locality and to confirm a city's importance as a regional focal point. Both bishops and kings had a natural interest in this process; dynastic and episcopal saints found their natural location in major cities, as Wenceslas did at Prague or Stephen at Buda. Like the Confessor at Westminster or St Louis at Paris, however, most such cults had meaning principally within particular national contexts.

Paris combined the attributes of a royal capital (like London) with those of a great university city (like Bologna). In addition it was one of several major transit camps for Santiago pilgrims from further north. Paris possessed notable shrines and relics, among them St Genevieve, the abbey of St Denis with the royal mausoleum which contained the tomb of St Louis, and the relic collection at the Sainte Chapelle, all of which would have attracted at least those foreign visitors who had other business in the city. The lofty tower, crowned by a statue of St James, which still stands just off the Rue de Rivoli, marked the point of departure for the pilgrim setting off from Paris to Santiago, and in what are now the southern suburbs the substantially rebuilt church of St Jacques du Haut Pas marked a further stage on his journey.[1]

London differed from Paris in that it was not, for pilgrims from elsewhere in Europe, on the way to anywhere else. Only Canterbury among English shrines had a real place in the wider European consciousness, and it was still attracting some foreign visitors on the eve of the Reformation. Among its other advantages was the simple fact that it *was* on the way to somewhere else: London. Indeed it was all but inescapable for the foreigner who landed at Dover or Sandwich. Once at London for other reasons, visitors doubtless visited the city's most notable churches. Those who waited on the king at Westminster probably found themselves having to do reverence to Edward the Confessor at the Abbey.

The constant commercial presence in the capital also fostered incidental pilgrimage. When a cult briefly sprang up around the demagogue William fitz Osbert, executed by the justiciar Hubert Walter in 1196, interest was shown in it by people who had come to London on business. Henry III caused some ill-feeling by forbidding any other fair in the country to coincide with the fair held to mark the feast of the Confessor in October. London was also unavoidable for English pilgrims to Canterbury (except those from the far south of England or those who crossed the Thames estuary from Essex to Kent, below London) and this helped nourish the city's own cults. There were several venerated crucifixes and shrines of the Virgin to be found in and around the city in the later middle ages. The Cross at the North Door of St Paul's, which was the cathedral's principal attraction in the fourteenth and fifteenth centuries, was particularly well known, and did attract some custom from further afield in England.

Peripheries

Regions on the geographical periphery of Latin Christendom – Scotland, Ireland, Scandinavia, eastern Europe, southern Spain and southern Italy – generated their own domestic pilgrimage networks and supplied pilgrims to famous shrines elsewhere, but probably attracted relatively few pilgrims from the 'core' area. One guide to awareness of the existence of shrines throughout Europe is furnished by the lists of penitential destinations used by several Netherlandish cities. The compilers of these lists, like their counterparts in the Hanseatic cities and in eastern England, Scotland and Scandinavia, belonged to a north Atlantic world, bonded by the sea. Their cities enjoyed lively commercial contacts virtually throughout Europe, and some of the lists were of considerable length and furnish an interesting guide to awareness of distant shrines. They include the names of places which have not left any great mark on the history of medieval pilgrimage, but reflect the professional knowledge of the men who drafted them, for example Baltic cities such as Königsberg and places in eastern England such as Peterborough and Louth, as well as the more obvious Walsingham; the shrines of the Virgin at Salisbury and Oxford were also mentioned. Among the Italian shrines included were several in the south, at Benevento, Gaeta, Salerno and at Naples and its vicinity. In Spain, apart from Our Lady of Barcelona (that is, Montserrat), the lists name Santiago and a few shrines in northern Spain which could be taken in on the way there. In central Europe only St Wenceslas at Prague, St Stephen at Vienna and St Peter at Warasdin in Hungary are included; in Scandinavia only St Olaf at Trondheim.[2]

The 'peripheral' areas of course varied considerably. Santiago de Compostela would have looked like a place on the fringes of Christian Europe until it became celebrated. Parts, at least, of Italy south of Rome were well known to pilgrims who embarked for the Holy Land from the Apulian ports and who, as we have seen, sometimes visited St Nicholas at

Bari or St Michael at Monte Gargano. By transplanting herself to Rome
from Scandinavia in 1350 Birgitta of Sweden become an honorary native
of a distinct pilgrimage world. Between 1350 and her death in 1373, she
visited Assisi, Bari, Monte Gargano, St Andrew at Amalfi and St Thomas
at Ortona, as well as going to Jerusalem. In the 1520s, Master Robert
Langton, fellow of Queen's College Oxford, covered much of the same
ground, although he did not go on to the Holy Land.

Langton, like an earlier Englishman, Purchas's Pilgrim in the 1420s,
also penetrated deeply into Spain. Their travels reflect the long-term
recession of the Muslim threat, the relative pacification of the country
after the murderous Castilian civil wars of the 1360s and the ending also
of the antagonisms caused by the Great Schism, in which both Castile
and Aragon had supported the Avignonese pope. Both men went not
only to Santiago, but to Our Lady of Montserrat near Barcelona and as
far south as Seville and Cadiz.[3] Langton in the early sixteenth century
went also to Our Lady of Guadalupe and to Granada, now reconquered
for Christendom by the Catholic Kings.

A few pilgrims to Compostela from as far afield as Italy and Hungary
also visited St Patrick's Purgatory in Ireland while they were at the western extremities of Europe.[4] We are told that the Hungarian Laurence
Pazthó took the opportunity to venerate the relics of Patrick, Columba
and Brigid at Dublin. St Andrew's on the east coast of Scotland was in a
different world. It drew pilgrims from England and also from Flanders;
it appeared in some of the Flemish lists of penitential destinations mentioned above. A few English pilgrims also penetrated to St Ninian's
shrine at Whithorn in Galloway. From a European perspective Scotland
must have had much in common with Scandinavia, seeming remote and
inhospitable, and Scandinavian pilgrimage places similarly seem to have
exerted little pull beyond the region. Pilgrimage to Scandinavia, as to
most of the British Isles, paid no additional dividend. The Swede or the
Dane setting out for Santiago was not only aiming to visit one of the chief
shrines of Christendom; he or she was also potentially able to visit a
number of others en route. A Norwegian on his way south by sea might
call at Canterbury, but an English pilgrim had little incentive to return
the compliment. Some interest was taken in the shrine of St Olaf at
Trondheim by members of the trading company of Bergenfahrers at
Lübeck; four surviving Lübeck wills mention pilgrimages to Trondheim. There were allegedly penitential pilgrims to Trondheim from as
far afield as France and Spain in the twelfth century, but the relevant
stories have a suspiciously stereotypical look.

The early records of domestic Scandinavian pilgrimage suggest that the highest level of activity was, predictably, in Denmark, the most densely populated part of the region, with the most numerous markets, and the most open to influences from continental Europe. With time, the development of Sweden was reflected in an intensified pilgrimage culture. The ecclesiastical and cultural centre of Sweden was and remained at Uppsala, where King Erik (d. 1150) enjoyed some fame in the thirteenth century as a healer, especially of the possessed. In the early fifteenth century a flourishing cult grew up around the image of the Deposition of Christ from the Cross in the Dominican church at Stockholm. This was one of several new cults to flourish in fifteenth-century Sweden, but all were restricted to a Swedish or at most Scandinavian public.

Birgitta of Sweden (herself once a pilgrim to Trondheim) died at Rome in 1373. Her relics were promptly brought back by her daughter Katharina, or Karin, to the house she had founded at Vadstena.[5] Birgitta's cult, like Olaf's, had a wider public, and she was known far beyond Scandinavia, but there is, again, little evidence for non-Scandinavian pilgrimage to Vadstena. English enthusiasts could go to Syon Abbey, a Bridgettine foundation at Isleworth just west of London, and her house in Rome was shown to visitors (Margery Kempe, who also went to Syon Abbey, was one). Other regional centres were established. In 1402 the archbishop of Magdeburg sought relics from Vadstena, in consequence of certain miracles that had occurred at a chapel built in Birgitta's honour; almost simultaneously, the abbot of the Cistercians of Zinna, near Brandenburg, put in a similar request for similar reasons.

Only an incomplete picture is as yet available of the network of eastern European shrines. Like their Scandinavian counterparts they attracted few pilgrims from beyond the region, although increasing numbers of Poles and Hungarians were participating in pilgrimage to Rome, Santiago and the Holy Land in the later middle ages, as well as going to Wilsnack, Cologne and Aachen. Bohemian pilgrimage suffered as a result of the Hussite revolt in the fifteenth century and Bohemia's miracle collections were destroyed. Pilgrimage in Poland bore the marks of the long division of the country into distinct principalities (Greater Poland, Little Poland, Silesia). Most of the cults centred on Cracow, for example, were for very local consumption, with the partial exception of that of St Stanislas, the eleventh-century bishop who was canonised in 1253. The image of the Virgin at Czestochowa already enjoyed a popular cult, destined to increase and endure to the present day, but little evidence survives from the medieval period.

At Monte Calvo (Łysa Góra) a piece of the wood of the True Cross enjoyed regional celebrity, and at Poznan there was a popular cult centred on a miraculous Host, whose fame extended into Lithuania and between 1493 and 1529 attracted a high proportion of pilgrims from relatively long distances (over 60 km). Poznan could not, however, rival its Prussian counterpart at Wilsnack for international pulling power. A merchant of Bratislava, in peril at sea on his way back from the Holy Land in 1496, vowed to go on pilgrimage to the Silesian saint-princess Hedvig (canonised in 1267) at Trzebnica and also to offer masses to St Barbara at Torún and to St Nicolas, that notable friend of seafarers, at Bratislava itself. There are instructive glimpses of rivalry between neighbouring centres, for example Bratislava and Trzebnica, only 27 km apart, which sought to offer competing attractions on the same dates. As everywhere in Europe, all these shrines assiduously sought and offered indulgences, and as elsewhere they were the currency of an essentially local traffic.[6]

Competition and the Passing Trade

For many shrines of the second or lower ranks, a position on or near a major route was crucial. Conversely, such a location doubtless often also stimulated the development of subsidiary shrines to tap the passing trade, which would be the more successful if the place was equipped with good inns and could obtain attractive indulgences. The Volto Santo, the celebrated miraculous crucifix of Lucca, was a conspicuous example of this exploitation of situation. Lucca was an important stop on the road to Rome already in the early eighth century, as a wave of hospital foundations by local notables testifies. Legend ascribed the coming of the Volto Santo to Lucca to the year 782, but it is not certainly documented until the very end of the eleventh century, another great growth period in the history of pilgrimage and another period of hospital foundation at Lucca. Pilgrim-badge finds indicate that it was commonplace to stop at Lucca and venerate the Volto Santo.

Assisi, the burial place of St Francis, was differently situated. It was not on the major road that brought travellers from north-western Europe to Rome, the Via Francigena, which ran to the west of Lake Trasimeno, but it lay near another major Roman road, the Via Flaminia from Rome to the Adriatic. The popes in the thirteenth century sometimes resided at Assisi for prolonged periods, which enhanced its attraction for visitors such as Eudes Rigaud, archbishop of Rouen, who spent a month there on business with Innocent IV in the summer of 1254. Francis's tomb in the church of San Francesco was less accessible to visitors than one might expect, however, and from the fifteenth century it was not accessible at all.[7] The great draw for pilgrims was rather the little church of the Portiuncula in the plain below the town, where the saint had died. Now enclosed in a vast and chilly sixteenth-century basilica hard by the railway station, it offered a plenary indulgence, at the beginning of August, which drew crowds from far afield: Margery Kempe was one visitor. A slightly earlier pilgrim to Assisi, Birgitta of Sweden, came from Rome in response to what she took to be a personal visionary invitation from St Francis, only to discover that he had intended it metaphorically.

Assisi's neighbour and enemy, Perugia, then as now, was the most considerable city in the region, but not itself a pilgrimage centre.[8] When lavish indulgences became available at the Portiuncula, the Perugians took steps to ensure that they benefited as far as possible from the flow of pilgrims, enacting measures to ensure the supply of bread and water for the increased numbers of persons passing through the city and issuing permissions to their own citizens to go to Assisi for the indulgence. It was sometimes even stated that these demonstrations of piety were intended 'to the shame and opprobrium of the city of Assisi'. In 1433 the Perugians exempted foreign and native merchants from tolls on most merchandise, hoping thus to encourage traffic through their territory to the fairs which accompanied the indulgence. Pilgrims might also pass by or near Perugia on their way to Rome from north-eastern Italy, including the port cities of Venice and Ancona. In 1450, a Jubilee year, the Perugians hired a guide (*interpres*), who was stationed at Gubbio in the mountains to the east to direct intending pilgrims from that region onto the road that went by Perugia, and they also remunerated a craftsman of Gubbio for setting up an image to serve as a signpost pointing pilgrims in the right direction. Not themselves in possession of a major spiritual attraction, the Perugians could at least try to exploit their proximity to one important shrine and their situation on or near a route to another still more important.

Sigal's analysis of eleventh- and twelfth-century French miracle stories reveals a contrast between different shrines, which, it can be argued, depended on geographical situation. Most shrines appealed to a local or at most regional public; the principal exceptions were St Gilles du Provence and Rocamadour, both of which lay along the roads to Spain and Santiago de Compostela. The St Gilles miracles benefited numerous

Germans; one Polish pilgrim is mentioned by name, and there were other pilgrims from that country. Among the pilgrims recorded at Rocamadour between 1148 and 1172 were five from Germany and four from the Low Countries, all of whom might plausibly have been on their way to Spain. The five pilgrims who are mentioned from northern Italy, had they been intending to go to Compostela, would however have had to make a substantial detour from their most direct route in order to visit Rocamadour. Natives of Tours and Poitou were explicitly described as pilgrims both to Our Lady and to St James, but otherwise the miracle stories do not betray any direct connection between the shrines.

This silence is perfectly consistent with the conventions of the genre: authors preferred not to mention other churches unless it was to demonstrate the superiority of their own. Oft-repeated and stereotypical stories told how a frustrated suppliant went to a famous shrine, sometimes to Rome, Santiago or even Jerusalem, and failed to receive release from his affliction or his penitential fetters, only to obtain it at the usually much less noteworthy shrine (for example, St Aldhelm's at Malmesbury) which was being publicised by the writer. The miracles of San Prospero of Reggio, between Piacenza and Bologna on the old Roman Via Emilia, which remained a major artery of traffic across northern Italy, were recorded in the eleventh century. The saint, who is unlikely to have been of much interest to anyone outside the immediate vicinity, was credited with several cures of French pilgrims who were on their way to or from Rome and one of a native from Benevento who was allegedly setting out for Tours. Such stories at least delineate the mental map of their authors.

Several 'competitive' miracles were generated by the sudden success of Becket's cult at Canterbury in the 1170s. Clergy whose business it was to look after the interests of the Hand of St James at Reading Abbey, of St Frideswide at Oxford or of St Cuthbert at Durham knew, after 1171, that a new power had arisen in the land and that it was their duty to respond to it. One theme of the propaganda that resulted is well illustrated by the miracles of St Cuthbert and of St Godric of Finchale, who died only a few months before Becket. The author of both collections, Reginald of Durham, lays great stress on the power and claims of locality, even putting words into Becket's own mouth, when he appears in a vision to one pilgrim, to support the view that the north-countryman should apply to the north-country saint. The pilgrims who went to St Frideswide's shrine at Oxford were with few exceptions local people, and it is possible to infer that when she did miracles for pilgrims who had been disappointed at Canterbury she was gently rebuking them for not having come to her first, as the presiding genius of the neighbourhood. This homely doctrine was in effect making a virtue out of what for many people was a necessity. If in general shrines everywhere drew most of their pilgrims from the immediately contiguous area, it follows that the generality of pilgrims went only short distances. Age, wealth, health, social status and other circumstances (including gender) would either open up or restrict the possibilities open to the individual. The servant Zita of Lucca (d. 1278) was assiduous in all her devotions, as might be expected of a future saint, but circumscribed by her means and her duties as a housekeeper. Although we do not hear of her making any lengthy pilgrimages, she visited local churches of St Mary Magdalen and of both Peter and St James in the neighbourhood of Pisa. Was it coincidental that these were all saints whose best-known churches were major centres of 'international' pilgrimage? The church of San Jacopo di Podio which Zita visited, just north of Pisa, was built, early in the thirteenth century, by Bona of Pisa, a local saint who was herself a frequent pilgrim to Compostela, and it was clearly intended to serve as a local outpost of devotion to St James (who helped her with the design and building). Zita, unable to absent herself from her domestic responsibilities, took advantage of what lay to hand.

Throughout the medieval period, subsidiary shrines, centred on secondary relics or on portions of a saint's bones begged or purloined from his or her principal burial place, were important focuses of pilgrimage. Although competition between shrines is a common motif of miracle stories, their interdependence was often a matter of observable fact. A monk of Worcester said in 1307 that he knew about the sanctity of Thomas Cantilupe because the church of Worcester had benefited from offerings made by pilgrims passing through on their way to Hereford. Occasionally pilgrim souvenirs were made to commemorate two shrines jointly: badges were made showing both the Yorkshire saints, John of Beverley and John of Bridlington, for example, and the Virgin and Charlemagne (venerated at Aachen) were similarly shown accompanied by St Cornelius (at nearby Kornelimünster).

Routes and Destinations

Before the fifteenth century few medieval pilgrims had a green or red Michelin guide to the roads they were going to traverse and the facilities available along them. Although several itineraries and descriptive accounts of pilgrimages survive from earlier centuries and provide invaluable sources for the modern historian, there is little direct information about the use that was made of them by other pilgrims. The impulse to record something of one's pilgrimage experience in writing was clearly felt from early times, and the resulting accounts seem sometimes to have been written as much for the benefit of interested stay-at-homes as for intending travellers. They vary considerably in the quantity and character of the practical information they include. There are, however, occasional references to the use, or at least the possession, of them by other pilgrims. In 1285, a deacon of Lund referred in his will both to his pilgrim staff and to 'my itinerary in two parts'. This might conceivably have been a copy of an earlier account such as the one by the Icelandic abbot Niklas of Munkathvera, who went to Rome and the Holy Land around 1150. Two later English pilgrims to Rome, Purchas's Pilgrim and Master Robert Langton, said that they had read a slightly earlier English guidebook, *The Stacions of Rome*, and Langton had also consulted the *Mirabilia Urbis Romae*.

Reference has already been made to the so-called *Pilgrim's Guide* to the roads to Santiago, compiled some time around 1140. As the most recent editors of the text have stressed, there is no evidence that it was ever widely known within Spain or without, still less that it was at any time actually used as a *vademecum* by pilgrims. The strongest negative indicators are that there are no surviving non-Spanish manuscripts from before the fourteenth century and that even then the *Guide* always occurs as part of the whole *Codex Calixtinus* or a substantial part of it, never in a reduced or portable form. In the thirteenth century, Matthew Paris, monk of St Albans, provided a description, with maps, of the routes that might be followed from England to Rome and the Holy Land, which bears witness to some circulation of information in the circles to which he had access. Maps of course were particularly difficult to reproduce in large numbers before the age of print. Even before the advent of printing, guidebooks were almost certainly in wider use by the fifteenth century.

What information the early pilgrim possessed when he (or she) started out was presumably obtained for the most part by word of mouth. In so far as he needed to know in what direction and by what route to proceed, and what overnight stops to make, the pilgrim was in the same position as the merchant or any other traveller, and like them derived intelligence from those who had gone before him or accompanied him, and subsequently, of course, from his own experience, if he was a frequent pilgrim. His unwritten Michelin may have included assessments of inns and other facilities en route, but it certainly included something far more fundamental, which is paralleled in its modern descendant, the evaluation of likely destinations as 'Interesting', 'Worth a detour' and, on the topmost rank, 'Worth a journey'. It was the choice or choices made from the last category that ultimately determined the direction the pilgrim took, whether over a long or a short distance, but his selection of one or more shrines in the 'Worth a detour' class did much to influence the precise route. The merely 'Interesting' would be viewed if the pilgrim came across them.

In the heyday of medieval Christian pilgrimage after the eleventh century, there could be little doubt that, for those whose capacity matched their inclinations and their opportunities, there was a handful of shrines of the highest rank which the serious pilgrim would aspire to visit in his or her lifetime: Rome, Santiago, the Holy Land. There were many others that would also have merited inclusion in the 'Worth a journey' category, if only at certain periods when they were new or fashionable: Becket at Canterbury, the Three Magi at Cologne, Our Lady at Aachen, the Holy Blood at Wilsnack. For some pilgrims any one of these shrines would have meant the journey of a lifetime, the most that they could aspire to achieve, requiring careful preparation and the disposition of their affairs before departure. Journeys that seemed minor to the professional frequent traveller might seem epoch-making to others. In 1508 Elizabeth Wilson of Gisburn, in what is now Cleveland, made her will on the eve of departing for Canterbury. It was not apparently usual to make a will before going on what would have been regarded by many as a normal, domestic pilgrimage; perhaps Elizabeth was elderly or nervous about her health or about the hazards of the road, or this was, for her, simply an unparalleled event. For more ambitious pilgrims, shrines of similar standing would be integrated into a longer journey, perhaps helping to determine the precise choice of route. The English pilgrim to Rome or the Holy Land who departed from Dover could scarcely avoid Canterbury en route.

The Compostela *Pilgrim's Guide* is the classic, and certainly the most quoted, description of an important cluster of pilgrim routes, dotted with subsidiary shrines. It describes, in a somewhat uneven wealth of detail, four principal routes through the more southerly parts of France, which met south of the Pyrenees and proceeded as one to Santiago. Their points of departure were, from east to west, St Gilles in Provence, Notre Dame of Le Puy in the Auvergne, the great Burgundian abbey of

Vézelay, and St Martin of Tours, all themselves established shrines of consequence. The author of the *Guide* recommended a number of other notable holy places to the pilgrim's attention, but his personal knowledge of them seems to have been variable, and there are some odd omissions from his lists, notably St Martial at Limoges.

Whatever the purpose for which it was originally written, it is clear that the *Guide* gives us only a partial view of the web of roads which linked Santiago to other shrines and into what can loosely be called the European road network. In the first place, it cannot and does not convey an adequate impression of the maze of side-roads and by-ways which pilgrims everywhere undoubtedly used opportunistically according to their individual places of origin and incidental purposes. The state of the going or the collapse of a bridge could enforce a diversion, rather as an accident or major road-works may today enforce the use of minor roads. It was rare for there not to be more than one possible path between two places that were any distance apart, even if one of them was the more or most frequented.

Secondly, the *Guide*'s overall geographical scope is inevitably limited. It does not and cannot tell us how the thousands of pilgrims who came from all parts of Europe to Santiago arrived (if they did) at one or another of the starting-points postulated by the author. For those Englishmen, Netherlanders, Germans or Scandinavians who did not come by sea, and for the Pole, Hungarian or Italian, there was a great deal of ground to cover first, and that probably meant visits to shrines which lay beyond the ken of the author of the *Guide* but benefited from their position on a long-distance route to Santiago. Pilgrims from England could, for example, easily visit Our Lady of Boulogne and St John the Baptist at Amiens on their way to Paris. Amiens seems to have been a particularly popular destination in its own right for Scots in the fourteenth and fifteenth centuries, to judge from the permissions the English kings granted them to cross the kingdom of England en route. Einsiedeln in Switzerland, itself a major shrine, has been described as a meeting place for Santiago pilgrims from southern and eastern central Europe: the German Servite friar Hermann Künig von Vach, late in the fifteenth century, as a devotee of the Virgin regarded it as the desirable starting-point.

Italians necessarily followed their own trajectory. It was possible for them to perform part of the journey by sea from one of the ports on the Tyrrhenian coast, notably Genoa; a Venetian who did so in the first half of the fourteenth century landed near Fréjus and proceeded by land to join the road that went via Toulouse. Two Florentine pilgrims whose (separate) itineraries survive from the late fifteenth century went overland via the Mont Cenis pass, coming down the valley of the Isère via Grenoble. An early twelfth-century document mentions the road at Grenoble, which led either 'to Rome or to St James'. At Romans, a little beyond Grenoble, many Italians made a detour to the shrine of St Antony at La Motte, just to the north of the main line of their journey. The first Italian pilgrim known to have done so was Raimondo 'Palmario', who visited St Antony on his way back from Compostela in the late 1170s; the two fifteenth-century Florentines just mentioned made the detour on their outward journey. St Antony was a popular destination for Italians, mentioned in wills and sometimes sought in his own right. The itinerary of Niccolò d'Este's pilgrimage to St Antony in 1414, mentioned in the preceding chapter, survives. On the outward journey he went from Ferrara to Parma, then crossed the Apennines and took ship from Genoa to Nice, making his way thence via Aix, Avignon and Orange to St Antony and subsequently Paris. Returning from his interview with Charles VI, he passed once more through Lyon and returned to Italy via the Mont Cenis, 'where there is a good ascent and a bad descent'.

Although the brethren of St Antony had property in England and conducted collections there, there is little direct evidence of English pilgrimage to La Motte, at least before the fifteenth century, perhaps because pilgrims to the saint went instead to his hospital in London. The future St Hugh of Lincoln went to La Motte on the tour he undertook in 1200, not long before his death, to the birthplace of his order, the Grande Chartreuse. English pilgrims generally, whether they were going to Santiago or to Rome, went by routes which did not easily lend themselves to a detour to La Motte. If going to Rome they would have turned eastwards much further north to approach the Great St Bernard, if going overland to Santiago they would have come by one of the more westerly routes, by Paris or perhaps Tours, before crossing the Pyrenees. However, both Purchas's Pilgrim and Master Robert Langton visited La Motte. They did so because they had gone first to Spain and then crossed into Italy from Provence by the Mont Cenis, as Italians did going home from Santiago.

Roads to Rome

Italians who went to Santiago, or indeed to any other transalpine shrine, were likely to use some part of the greatest of all European pilgrim roads, the Via Francigena, the 'Frankish road' from north-western Europe to Rome. There is no single source for the Francigena to compare with the *Pilgrim's Guide*, which may help to account for the fact that outside Italy it has not received quite the concentrated (and sometimes rather romantic) attention which has been focused on the roads to Santiago.[9] The Francigena was, of course, mapped out rather earlier. In large part, like most European 'major roads', it rested on pre-Christian and Roman foundations. As the recent work of Renato Stopani, A. C. Quintavalle and others in Italy has amply demonstrated, there is a wealth of written material bearing on its course, its variations and diversions and the stopping places along it. These include the itineraries of pilgrims and other travellers and a host of incidental references in chronicles, letters, *chansons de geste* and archival sources. Surviving churches and other buildings along the road supply further evidence, and in some places there are substantial tracts of road surface surviving from the Roman or medieval periods.

The course of the central portion of the Francigena, from the north Italian plain to Rome, was decisively affected by the political and military division of the peninsula, between the sixth and the eighth centuries, into areas of Lombard and Byzantine power. The Lombards, as they turned Christian, sought a route to Rome which as far as possible avoided areas still in Byzantine occupation. Masters of much of the Po Valley, with a capital at Pavia, they could use the more westerly portion of the old Roman consular road, the Via Emilia (later called Strata Claudia), which ran from Piacenza in the west to Rimini on the Adriatic coast. The tracks they developed across the Apennines were dotted with monastic foundations, which were partly intended to serve the roads and their travellers. This Apennine section of the 'road' came to be known collectively as 'Monte Bardone', a reminiscence of its Lombard origin. South of the Apennines, in Tuscany, it was not always possible or desirable to follow the line of the Roman Via Cassia and alternative routes were developed which helped to shape settlements, such as San Gimignano and Siena, which lay along them.

When the Carolingians in the later eighth century supplanted the Lombards in northern Italy and established their dominance over the peninsula as far as Rome, traffic into Italy from beyond the Alps increased. It had of course never altogether ceased, as the travels of Anglo-Saxon pilgrims in the seventh century indicate. The westerly Alpine passes (principally the Mont Cenis and what would later be called the Great St Bernard) and the pathways to and from the crossing of the

Po at Piacenza had remained in use, but now there was once again a political power straddling the western Alps which had a keen interest in communications between France and Italy. The great monastery of Novalesa on the Mont Cenis, where Louis the Pious endowed a hospice early in the ninth century, could be taken to symbolise this interest. Epic poems of twelfth- and thirteenth-century date, the *chansons de geste*, preserve numerous reminiscences of the Carolingian association with the road to Rome. These are especially numerous in the epic of *Ogier the Dane*, which, for example, preserves the tradition that the companions in arms Amicus and Amilius were buried at Mortara, on the road between Vercelli and Pavia, where they were venerated as saints.

Several other places in this Piedmontese–Lombard region are associated with what may be termed pilgrimage folklore and with saints who were in effect the products of the pilgrim roads. The St Bernard passes take their name not from the great Cistercian saint but from Bernard of Aosta, who for forty years or more in the eleventh century devoted himself to the needs of travellers over the Alps. The tenth-century Provençal knight Bobo or Bovo is venerated as a patron saint of Voghera, southwest of Pavia; having dedicated himself to the struggle against Saracen piracy around Fréjus he laid down his arms and performed annual pilgrimages to Rome, dying at last on the road. Further along the road towards Piacenza, Contardo d'Este is similarly venerated at Broni, where he died in 1233 on his way to Compostela. Ejected from the inn when he became inconveniently ill, he was cared for in a neighbouring house until he died. He was buried in the 'pilgrims' burial place' until unmistakable signs of his sanctity prompted his removal into the church. The phrase *peregrinorum sepultura* might conceivably mean a burial place for foreigners or outsiders rather than for pilgrims as such, but it remains interesting testimony to the provision made for travellers in a very small but strategically sited settlement.

The earliest full description of the Francigena that we have is the list of the overnight stops (*mansiones*) made by Archbishop Sigeric of Canterbury on his return journey from Rome, where had gone to receive his *pallium* from the pope, probably in the summer of 993. The itinerary revealed in this list, both in Italy and beyond the Alps, is confirmed by abundant later testimonies, but, as Sigeric's choice of it might itself suggest, it was already well established. Reference was made earlier to Lucca's prominent position on this road. The nameless father of Sts Willibald and Winnebald, who accompanied his sons on their pilgrimage in the early 720s, died and was buried at Lucca; here in the twelfth century he was transmogrified not only into a saint but into a king, with the unlikely name (for an Anglo-Saxon) of Richard. The account of the pilgrimages of the ninth-century noble saint Gerald of Aurillac given by Odo of Cluny mentions several of the places later included in Sigeric's itinerary, including Piacenza, Lucca, and Sutri, but Gerald, coming from the Auvergne, clearly followed the Rhône valley on the first stage of his journey. Whatever alterations the road underwent, there were certain constants. Nearly six hundred years after Gerald of Aurillac, Anthony Woodville, the brother-in-law of Edward IV of England, was robbed of his valuables at Sutri when he went to Rome for the Jubilee indulgence of 1475.

The very varied testimonies to the history of the Francigena and its tributaries implicate pilgrims from the remoter parts of European Christendom. The Irishman Donatus, who became bishop and patron saint of Fiesole near Florence, in 850 founded a hospital at Piacenza for the reception of other Irish pilgrims. In the late eleventh century Erik I, 'the Good', king of Denmark, is supposed to have founded a hospital at Fiorenzuola d'Arda, south of Piacenza, for the reception of Scandinavian pilgrims, and also to have made provision at Lucca for them to have an adequate supply of wine. A little later, in 1106, Duke Sviatopulk of Bohemia made a gift to the Volto Santo of Lucca. There were several Germans among the beneficiaries of the twelfth-century miracles of both the Volto Santo and 'St Richard'. Just a few years before Sigeric made his journey, the first known pilgrim to go from Italy to Compostela, the Armenian hermit Simeon, followed part of the same route, crossing the Apennines from Lucca and proceeding by way of Piacenza. The river crossing at Piacenza is repeatedly mentioned in narrative sources, in the lives of both Gerald of Aurillac and Simeon, for example, and in the miracles of St Thomas Becket. From Piacenza Simeon branched off through Pavia to cross the Alps not by the Great St Bernard, as Sigeric did, aiming further north, but by the Mont Cenis. Unfortunately his *Life* gives no particulars of his route through France towards Santiago, which would have furnished a most valuable addition to our knowledge a century and a half before the *Pilgrim's Guide*.

One of the most comprehensive and informative of surviving itineraries was composed by the Icelandic abbot Niklas of Munkathvera *c.*1150. The value of this account is not only that the abbot's travels were particularly extensive, but that he comments from time to time on alternative routes and connections which were in current use, and that cross-reference is sometimes possible between his observations and other Scandinavian and German sources. Having traversed Norway and Denmark on his way south, the abbot continued from Stade, on the east of the neck of the Jutland peninsula, to Paderborn and Mainz. Mainz, according to his account, was a major junction, for here there were alternative routes to both east and west; the pilgrim could come from Stade via Hanover and Hildesheim, or he could take an entirely different route, crossing from Norway by sea to Frisia and coming on via Deventer or Utrecht, where, Niklas said, the ceremony of blessing of the pilgrim's staff and satchel was performed. This westerly route to Mainz lay via Cologne. From Mainz, Niklas implies a single main route down the Rhine as far as Basel. Here pilgrims left the valley, making for Vevey on Lake Geneva, which was a mustering point for all, French, Flemish, English, German and Scandinavian, who wanted to cross the Alps by the St Bernard. A century later, the traffic was beginning to flow over the St Gotthard pass, to the benefit of both pilgrims and merchants who wanted access to the Rhine valley via Switzerland.

There are references to the 'eastern' and 'western' routes from Scandinavia to Rome in other northern sources, and it is evident that there were yet further options. At the end of *Njal's Saga* two of the major protagonists in the deadly feud which furnishes the main thread of the story, set around the year 1000, make separate penitential pilgrimages to Rome. Both started from Normandy, for they had previously been busy creating mayhem in the British Isles. The first, Flosi, returned from Rome 'by the east route, staying in many large cities'. The other, Kari, had come from Scotland to Normandy where he left his ships before proceeding to Rome on foot, so he returned 'by the west route' to pick them up and begin the voyage home. No further details of the precise route or routes are given. In *Orkneyinga Saga*, Earl Rognvald of the Orkneys, returning from the Holy Land in the mid-twelfth century, rode from Apulia to Rome and then followed 'the usual pilgrim-route all the way to Denmark'. This may well mean the route via the St Bernard and the lower Rhine valley, which Niklas of Munkathvera contemporaneously describes in the reverse direction.

Once in Italy, Abbot Niklas noted that Milan was a day's journey off the main road to Rome and that at Piacenza, at the crossing of the Po, there was a junction with the road 'taken by those who have taken the road of St Gilles'. This must presumably signify the more southerly road to and from the Mont Cenis, which from Piacenza went via Tortona and Asti. A day's journey further on from Piacenza, Niklas noted the hospice reputedly founded by King Eric of Denmark. Having crossed the Apennines, he came down to the Tyrrhenian shore at Luni, where he remarked on the junction with 'the roads coming from Spain and the land of St James'; he was more probably referring to the sea passage from that coast to Spain than to a land route around the Ligurian coast. From Luni to Rome his itinerary substantially agrees with Sigeric's, but, unlike the archbishop, Niklas was going on to the Holy Land.

Between Rome and Capua the abbot again notices alternative routes, and here further comparisons are possible, for example with the itinerary followed by Philip II of France on his return from crusade in 1191 and with the route suggested by Matthew Paris in the mid-thirteenth century. From Rome southwards the main road was supplied by the ancient Via Appia as far as Capua and Benevento, although Niklas again indicated the existence of an alternative way to Capua, via Terracina. Beyond Benevento the medieval sources indicate a preference for the Via Traiana, which followed a more northerly trajectory than the Appian Way, arriving at Bari on the Adriatic coast. It was an important consideration that the greatest European shrine of St Nicholas was to be found here. If one followed this route it was also possible to make a detour to the shrine of the Archangel Michael on the Gargano peninsula still further to the north in Apulia. From Bari the road followed the coast to Brindisi and Otranto, both embarkation points for the eastern Mediterranean. Philip Augustus in 1191 landed at Otranto and followed this route to Benevento and Rome.

Routes were obviously not changeless. Like other medieval roads, the Francigena was more properly a complex of routes, incorporating alternatives, diversions and junctions for other destinations. The pilgrim (or merchant or diplomat) on his way to Rome could turn off between Piacenza and Bologna at one of several points to make his way across the Apennine passes. On one of his journeys to Rome the paranoid Gerald of Wales believed that his enemies were lying in wait for him at Bologna so, having changed his money at Modena, he skirted Bologna and continued down the Emilia to Faenza, branching off here by a most arduous route across the Apennines to Spoleto, a story which struck all with wonder when they heard it, as he reported with satisfaction. A little later Matthew Paris of St Albans also described the possibility of following the Via Emilia beyond Bologna to Faenza and Forlì before turning definitively south, as an alternative to crossing 'Monte Bardone', which suggests that he had heard about this route from Englishmen who had used it. A visit to Assisi could thus be included.

William Brewyn's itinerary from England to Rome, dated 1469, is an anthology of possibilities. Evidently seeking to avoid France, he described a route from Calais to Ostend, proceeding via Bruges, Ghent and Maastricht to Aachen and Cologne (unless one wanted to avoid the archbishop's taxes, in which case there was an alternative route via Trier). From Cologne, Brewyn followed the Rhine valley but then turned east through southern Germany and crossed into Italy by following the valley of the Adige, that is the Engadine pass, to Merano, where the market was noteworthy, and Trent. He calls Verona 'a fine city' where 'one is given *baculos*', presumably meaning pilgrim staves. Verona was indeed an important halt for pilgrims coming via the Brenner or (like Brewyn) other easterly Alpine passes. He proceeded thence via Bologna and Florence to pick up the traditional road to Rome.

By 1469 the 'road revolution' caused by the rise of Florence to commercial pre-eminence and dominance within Tuscany was a long-accomplished fact. From the thirteenth century it became increasingly common to diverge from the ancient course of the Francigena through Tuscany to the Apennines via Lucca and to go instead by Florence and Bologna. Towards the end of the century the poet Dante recorded seeing Rome-bound pilgrims in the centre of Florence, who were on their way to see the 'Veronica'. Further south the increasing importance of Viterbo as a papal city had a not dissimilar impact on the road through Lazio. The power of the counts of Savoy owed much, historically, to their command of the more westerly alpine passes, but by the later middle ages a significant proportion of commercial traffic to and from Italy had shifted eastwards to the St Gotthard (rendered more easily passable in the first half of the thirteenth century) and the Simplon, and some pilgrimage traffic also went by these routes. Eudes, archbishop of Rouen, went via the Simplon to Rome in 1253, but returned via the Mont Cenis.

Much of the traffic from further east, from Bavaria, Austria and eastern Europe, came over the much lower and easier Brenner. The economic, commercial and urban development of central and eastern Europe was reflected in a dense and better used road network. The popularity of Roman pilgrimage with the Hungarians, for example, is well documented. From the thirteenth century onwards it seems that Scandinavian pilgrims were increasingly availing themselves of their Hanseatic trading connections and the development of routes further east through Germany than Niklas of Munkathvera had envisaged. This might involve taking ship to Lübeck on the east of the Jutland peninsula and proceeding via Würzburg, Rothenburg, Augsburg and Innsbruck to the Brenner. Such a route intersected at many points with the paths taken by pilgrims from eastern and central Europe not only to Rome but to Compostela, and not unnaturally places situated on these routes, such as the picture-book town of Rothenburg on the Tauber, developed their own pilgrimage attractions.

Rothenburg's principal church (rebuilt in the late fifteenth century) is dedicated to St James, and the saint figures prominently on its main altarpiece. On the predella he is depicted next to a rather worried-looking, bespectacled St Peter, which seems appropriate if pilgrims to both Rome and Compostela were expected to pause before the altar. The adjacent chapel of the Holy Blood, built by the knights of the Teutonic Order, was consecrated in 1266 and attracted pilgrims, for whom indulgences were available.[10] Regensburg too was an important crossroads; here the church of St Jakob (where a fourteenth-century statue of the saint can still be seen) was a *Schottenkloster*, a centre of missionary Irish monasticism in Germany. In 1519 a new pilgrimage sprang up at Regensburg to an image of the Virgin and Child painted by Albrecht Altdorfer. This doubtless benefited from the city's position and seems to have been briefly profitable, stimulating a busy pilgrim souvenir industry; it was one of the cults which incurred the wrath of Martin Luther.

Aachen and its Influence

Pilgrimage across Germany did not merely go east–west towards Compostela or north–south towards Rome and the ports of embarkation for the Holy Land. The shrines of the Rhine–Meuse region too exerted an attraction. The cathedral of Aachen is an excellent example of a shrine which was visited both in its own right and in transit; it also nourished subsidiary and imitative pilgrimages in its vicinity.

Aachen offered many-layered attractions. The coronation place of the emperors as kings of Germany, it possessed the 'relics' of Charlemagne as well as the garment worn by the Virgin Mary at the Nativity of Christ, Christ's own swaddling-clothes, the loincloth He wore on the Cross, and a cloth used to wrap the head of John the Baptist. Badges sold at Aachen depicted Charlemagne venerating the Virgin's garment, and the pilgrimage doubtless drew part of its nourishment from the city's imperial associations. In 1357 Charles IV, Holy Roman Emperor and king of Bohemia, came on pilgrimage to Aachen, where he had been crowned in 1349, together with his wife Maria and Elizabeth, the queen mother of Hungary. Elizabeth took the opportunity to found a Hungarian chapel in the cathedral, which was completed ten years later, and Charles later established an altar of the Bohemian St Wenceslas there.

The public exhibition of the major relics, which took place at Aachen between 10 and 24 July in every seventh year, was an attraction for pilgrims from all parts of Germany and central Europe and also from France, the Netherlands and Scandinavia. There is abundant evidence for Aachen's appeal to pilgrims from a wide area of northern Europe. A Swedish nobleman was on his way to Aachen in 1374 when he was persuaded by an ecclesiastical acquaintance to go to St Birgitta's burial place at Vadstena first (or instead). Testators from Hanseatic cities such as Hamburg and Lübeck left money for pilgrimages to Aachen, and Dorothea of Montau and her husband made the journey from Gdansk more than once. Reference was made in an earlier chapter to the poor pilgrims with whom Margery Kempe entered Aachen in 1433, and to the baths provided at Hildesheim in 1474 for the benefit of Aachen pilgrims. Some of the traffic through Hildesheim was from eastern Europe; the magistrates early in the sixteenth century endeavoured to establish rates of exchange, for the protection of pilgrims, including one for the Hungarian penny. Vienna was a mustering point for Hungarian and Slavonic pilgrimage to Aachen, which clearly assumed significant dimensions; areas of Aachen itself were allocated to provide lodgings for pilgrims from these regions. In 1447 it was discovered that a group of pilgrims from Hungary were descendants of Walloon-speakers who had emigrated from Liège to escape starvation; they went on from Aachen to Liège and were indeed still able to converse with the inhabitants. A longer haul from Aachen was the Swiss shrine of Einsiedeln, which rose to prominence in the fourteenth century and which Dorothea of Montau visited twice with her husband between 1384 and 1387, making their way there from Aachen or Cologne.

Kings, queens and lesser mortals alike would get the best value out of their time and effort by combining pilgrimages. Charles IV's pilgrimage to Aachen in 1357 also took in the Three Magi at Cologne and the tomb of the Hungarian-born Franciscan saint Elizabeth of Thuringia at Marburg, which on pilgrim-badge evidence also attracted pilgrimage from both Scandinavia and the Netherlands. To go to Cologne as well as Aachen was normal; in 1434, Philip, count of Katzenellenbogen, came from Wilsnack to Aachen in thirteen days via Magdeburg and Cologne. Scandinavian or German pilgrims who took such a route might be going on to Rome or to Santiago, although much Scandinavian traffic for Santiago probably went by sea. When Margery Kempe arrived at Aachen on her way back from Wilsnack she met an English monk who was on his way to Rome, and a little further on she came to an unnamed place where she encountered English pilgrims who were returning from Rome. One of them was the poor friar who then accompanied her to Calais; he said that he knew the area well, because he had often been that way to Rome. The immediate usefulness of this was that he knew a hostelry 'a little hence'. The long drawn out war between the English and the French was now in its latter stages, and a route through western Germany was preferable, for English pilgrims, to the familiar one down through eastern France to the St Bernard pass; so it evidently still seemed to William Brewyn in 1469.

Some Aachen pilgrims will have gone on to Maastricht, only twenty miles away (although now in a different country). Here the shrine of St Servatius surely benefited from its proximity to a major trans-European route. Unlike the Virgin at Aachen or the Three Kings at Cologne, Servatius was, intrinsically, a saint of limited interest beyond the Low Countries, but the discovery of pilgrim-badges from Maastricht not only elsewhere in the Netherlands but in London, Scandinavia, Bremen and Brunswick suggests that he attracted interest from further afield, even if it was by way of the passing trade; Brewyn's itinerary suggests one way that this might have occurred. Hermann Künig von Vach proposed a return route overland from Santiago which went via Tours, Arras and Brussels to Maastricht and Aachen.

Maastricht was only one of a number of shrines in the Rhine–Meuse region which have been classified as belonging to Aachen's 'family' and which held seven-yearly relic exhibitions, accompanied by indulgences, to coincide with the Aachen *ostensio* and to tap the flow of pilgrims to the region which that attracted. Some of these places were quite insignificant. In 1396, the Hospitaller Commandery of Kieringen, just to the north of Jülich, which displayed its relic collection during the Aachen pilgrimage, reported offerings of more than one hundred gulden. An exhibition began at Düsseldorf in 1394 and one at Düren in 1510, when the church acquired a portion of the skull of St Anne. At Trier there was a seven-yearly exhibition of relics of the Passion at the abbey church of St Maximin; in 1354 Charles IV acquired some of these relics for his cathedral at Prague. Closest of all to Aachen was the Benedictine abbey of St Cornelius at Kornelimünster, which claimed to have possessed the head of the saint since the ninth century. Not only was an exhibition held here to coincide with Aachen's, but, as already noted, pilgrims could buy badges which commemorated the two shrines together.

Aachen drew pilgrims from far and near. The dimensions of the pilgrimage were impressive still at the very end of the fifteenth century: in 1496 the gatekeepers of the city counted 147,000 incomers during the fifteen-day period of the indulgence, that is something under 10,000 per day. What proportion of these crowds came from what distance it is of course impossible to say.

A Regional Case History: Our Lady of Den Bosch

The *Mirakelboek* of Our Lady of 's-Hertogenbosch (familiarly and rather more shortly known as Den Bosch) makes it possible to get some idea of the catchment area of a regional pilgrimage that originated in the late fourteenth century in a closely neighbouring region. Den Bosch lay in the duchy of Brabant and is now in the province of Noord-Brabant in the south of the modern Kingdom of the Netherlands. Its cult of the Virgin was typical of many that arose in the fourteenth and fifteenth centuries in that it was centred on an image – in this instance a wooden statue of the Virgin and Child, dating from between 1280 and 1320, in the church of St John. Between February and November 1381, this statue performed twelve miracles, but the flow recorded by the *Mirakelboek* began a year later, in November 1382. In all, 481 miracles are recorded, of which a few took place in the sixteenth century, with an out-lier in 1603; 461 took place between November 1382 and 10 July 1388, and it is on this chronologically concentrated sample that the following observations are based. It should be noted that the figures given here refer to pilgrimages rather than to individuals: many pilgrims came in family groups and others, notably merchants who had been rescued from some unfortunate experience on land or water, also sometimes made up a party. Many questions could be asked of this material, for example about the gender and social class of the pilgrims and the nature of their problems, but interest here focuses on their geographical origin and also on what awareness of other shrines their stories reveal.

It is necessary first of all to dismantle mentally the modern national boundaries which cut across the region. The historic duchy of Brabant embraced not only the present Netherlandish province of Noord-Brabant but the modern Belgian provinces of Brabant and Antwerp. Most of the more considerable cities of the duchy (Brussels, Antwerp, Leuven, Mechelen) lay in this more southerly area and a steady trickle of pilgrims came to Den Bosch from these places and many others in their neighbourhoods, as well as from Flanders to the west. About 16 per cent of the total number of pilgrimages originated in the area of what is now Germany which is immediately contiguous to the Netherlands on the east: from Aachen, from Cleves and Jülich and from the vicinity of places such as Münchengladbach, Düsseldorf, Dortmund and Cologne. The pilgrimage also attracted custom from a string of places in northern Germany and along the Baltic coast which were linked to the Netherlands by the Hanseatic trading connection, from Bremen and Hamburg in the west, to Elbing and Königsberg in Prussia, and Gdansk, in what is now Poland, to the east.

It is apparent that the Virgin's catchment area constituted a cultural and economic zone rather than a national one. This perception is strengthened when one considers that the pilgrims were to a man (and woman) native speakers of Germanic dialects, principally though not solely Dutch, the language in which the *Mirakelboek* was composed. No pilgrim seems to have come from the French-language zone south of Brussels; a couple of apparent exceptions were in fact natives of Den Bosch or its vicinity who now lived in Paris and Liège. Pilgrims from the Baltic region and the Hanseatic trading cities would have understood one of a group of more or less mutually comprehensible Germanic dialects. Of the handful of pilgrims who came to Den Bosch from this region, one who was now living in Prussia had been born in Harderwijk in the north of Holland and another was a native of Kampen in Overijssel, a place with strong Hanseatic connections.

A rough calculation shows that in the period under review nearly 39 per cent of the pilgrimages originated within Brabant. The other regions of what is now the Netherlands contributed as follows. Holland (meaning both the present provinces of North and South Holland) accounted for 16.05 per cent; Gelderland, 13.23 per cent; Zeeland, 5.64 per cent; Friesland (including the city of Groningen, which today has its own province), 3.47 per cent; Overijssel, also 3.47 per cent; and the tiny ecclesiastical province of Utrecht, 1.95 per cent. Limburg, which like Brabant is today divided between the Netherlands and Belgium, accounted for 4.12 per cent. Pilgrims came from an enormous number of small places, some of them no longer in existence. Of the larger towns of Holland, Dordrecht sent nine pilgrims (or parties) during this period, as did Groningen, while Leiden, Amsterdam, Haarlem and Gouda all sent five or six. Only twelve individuals or parties are recorded from Den Bosch itself; Brussels, with eleven, did almost as well.

There are occasional references to other pilgrimages which suppliants to Our Lady had previously attempted without success, and these for the most part maintained a strongly regional colouring. Vows to Aachen and to the Three Kings at Cologne are mentioned. Our Lady was not, it seems, in competition with St James, for there is no reference to Compostela (which certainly does not mean that natives of the Low Countries did not go there). One native of Brussels was returning from Rome when he ran into trouble between Assisi and Perugia; his journey is simply called a *reis*, and it is not explicit that it was a pilgrimage. The only other possible reference to a far-distant shrine occurs in the story of a pilgrim from Gelderland who had been to 'St Antony' and to 'St Cornelius', but in neither case is it made clear where these shrines were. St Antony presided over shrines rather more accessible to Netherlanders than his headquarters in the Dauphiné; they included Borsbeke in West Flanders and Bailleul in what is now France. Dutch pilgrim-badge finds suggest that the pope-saint Cornelius, a specialist in the treatment of epilepsy, was often sought at the Premonstratensian abbey at Ninove in modern Belgium, founded in 1137, but no fewer than eight of the stories in the *Mirakelboek* refer to pilgrimages, sometimes repeated fruitless pilgrimages, to Kornelimünster near Aachen. A woman of Tienen (now in Belgium) had been not only to St Cornelius but to St Quentin at Leuven and to Our Lady at Halle just south of Brussels (where her shrine still flourishes). St Quentin, who was supposed to be good for dropsy, was principally associated with the place which bears his name, near Noyon in northern France.

It must have been an important factor in the calculations of many pilgrims, especially those who could not afford a prodigal outlay of time and money, that so many saints, including specialists in particular diseases, were available in more than one place. The pilgrim did not have to go to Bari for St Nicholas or to the Dauphiné for St Antony. An inhabitant of Nieuwpoort in Flanders had returned from a pilgrimage to St Nicholas du Port in northern France when he was struck blind. This was probably the most frequented of shrines of St Nicholas as far as Netherlanders (and probably other northern Europeans) were concerned; it was believed that a finger-joint of the saint had been brought there in the later thirteenth century.

The Virgin herself, the greatest of all general practitioners, could be found almost everywhere. As pilgrimage to her was most commonly focused on images, there was nothing to prevent the multiplication of Marian pilgrimages, which would for the most part be local in character, because there was bound to be another Virgin, at least as potent, not too far away. As the more recent history of wonder-working Virgins shows, however, there have always been some manifestations of her cult which, for whatever reason, have exerted an exceptional degree of magnetism (now of course potentially intensified by the speed of modern transport and communications). The *Mirakelboek* in a sense documents the claim of the shrine of Den Bosch to be a cut above the run of local Marian cults. A woman from Elburg, in the north of Gelderland, made a vow of pilgrimage to the Virgin, but did not specify where she would go; only later was it made known to her that it must be to 's-Hertogenbosch. A father from Arnhem, who had already once obtained the cure of his whole family from blindness by vowing a pilgrimage to Den Bosch, made another such vow when his daughter became deaf. He registered his vow before the image of the Virgin in the church at Arnhem.

Virgin could sometimes compete with Virgin: the resuscitation of the same drowned boy at Delft was claimed for the Virgin of Den Bosch and also (in a Delft source) for the Virgin of Delft. When Pauwel Boyken was imprisoned at Leuven and released through the intercession of Our Lady of Den Bosch, he went with his fetters to the Dominican church at Leuven. The brethren there wanted to hang up the fetters as an ex-voto before their own image of the Virgin, who was, surely, as powerful as her rival to the north, but Pauwel was insistent that he must take them to Den Bosch and at last fulfilled his pilgrimage with many pilgrims from Leuven, including, the *Mirakelboek* triumphantly relates, some of the Dominicans themselves. It seems a little bizarre that the Virgin should compete with the Holy Sacrament, but when a drowned girl of Amsterdam was not restored to life by the Holy Sacrament venerated in that city, the Virgin of Den Bosch obliged, as she did in a similar case at Dordrecht.

As these stories indicate, every major centre of population boasted cults and relics which, it was to be hoped, might satisfy the needs of the local population. The *Mirakelboek* supplies still more evidence for the density of devotions which were available sometimes within the space of a few miles. New ones were springing into life in the same region and at very much the same period as the cult of Our Lady herself did, around 1380. One was the cult of the Holy Cross at Asse, in what is now the Belgian province of Brabant. In March 1383, Our Lady was successfully invoked by Peter Poelman from Gdansk, who had vowed a pilgrimage to Asse but was arrested as a spy when he reached Mechelen and imprisoned for seven weeks. Another of her pilgrims was described as 'dwelling by the

Holy Cross at Asse'. Also new in the early 1380s was the veneration of the Holy Blood of Christ at Boxtel, which is only about 10 kilometres due south of 's-Hertogenbosch and which flourished sufficiently to support a pilgrim-badge trade. Two pilgrims came from Boxtel to Den Bosch during the period under review, but the only mention of the cult itself in the *Mirakelboek* occurs in a later story, dated 1520, which relates that a pilgrim to Our Lady had been unavailingly to Boxtel and also to the Holy Cross of Kranenburg, in modern Germany but only a few miles from the border with the Netherlands.

It would be rash to presume either that the picture given in this one source of a regional network of cults could serve as a model for similar networks elsewhere in Europe or that it was altogether exceptional. Most of these centres of devotion catered, and presumably expected to cater, only for devotees from a more or less circumscribed area. We hear little or nothing, in the *Mirakelboek*, of pilgrims in transit across the Netherlands to greater shrines further south, of whom there were undoubtedly many. Nor do we hear of the pilgrims from central and eastern Europe who helped to sustain the fortunes of Aachen.

By Land and Sea

Such professional globetrotters as the seafarers and merchants of the Baltic, Atlantic and Mediterranean worlds represented one extreme of geographical awareness, but comparable levels of experience could be achieved by different means. Chaucer seems to have expected his Wife of Bath to be accepted as a plausible if satirical image of a type, the vulgar woman of means, bold as brass, for whom her frequent long-ranging pilgrimages added to her status in local society. The fictional Wife had been not only to Rome, Jerusalem and Santiago but to Boulogne and Cologne; in the next generation, the real Margery Kempe of Lynn, a woman of not dissimilar social standing, did just as well, performing the three major pilgrimages, going to Assisi for the indulgence of the Portiuncula and also visiting Wilsnack and Aachen late in life. She must also have visited all the principal English shrines, including the ones that were new, or newly fashionable in her time: St John of Bridlington, the Blood of Hailes in Gloucestershire, the Bridgettine convent of Syon in Middlesex.

Margery was not a great lady, but by birth and residence she had connections with the maritime world centred on the North Sea. Her son was married to a German woman and it was when she escorted her widowed daughter-in-law back to her homeland, taking ship with her from Ipswich to Stralsund, that she had the opportunity to visit Wilsnack. A handsome pilgrim badge from Wilsnack has been found at Lynn itself, and a century after Margery's time another inhabitant of an east coast port, Richard Wilfit, mariner of Hull, left money to two shrines: Our Lady of Walsingham and the 'Holy Blood of Welslayk', *recte* Wilsnack. We cannot know whether he had been there in the course of business, but it is not improbable. Both Hull and Lynn were outposts of the Hanseatic connection in England.

The geographical perspectives and awareness of Dutchmen, Danes or Englishmen must have been somewhat different from those of an Italian merchant or pilgrim, although there was some overlap. There is no evidence of Italian pilgrims in Scandinavia, but the significantly surnamed Antony the Pilgrim of Padua in the thirteenth century got as far as Cologne; there was a Tuscan woman among the twelfth-century clients of St Erkenwald at St Paul's in London and some Italians certainly came to Canterbury, including Venetian captains of the Flanders galleys, who early in the fifteenth century obtained the Senate's permission to leave their ships for as long as it took to make the pilgrimage. These particular shipmasters were members of the Contarini family, which was also deeply involved in the pilgrimage traffic between Italy and the Holy Land.

During the early centuries of Christian Holy Land pilgrimage, ships from the east coast of Italy provided the only feasible route, but by around 1000 the Christianisation of east-central Europe was opening up an alternative possibility. The chronicler Ralph Glaber, noting what seemed to him an enormous increase in the volume of Holy Land pilgrimage at this date, commented on the opening of a land route across Hungary. Later eleventh-century Jerusalem pilgrims seem to have taken their choice, many still preferring the maritime option via Cyprus, others going overland via Constantinople, which was itself an attraction. The Anglo-Norman Orderic Vitalis, early in the twelfth century, commented on a fine hostel which was available to pilgrims on the borders of 'Hungary' and 'Bavaria'. The security and attractiveness of the overland route deteriorated, however, in and after the thirteenth century in face of the expansion of the Mongols and subsequently, and more permanently, the Ottoman Turks. Western pilgrims who went to the Holy Places in the fourteenth and fifteenth centuries took ship, most often from Venice.

The inevitability of the sea route to the Holy Land was obliquely referred to in a late fourteenth-century English guidebook, *The Stacions of Rome*. The author laid great stress on the wondrous indulgences which were to be had at Rome: there was no need to go either to Santiago or to Jerusalem 'over the sea'. Individual narratives, which survive in considerable numbers, provide abundant and picturesque details about the organisation of this traffic and the rigours of the journey. The route was not always directly to Palestine. Leonardo Frescobaldi and his companions in 1384 aimed for Alexandria, intending to approach the Holy Land via Sinai. They carried with them letters of credit addressed to the Portinari company agents in both Alexandria and Damascus. One of the company, Andrea di Francesco Rinuccini, in fact died and was buried at Damascus. Not all pilgrims, however, chose the arduous Sinai option and those who did often went there from the opposite direction, after seeing Jerusalem and the other Holy Places.

For many centuries, it was virtually obligatory to make the return journey from Rome or the Holy Land to northern Europe overland, for the passage from east to west through the Straits of Gibraltar was not often undertaken before the later thirteenth century, when the Genoese and the Venetians began regular direct sailings to Bruges and Southampton. The sea journey from west to east, as the Vikings had demonstrated, was possible much earlier, and some at least of the crusaders who accompanied Richard the Lionheart in 1190 also performed it, although others crossed France overland and embarked at Marseille. As already noted, Earl Rognvald of the Orkneys went to the Holy Land in the 1150s by sea, but returned to Denmark overland from Apulia.

One of the many indicators of the international pulling power of Santiago de Compostela is the published list of safeconducts and letters of recommendation, numbering 134 in all, issued by the royal chancery of Aragon between 1378 and 1422. There are large chronological gaps in this record, and it clearly only recorded pilgrims approaching Santiago from a certain direction, as the relatively large numbers of letters issued for Sicilians and, still more, Neapolitans, who were most probably coming by sea, suggest. Only five letters are recorded for English pilgrims, which can give no idea of the volume of English pilgrimage that was reaching Galicia either overland or by sea from other directions. No Scandinavians at all were noticed, but there were small numbers from Poland, Bohemia and Hungary as well as from Germany, and a few named Flemings. A majority of the pilgrimages documented in these records originated in France, Italy and the kingdom of Aragon itself, specifically Catalonia. Later in the century Hungarians were passing through the Tuscan city of Pistoia on their way to Compostela. Such a trajectory may well suggest that they intended to take ship from the Tyrrhenian or Ligurian coast to Spain; they may, not improbably, already have been to Rome. The same may apply to the one English pilgrim to Compostela mentioned in the Pistoiese records, the 'Tommaso' who passed through in 1394.

A significant proportion of the pilgrimage traffic for Compostela was carried by sea, whether it was to the nearby Galician coast, to Marseille and its neighbourhood or to the the eastern seaboard of Spain. Pilgrims from the British Isles and Scandinavia had to cross the sea at some point, even it was only across the Channel or the Sound or the Baltic respectively. Many late medieval English pilgrims to Santiago went by sea, principally but not exclusively from west-country ports, and royal licences to shipmasters to carry stated numbers of pilgrims give at least a notional impression of the volume of traffic. A fifteenth-century poem, *The Pilgrims' Sea Voyage*, sardonically describes their sufferings, but the relative speed and cheapness of the journey may well have appealed. Other English pilgrims went overland, which of course afforded the opportunity to visit many subsidiary shrines en route. St Birgitta returned to Sweden overland from her Compostela pilgrimage in 1341, perhaps following a route similar to that recommended a century later by Künig von Vach, for her husband fell sick at Arras.

Land and sea of course did not exhaust the possibilities open to pilgrims. River transport was also used and presented its own hazards, as an Englishwoman discovered when, setting out in 1330 for Santiago, the Holy Land and Assisi, she was one of a party of pilgrims in a boat which foundered in the Rhône on leaving Valence. Some were drowned, and she lost all her money and was unable to continue with her pilgrimage. Long-distance pilgrims must commonly have used a variety of means of conveyance, as Dorothea of Montau and her husband clearly did when they went from Aachen to Einsiedeln and from Einsiedeln back to Gdansk. From time to time they hired a horse and cart, of which they were robbed at least once; on other occasions it seems they simply had a horse, which Dorothea's husband rode as he was elderly and infirm. Water transport (along the Rhine?) was at least a possibility, for it is stated that 'sometimes, because of the perils of the roads, her husband sold the horse and then, finding neither a cart nor a boat, he walked alongside her'. Their second return journey to Gdansk took place in winter, early in 1387, and there is a vivid description of the peril they incurred crossing a frozen river (the Elbe?) at Horburg on their way to Hamburg. They were in a cart pulled by three horses, of which the middle one went through the fragile ice and nearly took the entire equipage after it. From Hamburg we may presume they crossed the neck of the Jutland peninsula overland; they certainly then took ship from Lübeck home to Gdansk.

It should be noted that some pilgrimage traffic continued to flow from east to west in the later middle ages. In the thirteenth century the St Albans chronicler Matthew Paris reported the visit of some Armenians to the shrine of their supposed compatriot St Ivo at Ramsey Abbey in Huntingdonshire and in 1364 Edward III extended his protection to some Armenian monks who had fled from 'Saracen' persecution in their native land; forced to lead 'a wandering life', they sought licence to visit the shrines of the saints in England. The most exotic of the pilgrims for which the kings of Aragon issued safeconducts were an 'Indian' and a couple of 'Ethiopians', including one who was described in January 1416 as 'a mass-singing clerk, native of the Indies'. In 1489, Innocent VIII granted an indulgence to all who should render assistance to a group who had arrived in Rome from Jerusalem. They had, supposedly, come from India and they proposed to go on to Compostela, Finisterre, Mont St Michel and Canterbury before returning to India, again by way of Jerusalem.

One of this group was described as a canon of the monastery of St Antony of Vienne. Is it possible that he had made his way to India in hopes of finding the shrine of St Thomas at Mylapore, near Madras, which Marco Polo claimed to have visited late in the thirteenth century? Marco said that Christian pilgrims carried earth from the apostle's burial place back home with them and effected cures with it. Thomas was universally believed to have preached and suffered martyrdom in India, and the continued reverence of western Christians for the Indian site was expressed by King Alfred, who in 883, according to the *Anglo-Saxon Chronicle*, sent envoys with offerings not only to Rome and to St Bartholomew at Benevento, but to 'St Thomas in India', in thanksgiving for victory over the Danes at London. It was, however, widely believed that the apostle's relics had been translated from India to Edessa in the fourth century, and thence, eventually, to Ortona on the coast of the Abruzzi. Birgitta of Sweden was authoritatively assured by Christ Himself that the relics were at Ortona. In the course of the centuries the western church appropriated the spiritual treasures of the east and made them available to European pilgrims.

Mental Maps: Wills and Souvenirs

Richard Wilfit of Hull remembered one shrine, Wilsnack, far from his home town, which he may have visited, and another, Walsingham, which was much nearer and probably the most popular shrine in England in the last years before the Reformation, drawing devotees from a wider area of the country than any other except Canterbury. Other wills, in England and elsewhere, are equally revealing of reminiscences and attachments which were sometimes limited to the local and familiar and sometimes combined the far and near. Wills preserved in the archives of Assisi include bequests for pilgrimages to shrines of the Virgin at Viterbo and Todi, which can scarcely have been heard of outside this region of central Italy, others for the ancient sanctuary of St Michael on the Gargano peninsula in Apulia, and others yet again for Compostela. A citizen of Faenza in the Romagna in 1478 was principally interested in pilgrimages to Italian Marian shrines, the Annunziata at Florence, Our Lady in the cathedral at Prato and above all the Holy House at Loreto, which he wished to be visited twice on his behalf. In addition, however, he wanted a pilgrimage to be made to St Antony of Vienne at the expense of his estate.

Inhabitants of the great Hanseatic city of Lübeck made frequent testamentary bequests for pilgrimages to St Matthias at Trier and above all to Aachen. One who was not German by birth struck a different note. In 1358 Niccolò Salimbeni, who had been mint-master at Lübeck like his father before him, wanted pilgrimages done on his behalf to Rome, Santiago, to another Spanish shrine, St Idelfonso at Zamora, and to St Josse in Picardy; but he also, significantly, included a bequest for Aachen. Another Italian who had been transplanted to a different clime was Lucia Visconti, who remained in England after her brief marriage to the earl of Kent was ended by his death. She died in 1424 and declared in her will that her seneschal had agreed to go to Jerusalem, Santiago and St Antony of Vienne for the souls of herself and her late husband. Awareness of the shrine of St Antony in the Dauphiné was, as we have seen, high in Italy and Countess Lucia seems to have brought with her from her homeland the remembrance of the shrine of the hermit-saint, who was, after all, one of the most widely venerated in medieval Europe.

A still greater lady, Queen Margrethe, who ruled over all three Scandinavian kingdoms between 1387 and 1412, included in her will, made in 1410, bequests for pilgrimages which embraced the whole of Christendom, from Santiago and Sinai to small shrines throughout Scandinavia and Finland: her responsibilities and her consciousness were different yet again. Wills such as Margrethe's can be very informative about shrines otherwise unknown to history which were evidently held in high esteem by testators. In 1472, William Ecopp, rector of Heslerton in north Yorkshire, left a string of bequests for pilgrimage to be performed in England, which ranged from the celebrated (such as Thomas of Canterbury and Our Lady of Walsingham) to a number of north-country shrines of the Virgin which are otherwise unknown as objects of pilgrimage. By and large the attachments evinced in wills were local; men of Somerset and Sussex took little interest in northern saints, while north-countrymen, although often aware of Canterbury and Walsingham, were less likely than their southern counterparts to leave money for a pilgrimage to, say, the Blood of Hailes in Gloucestershire.

If wills furnish a rough guide to mental pilgrimage maps, finds of pilgrim 'souvenirs' may shed some light on pilgrimages actually performed. There are, however, many problems involved in identifying the provenance of pilgrim badges, not least when they survive only in a fragmentary condition. Some are instantaneously recognisable but many are not. It is also often impossible to know from what shrines badges of popular saints such as Katherine, Barbara or Margaret came, if indeed they were not worn simply out of devotion to the saint rather than as souvenirs of a pilgrimage. Pilgrim souvenirs were not *objects de luxe* and they were made in relatively cheap and fragile materials: pottery, tin, and latterly, with the spread of wood-block and metal-type printing, paper. Not only easily destroyed, all such objects were easily lost and presumably also frequently discarded. Many have been dredged up from the beds of rivers, including the Thames and the Seine, and they have been found in the drainage ditches of medieval Salisbury. The distribution and discovery of the surviving examples is therefore the outcome of innumerable chances and there are doubtless many more to be found.

Any conclusions that can be drawn from existing catalogues have to be viewed with all this in mind, but it seems not unreasonable to suggest that a high apparent rate of survival means that the shrine in question was popular and that souvenirs were produced in large numbers. Similar conclusions may be drawn from a wide distribution of souvenirs from a particular shrine. Even if some ampullae and badges were bought and sold away from the shrine, they were presumably not major articles of trade, and a wide geographical distribution therefore seems to suggest fairly reliably that pilgrims from a correspondingly wide area made their way to the shrine in question and home again. With all these provisoes in mind it is possible to collect, from easily accessible sources, some data for a wide area of north-western Europe.

Material from southern England has been catalogued by Brian Spencer for the Museum of London, the Norwich Museum and the Salisbury and South Wiltshire Museum. Finds in Paris, mostly from the Seine, first catalogued in the nineteenth century, have more recently been published by the Musée de Cluny. Much work has been done in the Netherlands, especially on the rich finds that have been made in the mud of Zeeland, while excavations in cities, including Amsterdam, have also yielded material. Valulable data have been produced for Scandinavia. Together these sources list badges from over 140 certainly identifiable shrines, which range from places apparently visited only by natives of the country or even region (over two-thirds of the total) to those that seem to have had a public everywhere. No attempt has been made here to compute how many badges or fragments of badges have been recorded.

For the most part the results, however approximate, substantiate the impression that a large proportion of souvenir-buying reflected an essentially local, short-range traffic. A hundred of these destinations are represented by finds in only one of the four 'target areas' (southern England, Paris, the Netherlands, Scandinavia). Of these the vast majority were found in the same broad region as the shrine in question. (There are exceptions, some of which will be noticed below.) Badges from Bridlington, Bromholm, Doncaster, Ely, Pontefract or Syon Abbey, are found only in England, and this is no cause for surprise. With all due caution, some significance can therefore be attributed to a wider distribution where it occurs.

Souvenirs from nine of these shrines have been recorded in all four 'target areas'. These are, in alphabetical order: Aachen, Canterbury, Cologne, Lucca, Noblat, Rocamadour, Rome, Santiago, and Tours. There is a possible tenth, the shrine of St Nicholas of Bari, but the provenance of many St Nicholas badges is uncertain, and St Nicholas du Port, mentioned earlier, may sometimes be the more plausible source for Parisian and Dutch finds. Scandinavian and London examples, however, have been confidently attributed to Bari. In 1272 a Danish woman left money in her will for pilgrimages to be performed on her behalf to Rome, Jerusalem and Bari, but it transpired that she was well enough to undertake the journey herself. Bari would have been fitted in between Rome and Jerusalem, either on the outward or the return journey.

Of the other shrines, Lucca was almost certainly visited on the way to Rome rather than as a destination in its own right, while another three, Tours, Noblat and Rocamadour, could be visited by taking one or another of the principal roads to Compostela. For some Scandinavian pilgrims, Canterbury might be incorporated into a sea voyage south, while those who took the overland route to Rome or Santiago might well stop at Cologne and Aachen. Some places, notably of course Rome, boasted more than one shrine which produced souvenirs. Most of the Roman badges that have been found depict either the apostles Peter and Paul or the Veronica, but there have been English finds apparently recording visits to the Virgin at Santa Maria Rotonda (the Pantheon) and to St John Lateran. English pilgrims sometimes obtained souvenirs of St Mary Undercroft and St Blaise when they visited Canterbury, but the non-English finds suggest that, as one might expect, to other Europeans Canterbury meant Becket.

Leaving the difficult case of Bari out of account, badges from thirteen other destinations have been found in *three* of the four areas. These are: Amiens (St John the Baptist); Boulogne and Chartres (both shrines of the Virgin); Maastricht (Servatius); Mont St Michel; Noyon (St Eligius); Paris (where several churches, including St Denis and Notre Dame, sold badges); St Gilles du Gard; St-Hubert-en-Ardenne; St-Josse-sur-Mer; Tombelaine (a shrine of the Virgin near Mont St Michel); Vendôme (Holy Trinity or the Holy Tear); and Wilsnack (the Holy Blood, as English pilgrims called it). There are English and Dutch finds from all these sources.

It is notable here that northern French shrines, which could be visited by northern Europeans in the course of a journey south to Compostela or possibly Rome, predominate. Scottish pilgrims were going to St Denis, in homage presumably to the Auld Alliance, in the fourteenth century. Scandinavian finds however are often lacking, although there has been one find in Sweden of a badge showing the Annunciation which is thought likely to have come from Notre Dame, and there have been relatively numerous finds of badges from Maastricht in Scandinavia. Wilsnack shows a different pattern; here it is Paris finds which are wanting. This may substantiate the impression that, outside Germany and eastern Europe, this was a shrine likely to be known especially to natives of the northern maritime trading commonwealth. Even finds in only one or two of the target areas can paint an intriguing picture. Königslutter was a popular resting-place for pilgrims on their way south from Scandinavia, so it does not seem too surprising that there should have been a Norwegian find of a badge from this source, but it is perhaps more noteworthy that a fragmentary Königslutter badge should have been found in London. London finds in fact cover a wide range, including St Dominic's shrine at Bologna and St Mark's at Venice, the Virgin of 's-Hertogenbosch and St Cornelius at Ninove. This last may find an explanation in the fact that there was a flourishing cult of St Cornelius in London in the early sixteenth century. As late as 1536 Anthony Croskyll, a labourer of Enfield in Middlesex, was seeking royal permission to go overseas with one companion to St Cornelius (it is not specified where, but almost undoubtedly Ninove); perhaps he was or had been a sufferer from epilepsy. Many London finds are reconcilable with the idea that they were picked up on an overland journey to Compostela; there are badges from the shrine of Our Lady at Le Puy, St-Guilhem-le-Désert, St Jean d'Angély, the shrine of the Magdalen at St Maximin in Provence, the Virgin of the Carmelites at Toulouse, and what appears to be a unique specimen of a badge from Notre Dame des Tables at Montpellier.

Some of the Dutch finds also are from far-flung destinations, among which one of the more intriguing is the tomb of St Ubaldo at Gubbio in east-central Italy, not by any means on the usual high road to Rome. Here it may be wondered whether interest had been aroused by the shrine of the saint usually called Theobald at Thann in Alsace, who may be identical with Ubaldo; there have been several Dutch finds from Thann. The only known badge of Peter of Luxemburg, venerated at Avignon, was found at Dordrecht.[11] The only evidence for non-English interest in British shrines other than that of St Thomas at Canterbury also comes from the Dutch finds, which include badges from Walsingham, St Andrews and St Edward the Confessor at Westminster. More striking still is the attribution of a badge of St Margaret, found in Zeeland, to her church at King's Lynn, which would surely have been visited in the course of a pilgrimage to Walsingham.

Both Dordrecht and Lund in Sweden have yielded badges from Marburg, showing St Francis and St Elizabeth of Thuringia together. There is also both Dutch and Scandinavian evidence for knowledge of St Quirinus at Neuss and the Virgin at Einsiedeln. There is a peculiarity, however, in some of the Scandinavian evidence which may limit its significance. Images deriving from some German shrines which do not occur elsewhere in our sample, such as St Anne's at Düren, just east of Aachen, or St Walburga's at Eichstätt in Bavaria, are found in Scandinavia only as reliefs cast on church bells, and while these may commemorate pilgrimages by local clergy or patrons, they may also be accounted for by the fact that much bell-founding was done by travelling German craftsmen who carried patterns with them. There can be no certainty about this one way or the other; sometimes there are both bell-reliefs and original badges as well as other evidence. In 1331, a pilgrimage developed at Gottesbüren in Hesse after local people claimed to have seen Christ in the form of a bleeding host. Its appeal to Scandinavian pilgrims seems to be indicated not only by the discovery of a badge in Norway, perhaps at Bergen, and a bell-relief at Nyköping in Sweden, but by a reference in the will of King Magnus Eriksson of Sweden and his queen, Bianca, in 1346. They made bequests for votive offerings to be made on their behalf also at Aachen, Gustrow, Rocamadour and Compostela, all of which, except Gustrow, are attested by Scandinavian pilgrim-badge evidence.

We usually have little or no idea how a particular badge arrived at the spot where it was found. A lot were dropped (or thrown away) in rivers, but we cannot know how, why, or by whom. Might a German merchant have lost his Königslutter badge while in London on business? There are, however, exceptions to this rule of uncertainty when souvenirs are found as 'grave goods'. Here there have been some intriguing Scandinavian discoveries. The presence of badges in a grave does not convey complete assurance that the occupant was a pilgrim. A Santiago shell was buried with a three- to four-year-old boy at the church of St Stefan in Lund, which suggests that it may have been intended as a talisman for the afterlife. Such shells are the commonest of all 'pilgrim souvenirs' to be found in graves over Europe, including Scandinavia, and their significance in any one instance may be uncertain. Where several different badges are found with one burial it may constitute a more reliable indicator of the status of the deceased. In the Dominican convent at Helsingborg in Sweden the skeleton of a man about 175 cm (5ft 8 in) tall was discovered in 1952, buried with no fewer than ten badges, two each from Tours, Lucca and Rome, one each from Rocamadour and Bari, and three that remain unidentified. In addition there were the remains of a pilgrim's staff. Was the dead man a full brother of the convent or a lay brother or servant who perhaps performed pilgrimages on behalf of the community, like the individuals discussed in an earlier chapter?

No other grave yet excavated has revealed a quite comparable wealth of pilgrim souvenirs. A man aged 50–55, whose skeleton showed signs of tuberculosis, was buried at St Stefan in Lund with three tokens, one each from Rocamadour, Bari and Santiago. He could hardly have performed these pilgrimages if his disease was well advanced, but he may have done so earlier in life. One Danish burial contained an Aachen badge. Other finds are known to have come from graves, although the burials are not fully recorded. Excavation of a tomb in the monastic ruins at Selje in Norway in 1937, for example, uncovered badges from Maastricht, Noblat and Bari. The burial of an elderly male in the monastery of All Saints at Lund with three Scandinavian badges, one from Vadstena and two from Trondheim, is the only example so far found of Scandinavian souvenirs in a Scandinavian burial.

We sometimes have documentary evidence of pilgrimages (or at least, pilgrimages intended) which would have made it possible to acquire a mixed bag of souvenirs. In 1366 Edward III gave the abbot of Evesham permission to undertake a tour which was to include Amiens, Cologne, St Francis at Assisi and Santiago. Somewhat later Margery Kempe could have built up an impressive collection. In 1451 two Scottish clerks obtained the English king's safeconduct for a pilgrimage which was going to take them not only to Canterbury, Walsingham and the Holy Blood of Hailes, but overseas to Wilsnack. The inclusion of both Wilsnack and Hailes in their plans suggests that this was, at least in part, a 'themed' pilgrimage.

Numerous considerations helped to determine which pilgrims, and how many, went where: political and economic constraints, the local effects of warfare, plague and famine, all interacting with shifting fashions and the appearance of new foci for pilgrimage. Our conclusions are bound to be quantitatively imperfect and somewhat impressionistic, but it seems highly probable that, were it possible to count the pilgrimages of all kinds made by individuals, short journeys would preponderate. This does not alter the fact that thousands of medieval European men and women made long and arduous journeys by way of pilgrimage, and it certainly does not deprive long-distance pilgrimage of its importance. Pilgrimage was the sole justification many of its practitioners had for travel and it exposed an unknowable number of people to sights, sounds and experiences which would otherwise never have come their way. From a wide variety of viewpoints, some of which will be explored in the following chapter, pilgrimage was a cultural phenomenon.

5
PILGRIMAGE IN MEDIEVAL CULTURE

Pilgrimage did not lose its power over the imagination even when and where the Protestant Reformation brought its actual practice to an end. The opening lines of a poem once attributed to Sir Walter Ralegh can be quoted in evidence of this:

> Give me my scallop-shell of quiet,
> My staff of faith to walk upon,
> My scrip of joy, immortal diet,
> My bottle of salvation,
> My gown of glory, hope's true gage;
> And thus I'll take my pilgrimage.

These lines reveal an interesting duality. First there is the marvellous fitness of the pilgrimage journey as a metaphor for the progress of man's bodily life from birth to death and of his spiritual life from earth to heaven. Later still in Protestant England, John Bunyan famously so used it in *The Pilgrim's Progress*. Secondly, there is the panoply of visual emblems. The scallop-shell was specifically associated with the pilgrimage to Compostela, but was often used as a symbol of pilgrimage in general. The 'scrip' or satchel contained the pilgrim's necessaries; the staff was his indispensable prop (and perhaps even weapon) and the water-bottle was equally indispensable. The poem points us to two areas in which pilgrimage left a mark on European culture, the visual and the literary. The following discussion will consider examples in both these categories, but it does not present anything like a complete inventory of the cultural reflections of medieval pilgrimage.

Song and Dance

There is another cultural category to which the pseudo-Ralegh's poem makes no reference, but which was omnipresent to the medieval pilgrim, both on the road and at journey's end: music. Chaucer's Miller played the bagpipes and piped the party out of town; the Squire probably played the flute and certainly sang. The Friar too sang well and played the stringed instrument known as a 'rote'; when he was 'harping', his eyes twinkled like stars in a frosty night. All these instruments were highly portable and any party of pilgrims, even if they did not have musicians amateur or professional with them, could sing. If we are to believe the Lollard William Thorpe, arraigned before the archbishop of Canterbury in 1407 (seven years after Chaucer's death), they usually made a great deal of noise. He complained that before they set off pilgrims made arrangements

> to have with them men and women that can well sing wanton songs and some other pilgrimages will have with them some bagpipes, so that every town that they come through, what with the noise of their singing, and the sound of their piping, and with the jangling of their Canterbury bells and with the barking out of dogs after them, that they make more noise than if the King came there alway, with all his clarions and many other minstrels.

The archbishop replied that music was an entirely acceptable remedy for the tedium and toil of the road and a welcome distraction from the pain that a pilgrim might feel if he hit his foot on a stone.[1]

To critics of Thorpe's stamp, this rowdy display was one more proof of the ignoble and impious conduct of pilgrims in general, but the music that pilgrims brought with them was not necessarily irreverent. In the autumn of 1399, a German party, sixteen strong, passed through Pistoia on their way to Rome. They were clad in white, in conformity with the custom that had been adopted in much of Italy during the penitential excitement of the past few months, and they were 'very respectable'; 'they sang Stabat Mater and other songs of praise most devoutly and well'. They were not necessarily in any sense professionals, but it was possible for bands of musicians, knowing that there was a market for their wares wherever religious festivals took place, to follow a pilgrimage path and regard themselves, in all sincerity, as pilgrims too. The boundaries between amateur and professional music-making were anyway fluid, as they have been in much of European history, and many clergy had a quasi-professional competence. For Chaucer's musical pilgrims their singing and playing were obviously only part-time occupations. The Drummer of Niklashausen, Hans Behem, seems to have earned extra money playing his drum, and perhaps also a pipe, at local festivities. When he embarked on his ill-fated career as a preacher, he composed songs which the pilgrims he attracted to Niklashausen learned to sing; they had catchy but alarming refrains such as 'catch the priests and kill them all'.

These were not typical pilgrim-songs, but disapproval of popular music-making on pilgrimage or at shrines was not new in the fifteenth century. It was one of several aspects of popular devotion to St Foy at Conques that disquieted Bernard of Angers in the early eleventh century. It had long been the custom that the peasants should keep vigil overnight in the church with lights and candles, while the clergy chanted the office; but because the people could not understand the language of the liturgy, they passed the time by singing popular songs and indulging in other unspecified amusements. When Bernard objected to this as unseemly, he was told by clergy who had been at Conques for rather longer that attempts to keep the peasants out of the church for the sake of decorum had been divinely frustrated when the doors sprang open of their own accord. Bernard thus came round to the view that while these songs were not actually pleasing to God, they were acceptable as an earnest of good intent.

A century later, the author of the sermon *Veneranda Dies* (part of the *Codex Calixtinus*) painted a vivid picture of the throng of pilgrims of all nationalities that was to be seen around the altar of St James at Compostela. Some of them played musical instruments, pipes, drums, flutes and stringed instruments of several varieties, including the English 'rote', which Chaucer's Friar played 250 years later. Other pilgrims kept vigil by singing along to the music of these instruments. Exactly what music all these people were singing and playing, and what the total effect was, we are not told. A similarly varied ensemble was contemporaneously depicted in stone on the Portico de la Gloria of the cathedral, where the Elders of the Apocalypse are shown playing a range of accurately depicted musical instruments.

That there were always musicians in the vicinity of shrines is indicated by a reference to the alms that Edward I gave, in the summer of 1285, to a *citharista* whom he found playing at the shrine of St Richard at Chichester. Miracle stories sometimes dramatise the indulgence shown by the saints or the Virgin to humble musicians or strolling players. One of the most famous concerns a French *jongleur* who was on his way to Jerusalem when he stopped at Lucca to venerate the Volto Santo. Having nothing to offer but his professional skill, he played sweetly before the image. The Crucified Christ showed His appreciation by kicking the silver slipper off His right foot, which the astounded minstrel picked up, not knowing what to do; retiring for a moment from the chapel he was divinely inspired to return and offer the slipper once again to Christ. Thereafter God so disposed it that the slipper could never again be fixed on the foot of the image.[2]

If much of what pilgrims heard and played on the road and even at the shrine was the popular music of the time, they would also of course have heard the formal music of the liturgy and efforts were made to create a repertoire of sacred song which pilgrims could carry with them. The *Codex Calixtinus* includes chants for the feasts of St James, to which a number of French bishop-composers, including Fulbert of Chartres, seem to have contributed. It also contains more 'modern', tuneful and rhythmic pieces for processional use, which could readily be adopted by pilgrims, such as the hymn *Dum pater familias*, which sings the praises of the saint in a jaunty rhyming metre. A somewhat later Spanish source, the *Libre Vermell* or Red Book of the shrine of the Virgin at Montserrat near Barcelona, was compiled in 1399. According to the preface, pilgrims often wanted to sing and dance, not only while keeping vigil but in the square outside the church; songs appropriate to the setting had there-fore been composed, but pilgrims were exhorted not to disturb other worshippers who wished to pray and meditate. The author of the preface also optimistically urged pilgrims not to indulge in frivolous and improper song and dance, even when they had departed from the shrine.

Another pilgrimage shrine on the feeder roads to Santiago which possessed a distinguished musical tradition was St Martial of Limoges. The Spanish heritage of pilgrim-related music was particularly rich, partly because such a variety of influences, secular and sacred, from the French to the Moorish, converged on it. In the thirteenth century the clerk Gonzalo de Berceo composed a life of San Millán (Emilianus) for the instruction and entertainment of pilgrims to the saint's shrine at San Millán de la Cogolla at Berceo and at Santo Domingo de Silos. He referred to himself as 'a minstrel of spiritual subjects (*juglar de cosas espirituales*)' and as the saint's *juglar*. His twenty-five *Miracles of Our Lady* were also written for San Millán, and they include one story of a sinful pilgrim on the road to Santiago who was rescued by the Virgin. The *Cantigas de Santa Maria*, which were compiled under the direction of Alfonso X of Castile (1252–84), may not have been specifically intended for pilgrims, but several of the songs were related to pilgrimage in the sense that they too recounted the mishaps and miracles of pilgrims on the way to St James.

Saints' lives were clearly often presented to a popular audience as songs or recitations. We know that readings of saints' lives and miracles took place at shrines from early times, for example in North Africa at the shrines of St Stephen in the early fifth century and at the shrine of St Martin of Tours in the sixth, but there is little clue as to what form they took. Sometimes they may have been not merely straightforward readings but recitations or even performances accompanied by mime or music or both. The *Song of Saint Foy*, apparently composed in the Rouergue around 1070, was presented by its author as a Provençal rendering of a Latin song, which he said was well-known in the Basque country, Aragon and Gascony. The Latin song, itself derived from the narrative of the saint's martyrdom, which was read during her office, was 'beautiful to dance', but the author had also heard it 'read' by clerks; he thought his French version, which he clearly proposed to sing, might be a source of great profit, perhaps both monetary and spiritual. He was certainly not the only composer engaged on such an enterprise. Thibaut de Vernon, a canon of Rouen in the mid-eleventh century, rendered several Latin saints' lives into 'pleasing' rhythmic songs. Such songs, even if originally intended for use in church for the edification of an illiterate public, could easily find their way into the marketplace. A conspicuous example was the song of St Alexis, who abandoned his promised bride to follow Christ and went on a long pilgrimage to Rome, returning after many years to die incognito in his father's house.[3]

Images of Pilgrims

The religious drama of the medieval church provided opportunities for combining music with imagery. Stage directions to thirteenth-century plays which dramatised Christ's meeting with the disciples on the road to Emmaus show that the disciples were depicted as pilgrims, with purses and staves; they continued to be so represented in drama, and also in painting as late as the age of Caravaggio and Rembrandt.[4] Already by 1100 Christ Himself was shown as a pilgrim, wearing a purse with a scallop-shell on it, in a sculptural version of the same subject at Santo Domingo de Silos. On the Portico de la Gloria at Compostela the pilgrim was greeted by St James, identifiable not only by his central position beneath Christ, but by the stout walking stick in his hand. His distinctive iconography developed from these simple beginnings.

James had never hitherto been as distinctive as St Peter with his keys and white curly hair or Paul with his sword and long dark balding head; he was scarcely distinguishable from the other apostles, although he often carried a book. By the fourteenth century, by an enchanting trick of transference between the saint and his shrine, but also in homage to the belief that he had come a long way from his native place to Galicia, he was almost invariably depicted as a pilgrim, or at the very least sporting a pilgrim emblem, usually the scallop. Whether in freestanding statuary or painted in the company of other saints, he often carries his staff and sometimes a scrip, and sports the scallop-shell either on his cloak or on his broad-brimmed pilgrim hat. He may retain the traditional book and sometimes there is a scallop on the cover. The seated figure of the apostle in the centre of the altarpiece which adorned (and still adorns) the chapel of San Jacopo in the cathedral of Pistoia is a splendid example.

It evidently seemed logical that as new pilgrimage sites became fashionable, James the pilgrim should accord them recognition by wearing their badges. An extraordinary sixteenth-century painting at Pistoia, where he was frequently represented because of his standing as a civic patron, shows him encrusted with emblems, among them one from the now popular Holy House at Loreto. The fact that churches and images of St James were to be found everywhere in Christendom, and that everywhere he was portrayed as a pilgrim, by itself guaranteed that pilgrim imagery was omnipresent. To representations of the saint himself must be added the innumerable occurrences of his scallop, both as a natural object and as a manufactured substitute.

Saints other than James in whose lives pilgrimage had played, or was believed to have played, an important part, were also represented as pilgrims. Among them was St Judocus or Josse, a supposed Breton hermit whose shrine near Etaples was popular with the English, French and Flemish. The cult of the mysterious Roche or Rocco, supposedly a native of Montpellier and pilgrim to Rome, originated in the late fourteenth century and achieved a wide dissemination and poularity in art. Roche doubled as one of the most frequently invoked plague saints of the late middle ages and was distinguished by the plague sore on his thigh as well as by his pilgrim garb; he is often accompanied by the dog who licked his sores. Birgitta of Sweden, whose pilgrimages and the visions that accompanied them received wide publicity, was also represented with pilgrim attributes, as were other more obscure saints such as Sebald of Nuremberg.

Other saints possessed pilgrim associations, sometimes deriving from a more general protective function in relation to travellers. St Christopher and St Julian, patron of innkeepers and hostellers, were examples. The Three Magi were supposed to have been the first pilgrims of all, and for this reason they were depicted on early pilgrim ampullae manufactured in the Holy Land. The pilgrim who carried such an ampulla had it on gospel authority that the Magi had not only visited the infant Christ but had returned safely home, a heartening thought which may have given these objects a special talismanic power. Certainly not all representations of the Adoration of the Magi were associated with pilgrimage, but it may well be that their appearance in the decoration of a number of churches along the Via Francigena should be so interpreted. A similar significance has been attributed to dedications to St Martin, not because he was himself regarded as a pilgrim saint, but because his own shrine was an early cynosure of international attention for pilgrims, such as Simeon of Armenia, who took the road to France and Spain from Italy.

St Antony of Vienne was another saint who was both a goal of pilgrims and frequently represented in western art. There were many reasons for his popularity: as a patriarch of monasticism and the eremitical life; as a protector against diseases of both man and beast; simply as a name-saint. He was also the patron of an order which possessed properties and ran hospitals throughout Christendom. As we have seen, the diversion to La Motte was commonly undertaken by Italian pilgrims to Compostela, and some Italian images of him undoubtedly have pilgrimage associations, not least when he is found in the artistic company of St James.

Chief among these must be reckoned the fifteenth-century frescoes in the oratory which belonged to a fraternity founded at Assisi in 1418 for persons who had performed the pilgrimage to La Motte and Compostela. In the early 1990s, during work on the Franciscan church of Sant' Andrea in the little town of Spello, only a few miles from Assisi, frescoes of rather rough, provincial workmanship were uncovered which showed St Antony and St James presenting donors to the Virgin and Child (there was a Compostela fraternity at Spello, too). The two saints are depicted as a pair in a fresco in Orvieto Cathedral commissioned in 1399 and the prolific Tuscan artist Spinello Aretino in 1378 painted them flanking the Virgin and Child with the donor, a knight, kneeling before the group. Naturally, both Antony and James are frequently depicted with other saints (including St Julian) but the pairing is sufficiently frequent to suggest that it may sometimes be accounted for by a patron's personal reminiscence of a pilgrimage or membership of a pilgrimage confraternity. In Pistoia the brethren of St Antony possessed a chapel frescoed with scenes of the life of the saint: the cycle ends with the translation of his relics to La Motte and miracles at the shrine. Several of the pilgrims who were given alms by the Opera di San Jacopo were said to be going to St Antony rather than to St James.

The visual emblems of pilgrimage become commonplace in later medieval art, for example in representations of the Seven Corporal Works of Mercy, a subject which originated in the mid-twelfth century but was at its most popular in the fifteenth and early sixteenth, especially but not solely in northern Europe. The subject was principally derived from Matthew 25:34–46, which numbered hospitality to the stranger among the works of charity which would be rewarded on Judgement Day. The pilgrim was a *peregrinus*, literally and originally a foreigner or stranger, and artists represented the stranger with the instantly recognisable attributes of the pilgrim. One of the most striking versions of the theme is, once again, in Pistoia, on the glazed terracotta frieze of the Hospital of the Ceppo, near the centre of a city which handled an extensive pilgrim traffic. Artists identified pilgrims by the most popular badges of the time. The Veronica or the crossed keys of Rome were frequent alongside the ubiquitous scallop, and in German art at the end of the middle ages a pilgrim was likely to have the badge of Wilsnack, showing the three miraculous hosts, on his hat.

There are also some straightforward representations of pilgrims intended to commemorate and advertise their achievements. Several memorials to fifteenth-century German pilgrims to the Holy Land survive. A relocated tomb-slab depicting the alert figure of Bernhard von Breydenbach, dean of Mainz, is still to be seen in the cathedral. He made the pilgrimage in 1483, and a guidebook survives which bears his name, although it is thought to have been written by a Dominican friar. Breydenbach died in 1497; two years later the knight Konrad von Schaumberg died on his way back from Jerusalem, and his executors commissioned a tomb-sculpture from Tilman Riemenschneider which stands today in the Marienkapelle at Würzburg. The Holy Land pilgrimages undertaken by members of the Rieter family of Nuremberg received a permanent memorial in a stained-glass window commissioned in 1483 for the church of St Lorenz, which fittingly depicted the entry of Moses into the Promised Land. This was commissioned by Sebald Rieter who had made the pilgrimage in 1479; his travelling companion Hans Tucher, member of another prominent Nuremberg family, in 1485 commissioned an altarpiece depicting the equally suitable subject of Christ on the way to Calvary (still to be seen in the church of St Sebald), in which the donor is portrayed. In the sixteenth-century Netherlands, paintings were sometimes commissioned to immortalise the journeys made by members of Jerusalem brotherhoods. Around the year 1520 a small group from Amsterdam had a painting done of themselves as if in front of the birthplace of Christ at Bethlehem. Two paintings of somewhat later date at Utrecht and one at Haarlem depict the pilgrims, half-length, in a row, holding their palms. Below each figure is an identifying inscription with some biographical particulars; they include both clergy and laymen, and in one of the Utrecht panels there is a woman.

A Roman Image: the Veronica

The Veronica, an image of an image, had strong but not exclusive pilgrimage associations as an artistic motif. Before it became a popular attraction for pilgrims to Rome, the image received some publicity from the circulation of a prayer composed in its honour by Pope Innocent III, with indulgences for its devout recitation. The English chronicler Matthew Paris transcribed the prayer, accompanied by a 'copy' of the image, and such images achieved some diffusion in thirteenth-century Europe, which may conceivably have contributed to the growing interest taken by pilgrims in the original. In the wake of Innocent III's prayer and indulgence, hymns were composed and circulated in honour of the Veronica, most notably, in the fourteenth century, *Salva Sancta Facies* ('Hail, Holy Face'), which became immensely popular and was translated into the vernaculars. A painting by the fifteenth-century Flemish artist Petrus Christus shows a young man at prayer, with a paper sheet bearing the hymn (in Dutch) and an image of the Veronica fixed to the wall behind him.

Given this kind of private devotional use of the image, its appearance in stained glass (as at Great Malvern priory), painting or sculpture cannot necessarily as be taken as a specific reference to or reminiscence of the experience of actually seeing it at Rome. On the other hand, extravagant beliefs about the amount of remission that could be obtained by seeing the Veronica were widely current. Guidebooks reported how much indulgence it carried with it (especially for visitors from the north of Europe, who obtained more than Romans or Italians) and printed German editions of the *Mirabilia Urbis Romae* included woodcuts depicting the exhibition of it to pilgrims. There can be little doubt that the image was at its most popular in the art of northern Europe.

The legend which accounted for how the image had been made existed in a number of variants; the most popular, by the fifteenth century, related that Veronica had wiped Christ's face with the cloth as He staggered beneath the weight of the Cross on the way to crucifixion. This episode was sometimes included in dramatisations of the Passion and began to be represented in a variety of artistic media, including the great carved and painted altarpieces which were produced in wood and stone in northern Europe around 1500. Alongside these dramatic representations there developed various modes of depicting the Veronica as a devotional object, sometimes by itself, sometimes incorporated among the Instruments of Christ's Passion, and sometimes held up for exhibition by the saint herself. Rogier van der Weyden and Hans Memlinc were among northern artists to paint the subject.

It seems a reasonable contention that artists, patrons and spectators of these images knew about the Veronica's Roman associations, which were especially strongly emphasised when the cloth, with or without Veronica herself, was represented flanked by Sts Peter and Paul. Dürer and others produced engravings of this subject in the early sixteenth century. Pilgrim badges were also made in this form, but they also often simply showed the Veronica by itself, and cloth and paper replicas of it (which could easily be sewn or stuck on a hat or other garment) were also produced. The head of Christ was depicted both with and without the Crown of Thorns, presenting either an agonised or a tranquil aspect. The late fourteenth-century mystic Julian of Norwich can presumably never have seen the image, but she had heard about it and reported the belief that it changed its appearance. Already in the later fourteenth century, William Langland sardonically described the ignorant gadabout pilgrim who had been everywhere and had the badges (including the Veronica) to prove it, but had never heard of a saint called Truth; and that unpromising character, Chaucer's Pardoner, had a 'vernicle' in his hat, as if to guarantee the authenticity of the pardons he had brought from Rome.

Souvenirs as Objects

Several references have already been made to pilgrim souvenirs, to their possible economic significance and to their value as evidence for the popularity of particular shrines. Although some were larger, more splendid, more ingeniously designed and better made than others, they were not primarily works of art, nor were they simply 'souvenirs'. The human impulse to pick up some memento of places visited and memorable experiences certainly runs very deep, and the term 'souvenir' undoubtedly expresses one of the functions of the pilgrim badge, but it is misleading to interpret them too narrowly by analogy with the modern tourist souvenir. The places they called to mind were holy places, and the pilgrim's ampulla (especially if it contained water from the Jordan or oil from the lamps of the Holy Sepulchre) was to a degree analogous to the 'relics' which were often also procured by pilgrims, especially in the earlier medieval centuries.

Some individuals were quite ruthless in their pursuit of holy objects, even if few went to the lengths of the notorious Fulk, count of Anjou, who on a visit to Jerusalem early in the eleventh century is supposed to have bitten a piece off the Holy Sepulchre. It has been suggested that the production of custom-made souvenirs was in part at least intended to divert pilgrims from such depredations. They were produced in the east long before they appeared in the west. The cathedral treasury of Monza, north of Milan, possesses some fine specimens of sixth-century ampullae from the Holy Land. These miniature bottles might contain Jordan water or oil from the lamps of the Holy Sepulchre. They and their contents clearly brimmed with healing potential for body and soul, and their decoration too was more than merely decorative. Several, as already noted, were adorned with representations of the Three Magi. Eastern shrines outside the Holy Land produced ampullae which were also widely distributed; ampullae of St Menas, from near Alexandria, have been found as far afield as Chester and Norway.

The souvenirs which were produced in the west in and after the twelfth century might perform cures or manifest other miraculous properties, or they might more prosaically serve to identify the pilgrim as entitled to hospitality and the protection of the law. At their most basic, they simply affirmed that the wearer had 'been there, done that'. Henry II departed from Canterbury after his public penance there in July 1174 wearing a Becket ampulla, and a little later Gerald of Wales recorded that when he and some companions waited on the bishop of Winchester at Southwark, after a visit to Canterbury, he knew instantly where they had been by the *signacula* around their necks. Having been widely and rapidly imitated at other English shrines, the ampulla gradually gave place to the badge, which could be sewn or otherwise fastened on to the pilgrim's hat or other garments. Badges could take a wide variety of forms, at their most elaborate telling a little story about the saint, like the Becket examples which depicted the martyrdom itself, or the badges of the popular unofficial saint John Schorne, rector of North Marston in Buckinghamshire, whose chief claim to fame was that he had once conjured the devil into a boot.

There was some discussion in the previous chapter of pilgrim tokens found in graves. The possibility that they were being used as good-luck charms for the afterlife cannot be excluded, but even so the predominance of St James's scallop in such contexts suggests the special prestige attached to that particular pilgrimage.[5] Various explanations are possible for the association of the scallop with the pilgrimage to Compostela. The most down to earth suggests that pilgrims found these shells on the neighbouring sea-coast and perhaps even put them to practical use as small plates or scoops for drinking. Legends then grew up to associate the saint with the shell. James's presence in Galicia was anyway intimately bound up with the sea, for his body had supposedly been brought by his disciples to Spain in a boat which was steered by the winds and tides (the Virgin of Boulogne and the Volto Santo of Lucca arrived at their destinations by similar means). It is perhaps worth observing that the scallop was a funerary emblem popular with the Romans, as an opulent sarcophagus preserved in the Verulamium museum at St Albans and the more recent discovery of the burial of a woman in Spitalfields in London both indicate. The implied association may be with a hoped-for rebirth from the sea, into which the soul was launched at death; Botticelli's *Birth of Venus* displays an analogous motif. Whether or not any connection existed between old meanings and new, there can be no doubt that the scallop not only achieved a huge diffusion as the specific emblem of St James, but was often used generically to signify pilgrimage. The scallop was widely distributed both as a manufactured and as a naturally-occurring object, in burials and elsewhere.

Pilgrim souvenirs constituted a repertoire of portable and exportable religious imagery, but their importance was not solely visual. As with relics and reliquaries, we need to make allowance for the role of the tactile and the sympathetic value attached to handling, or simply being in the presence of, objects that had been in contact with the saint or the shrine.

Pilgrims liked to have their badges and other souvenirs (later their 'beads') blessed by contact with the shrine or the saint's altar; this does not mean that the badges had no purely visual importance, but it does suggest that they conveyed meanings in a variety of different ways.

Relics and Images

Pilgrimage at all times had a strong visual component. For Bishop Reginald Pecock, rebutting Lollard criticism of pilgrimage in the middle of the fifteenth century, this was one of its great merits. People went to see images, and because most people, even if they were literate, retained what they saw much better than what they heard or read, they learned far more than they otherwise would. Even when, as in most of the earlier medieval period, the focus was on relics rather than on images, these were presented visually in a number of ways. The tomb itself manifested the bodily presence of the saint to the onlooker, even if the relics themselves were seen rarely, and then only by a very privileged few when ceremonial 'expositions' or 'revelations' of them were performed (and that did not always mean they were removed from their container). In an age when the vast majority of men and women merited only a hole in the earth, the fact that the tomb was elevated above ground level was in itself a visual and symbolic statement.

For many saints the moment of his or her 'translation' to such an exalted position, often after a preliminary period of more obscure burial, marked the real beginning of the cult. How close public access to the tomb was permitted to be, varied; as we have seen, there was a strong current of feeling that a reverent distance should be maintained. A few surviving examples, such as the reputed tomb of St Osmund still in Salisbury Cathedral, show the apertures in the sides which permitted a hand or head to penetrate, not to the very bones of the saint, but to the inner casing. Becket's shrine at Canterbury is so represented in several of the 'miracle windows', and some of his miracle stories describe pilgrims taking every advantage of the opportunity to approach as close as they could to the saint's hidden presence. Shrines were sometimes elevated high above the ground on pillars and in this instance it might be thought meritorious to pass or rest under the tomb-chest. The faces of such a chest could be adorned by reliefs telling the story of the saint, which could be viewed by those who were able to circumambulate the shrine.

Only a small proportion of shrines contained whole burials. Body parts, such as arms and heads, mere fragments of bone, and also secondary relics such as vestments or other objects associated with the saint, were given suitable presentation in a variety of forms: caskets might be simple rectangles, or shaped like a church or the anatomical relic they contained, hand or arm, foot or head; some were head-and-shoulders 'portrait busts'. Obviously the oblong casket was, like a tomb, more abstract in general effect, but like a tomb it could be adorned with reliefs. The reliquary of the Three Magi made by the goldsmith Nicholas of Verdun for Cologne Cathedral is an imposing example. The head or bust reliquary was itself an image, a stylised representation of the saint. All were adorned with all the splendour of materials and craftsmanship, in metal or ivory, that money could buy and were often encrusted with jewels. Such reliquaries might be placed on altars or carried in procession. Small ones were suitable for private veneration. The enamel-workers of Limoges in the thirteenth century produced little caskets to contain relics of Becket, which were frequently decorated with a representation of the murder. So many examples survive in modern museums as to give a striking impression of how many must originally have been made. They may have amounted to a quite impressive secondary means of publicising the cult, even if only among the fairly restricted circles of those who saw and admired such objects.

Despite the pre-eminent importance of relics in earlier medieval pilgrimage, there were always images among the accompanying furniture. There seem to have been two moments at which the use of images underwent a striking development, one around the year 1000 and the other around 1300. There was an image of St Cuthbert at Durham which was adorned with jewels donated by William the Conqueror, but the focus of the miracle stories collected by Reginald of Durham a century later remains the saint and the relics, just as it was at Canterbury. Bernard of Angers mused rather unhappily on the new importance of images in the early eleventh century. He was perturbed by the image of the ninth-century nobleman Gerald of Aurillac, which he saw when visiting his shrine, observing that it seemed to the beholding peasants to see them and hearken to their petitions. Bernard was worried, as many later commentators and reformers were to be, about the risk of idolatry, of confusion between the image and its prototype, and he reconciled himself only with some difficulty to the proposition that these images were immovably fixed in the devotion of the people and did less harm than good. In part, this was once again anxiety about popular pilgrimage itself. The famous reliquary statue of St Foy at Conques, which re-used a Roman portrait head, was a magnet for pilgrims, as Bernard's miracle stories make plain. Word of mouth, rather than reproductions, must have been the means of publicising the image. St Foy had no time for people who were rude about it.

Images certainly multiplied in numbers after c.1300, and their ever-increasing part in Christian pilgrimage was a Europe-wide phenomenon. We think of the years around 1300 as the age of Giotto and Duccio in Tuscany, of the development of an art which painted the gospel story in the colours of human emotions. It is not easy to recreate the impact that such stylistic innovations had on early fourteenth-century spectators. The images that were provided by patrons and clergy elsewhere in Europe will not have had precisely the same aesthetic qualities, but one did not have to go to Tuscany to find, for example, statues of the Virgin with the child on her arm which were not only pictures of feminine grace but movingly evoked the intimate relationship between mother and child.

There is plenty of evidence, in England and elsewhere, for the multiplication of images at the parish level in the fourteenth and fifteenth centuries. Many of them were of the Virgin and many others of Christ, most notably Christ crucified. It is well known that in the course of the thirteenth century the crucified Christ as represented by artists ceased to be the wide-awake Christ Triumphant of earlier centuries and became the human saviour, slumped, even agonised, and definitively dead. By about 1400 the image known as the *Pietà*, which shows the dead Christ on the lap of His sorrowing Mother, was achieving a rapid diffusion: Margery Kempe went into paroxysms of devotion in front of one in a church in Norwich. Such images, of Christ, the Virgin or both (as in the *Pietà*), were the focal points of the majority of the new pilgrimages that sprang up all over Christian Europe in the later middle ages. Not all of the images which excited devotion, however, were newly made or new in style; many of the Madonnas still venerated in Italy are Byzantine icons, now often all but invisible under an encrustation of crowns and gilding.

Images went far to supply the demand for a means of visual and even tactile contact with Christ and His mother. They depicted, furthermore, the two spiritual powers which, in the understanding of most Christians, operated on a different level from the generality of saints. Even if, in calling upon them, one was visualising a particular Virgin or a particular crucifix and vowed one's pilgrimage and offering accordingly, their powers were beyond question universal. Images provided convenient local habitations for these devotions and contributed to a multiplication of cult sites. They surely also had a powerful effect on spectators who were brought up on oral renderings of the Passion story but in the rest of their lives saw few images of any kind, a fact which has to be remembered by the modern reader, who is so bombarded and saturated with images that few of them make a real impact. This impressibility may have contributed to the disposition to believe that images moved, wept or bled, although it must be admitted that this is still very much alive in the television age. In some places, at least, shrine custodians were not above ensuring their effects by mechanical means.

In the course of the fifteenth century the advent of the woodcut and of engraving made it possible to distribute easily portable 'reproductions' of images, just as printing made it possible to distribute written propaganda, such as indulgences, more readily than before. The effects were arguably diverse, on the one hand perhaps whetting the appetite of the prospective pilgrim, on the other (like portable altars, altarpieces and reliquaries) making possible image-focused devotions in the domestic setting.

The Larger Setting

Pilgrimage had an architectural and topographical setting with many important features: the roads which gave access to a church, the disposition of doorways into and out of the church itself, the provision for the flow of people around it and for access to the shrine, the decoration of the shrine and of the church as a whole, including of course the images. Much has been written about the architecture and decoration of the churches to be found along some of the major European pilgrimage routes – above all, those which led across southern France and northern Spain towards Santiago de Compostela, and the Via Francigena to Rome. That the contacts fostered by these roads and the passage not only of pilgrims but of masons and other master craftsmen along them helped to create fertile conditions for the dissemination and development of architectural and sculptural styles is beyond doubt, but there are still many controverted questions about the precise nature and sequence of these influences, and it is not a subject to which it is possible to do any justice in a book of this scope. It is perhaps sufficient to note that the key period, which saw the development of a monumental style of church building with many common features across a broad area of western

Europe, roughly coincides with the twelfth century. On many other grounds this can be seen as the great growth period of mass pilgrimage.

Building and all forms of artistic production were economic as well as aesthetic activities, and required investment before they could reap a return (if they did), but equally they could and did draw on the income provided by pilgrims and their offerings to generate further expansion. The cycle, like other economic cycles, was not always seen as benign. St Bernard of Clairvaux in the twelfth century complained that money was being misspent on such projects. He noted shrewdly that this money was being laid out in order to attract more money. To Abbot Suger of St Denis, one of Bernard's chief opponents on this issue, architectural improvements meant not vulgar profiteering but the creation of a setting in which the worship of God and the veneration of the saints could be carried on with fit splendour and decorum.

Grandiose programmes of church building or rebuilding and decoration could be initiated for reasons which were not obviously directly or closely related to the needs of pilgrims or the desire to attract them, and the timing of campaigns was often affected by accidental factors such as the great fires which ravaged Canterbury Cathedral in 1069 and 1174. The fire of 1174 and the destruction of the east end of the cathedral meant that access to Becket's shrine, which would have had to be managed anyway, was newly thought out. What happened to Becket was in fact a typical progress, from his original burial in the crypt to a shrine behind the choir, in an elongated apse approached by staircases at the north-west and south-west and surrounded by a processional way. The south-west staircase bears the visible indentations of thousands of pilgrim feet, and the new shrine was overlooked by the stained-glass 'miracle windows', many of which survive. These doubtless provided an edifying spectacle for the pilgrim who was prepared to listen to the explanation of them given by the shrine custodians, but any idea that their meaning was self-evident to the uninstructed is dented by the humorous description in the *Tale of Beryn* of the Miller and his cronies wandering around the church interpreting the windows as their fancy took them.

The needs of hospitality also entailed investment in building. All but the most important pilgrims, who might be welcomed into the guesthouses of cathedral and monastic churches, would find accommodation somewhere in the settlements around and near pilgrimage churches, in hospitals, perhaps, if they were poor and sick, in inns if they were averagely prosperous. Bishops and abbots founded and built both hospitals and inns. Some of the great inns built by monastic landlords for the accommodation of pilgrims still stand; a notable example is the imposing 'George and Pilgrim' at Glastonbury. The pilgrimage traffic thus helped to create monuments of domestic as well as of ecclesiastical architecture, although many of the buildings which served the needs of pilgrims have been destroyed, or transformed beyond recognition.

Pilgrimage often encapsulated miniature pilgrimages. A Roman pilgrimage included the circuit of the seven major basilicas and visits to other holy places; the Holy Land offered a long list of attractions, not all of which were seen by every pilgrim. Within a great church, as at Canterbury, there was a circuit of altars and attractions, each with its prayers and indulgences. Erasmus's metaphor of the householder going from room to room of his house attending to the welfare of his dependants and thus performing his pilgrimage exploited an underlying awareness that any movement from place to place, bodily or even mental, as in the practice of the armchair pilgrim, had the same possibilities. It was in part a compensation for the abnegation of pilgrimage in the ordinary sense that monastic life, firmly anchored to a place, the abbey church and its precincts, was punctuated by rituals and processions which themselves had a spatial dimension. For those ordinary folk who had not embraced religion, but could not realistically hope to go to Jerusalem, the creation of the Sacro Monte at Varallo in the far north-west of Italy late in the fifteenth century (much elaborated subsequently) made available a life-size representation of Calvary and its *dramatis personae*; this was a more dramatic, pictorial and colourful version of the idea much earlier embodied in churches built in the west on the model of the Holy Sepulchre.

Satire and Metaphor

There was a subtle reciprocal relationship between pilgrimage the physical activity, the actual journey, and the inescapable pilgrimage of life itself on which all men (and women) needed to recognise that they were engaged. From a monastic perspective, the monk's (or nun's) quest for the heavenly Jerusalem was the true pilgrimage, not a second-best reflection. The professed religious was urged to understand and embrace this greater reality rather than to hanker after the lower satisfactions of mere holy sight-seeing. Jerusalem the city was after all only a place in a world destined to pass away.

It was a general feature of late medieval religious culture that practices and contemplative techniques that in earlier centuries had been more or less confined to the cloister were exported to a widening circle of people with devout aspirations, who might either be living newer, looser forms of the religious life, or were still dwelling fully 'in the world'. A quasi-monastic view of pilgrimage, which had both negative and positive shadings, was among the exports. Negatively, the Christian was warned that bodily pilgrimage might be a distraction and even lead to spiritual deterioration; positively, he or she was exhorted to realise the great truth that life itself was, inescapably, the real pilgrimage. The task was to apply the determination and single-mindedness to this pilgrimage that worldly pilgrims all too rarely applied to their journeys. *Ancrene Riwle* (a thirteenth-century English guide to the spiritual life for anchoresses) makes frequent use of the image of life as a road, as a journey; it is conceded that pilgrimage as commonly understood may be good, but the alternative, the only one which was in fact appropriate to a recluse, was better. The thirteenth-century Flemish Beguine Hadewijch borrowed a series of images from the practice of pilgrimage (among them wariness of thieves, appropriate dress, and the right posture for both ascending and descending mountains) to illustrate how 'The Pilgrimage of Love' was to be undertaken.

Another strand in late medieval piety, and consequently in the evaluation of pilgrimage at least by some, was the part played by the Eucharist in the lives of all Christians after the Fourth Lateran Council in 1215 made annual reception and confession a minimum requirement of all adults. Sacramental relics, as at Wilsnack, were objects of pilgrimage, but was not any consecrated Host miraculous, was it not superior to any imaginable relic in that it was the Body of Christ Himself? What need could there be, therefore, to make long journeys to see the relics of mere saints, who for all their unquestionable greatness were inferior to their Master? The point, already made in the thirteenth century by the Franciscan preacher Berthold of Regensburg, was made forcefully in the greatest spiritual classic of the fifteenth century, *The Imitation of Christ* (IV, 1). Such thoughts and such writings penetrated the consciousness of a small, if growing, number of people, while for others the physical enactment of pilgrimage aspirations remained an authentic form of religious expression.

It is hardly possible to determine the precise extent of the diffusion of the practice of pilgrimage throughout medieval society. We can reasonably assert that no class of society was entirely excluded from it, but we cannot on the other hand positively affirm that every single member of every class participated in it. What we can assume with rather more safety is that knowledge of pilgrimage and its associated practices, and of particular shrines and saints, was sufficiently widely diffused for it to furnish a part of the mental environment within which artists, builders and also writers and their audiences operated. When we speak of the latter we are, in general, talking about a relatively restricted segment of society. More people will have seen images at one time or another, and may have recognised representations of pilgrims and pilgrimage in them, than will have read books or even heard books read. This was a point on which Bishop Pecock insisted when he defended the value of images. Chaucer could assume that his audience, predominantly a courtly and urban one, would be able to place his pilgrims mentally in the setting he had devised for them. He depicted a 'real' pilgrimage, but pilgrimage itself was not so much his subject as a narrative device, providing a frame for the stories that his mixed bag of pilgrims were to tell. The gap between pilgrim ideal and pilgrim reality was there to be perceived and enjoyed by the readers or hearers who noted that the Miller and the Cook seemed unlikely to derive much spiritual benefit from their journey, or that the Monk and the Prioress should perhaps not have been out of their respective cloisters at all.

The satirical possibilities of depicting grossly unsuitable pilgrims on the road were obvious, and were exploited, two centuries before Chaucer, by the anonymous author of the adventures of the rascally Reynard the Fox. Reynard, after a severely misspent life, repents and is sent by his dismayed confessor to Rome. He takes as companions the ram Belin and the donkey, the so-called 'archpriest' Bernard, whom he reminds, alluding to St Matthew, that 'Christ has bidden us to leave father and mother, brother and sister, land and pasture, for love of him'. In search of shelter for the night, they let themselves into the house of Reynard's old enemy (and brother-in-law) the wolf Isengrim, 'where they found a good supply of bread and also salt meat, cheese, eggs, and everything a pilgrim needs, as well as excellent beer' . The 'pilgrims' murder Isengrim when he comes back to the house and, having escaped from a pack of his fellow-wolves who give chase to them, they decide that pilgrimage is not for them. As Reynard sententiously observes, 'There's many a worthy man in this world who has never been to Rome, whereas some other has returned from seven pilgrimages worse than he was before.' The knowing reader, then and later, would recognise in these words precisely the objections that many critics had to pilgrimage as it was commonly performed: it was not necessary to salvation, and it often did more harm than good.

Chaucer's near-contemporary William Langland united this kind of criticism of pilgrimage as it was actually performed with the evocation of the true though metaphorical pilgrimage which consisted in living a good life. The bad real pilgrim is represented by the wayfarer, festooned with badges, who has never heard of Truth, and by Greed personified who has no idea what repentance meant, but thinks that going to Walsingham or Bromholm with his wife (who sells adulterated beer) will suffice to earn him forgiveness. Piers the Plowman adds further, more direct criticisms of workshy vagabonds, bogus hermits, monks out of their cloister and overseas pilgrims who waste the kingdom's substance. All will be reformed when Piers is permitted to institute true pilgrimage, which closely resembles a good everyday Christian life. This contrast between actual pilgrimage, which all too often did not benefit the soul, and metaphorical pilgrimage, that is living a good life, was a favoured theme of some of the Lollards who were arraigned in the early fifteenth century, but it is to be found also in the writings of orthodox critics. Criticism was not, however, the whole story.

Pilgrimage was a rich source of metaphor, as it was for the pseudo-Ralegh with whose poem this chapter began. It supplied the greatest of medieval poets with material for some haunting images. Dante mentions the 'Veronica' twice, first in his early *Vita Nuova* and secondly, over twenty years later, towards the end of the *Paradiso*. He uses the demeanour of pilgrims, whether they are on their way to see the Veronica or actually seeing it, as points of reference for his own state of mind. The pilgrims whom he saw in the centre of Florence making their way south to Rome looked distracted, and it cost him an effort to realise that this was not because of the death of Beatrice, of whom they had never heard, but because their thoughts were with their own people. The 'Croatian, perhaps' who actually beheld the Veronica embodied a simpler state of incredulous wonder. The sense of distance, detachment and loss suggested by the pilgrim's predicament appears in other images and Dante uses the figure of the pilgrim, trudging along the road and thinking that every house he sees must be the hostel, as an analogy for the constant human state of unfulfilled longing for a moral or spiritual goal.

Pilgrimage Narratives

Real pilgrims in increasing numbers wrote about their experiences. Occasionally this even became a family habit. Both Sebald Rieter the elder of Nuremberg and his son left accounts of their Jerusalem pilgrimages, undertaken in 1464 and 1479 respectively. In the sixteenth century these were incorporated into a family *Book of Travels (Reisebuch)* in which the pilgrimages of family members to Rome, Santiago and elsewhere were also recorded. This compilation was in German, but according to the younger Sebald his father had possessed 'a little book in Latin' which described the Holy Places. Furthermore, the younger Sebald's companion on his pilgrimage, Hans Tucher, wrote his own memoir. These and many other late medieval pilgrim narratives are monuments to both lay piety and lay literacy. We have already noted the Rieter window in St Lorenz at Nuremburg and the Tucher altarpiece in St Sebald; these patricians bequeathed to posterity memorials in both word and image of their Holy Land journeys.

Pilgrimage in fact provided the pretext for a very high proportion of what can be termed the medieval literature of travel. A fair amount of pilgrimage writing, it has to be said, has little pretension to be regarded as literature in any but the most basic sense; there are accounts which are little more than itineraries and there are guidebooks which tell the prospective traveller what are presumed to be the facts he needs to know, but do not offer any of the subjective reactions and reflections we tend to expect from the modern travel writer. Most of the more interesting accounts emerged from Holy Land pilgrimage, if only because the journey was effectively bound to introduce the Christian to people, places and things that were strange and indeed alien to him. Relatively few narratives are totally devoid of reaction to these stimuli. It is true that many pilgrims were able to contain their interests and their responses largely within a predetermined framework of belief and practice which conditioned what they permitted themselves to see and what they felt about it. Hostility to non-Christians (and non-Roman Christians) encountered along the way was commonplace. There was none the less a great deal of scope for individual variation, and many pilgrims clearly had the appetite for 'marvels', which helps account for the popularity of various translations of the thirteenth-century travels of Orderic of Pordenone, of Marco Polo's *Book* and of *The Travels of Sir John Mandeville*, all of which make some reference to places and routes frequented by pilgrims.

This taste linked 'travel writing' with the literature of chivalry and it was not, in essence, a new phenomenon in the later middle ages. As we saw in a previous chapter, curiosity about foreign parts has to be reckoned as a motive for pilgrimage from early times; St Willibald admitted to it in the eighth century. When Bede said that Adomnan's account of the pilgrimage of the Frankish bishop Arculf to the Holy Land was exceedingly useful to people who had no prospect of seeing Palestine with their own eyes, he seemed to hint at the existence a taste for what we might call 'armchair' pilgrimage. There was no explicit suggestion here that reading about the Holy Places was spiritually beneficial, except in the most general sense that you would put the book down better informed about the Holy Places than you had previously been, but by the fourteenth century a number of developments had combined to give it, potentially, a more precise value.

Techniques of pious meditation which encouraged the believer to visualise the scenes of the gospel story and follow Christ and the Virgin through their earthly lives in imagination were now achieving a wider popularity. To read, or hear read, a translation of the *Meditations on the Life of Christ*, originally written by a late thirteenth-century Tuscan Franciscan for the use of a Franciscan nun, was to be invited to perform an exercise comparable to following a guide around Bethlehem, Nazareth and Jerusalem. The pilgrimage narrative could assist such meditation and even make possible a 'virtual' pilgrimage. An anonymous Tuscan *Voyage to the Holy Land* of the fourteenth century opens with the rubric: 'These are the journeys that pilgrims who go beyond the seas to save their souls must perform and that everyone can perform, standing in his house, thinking at every place which is described below, and saying in every place a Paternoster and Avemaria.' The brief narrative which follows ends with a note of distances from one holy place to another, in paces or miles as appropriate, which might be intended for practical use but may also have been an aid to imagination.

Early in the sixteenth century Robert Langton exhorted the readers of his account of his travels in France, Spain and Italy: 'You who want to see whatever holy relics are venerated in all of Europe, read this book frequently. It will present everything to your eyes in its order. I do not ask much that you should be able to see everything, for the wish is sufficient; love conquers all.' He prefaces what in fact is little more than a list of places by referring the reader to 'Master Larke's book', 'wherein he comprehendeth all things concerning that holy pilgrimage, inasmuch that you, reading the same, shall seem rather to see it than read it'. Master Larke's book had evidently been of practical use, but it was also being recommended as an aid for armchair pilgrims.[6] If and when personal narratives of pilgrimage and guidebooks came into the hands of non-pilgrims, they had a potential value which qualitatively surpassed the combination of instruction and amusement that we expect from our travel writing, and this, it seems, was appreciated by some at least of the people who wrote them. A survey of writing about the Holy Land is scarcely possible here. It includes an immense quantity of chronicle material, much of it generated by the crusades, and hagiography, which affords insights into the way saintly persons like Willibald, Richard of St Vannes or Raniero of Pisa experienced Jerusalem. These two genres overlap to a not inconsiderable extent: there is, for example, a lengthy account of the pilgrimage of Richard of St Vannes in the later eleventh-century chronicle by Hugh of Flavigny. To these must be added the personal narratives and 'guidebooks' already mentioned. Here a distinction must be made between accounts produced in two very different phases of Christian pilgrimage. First, there is what can be regarded as the heyday, the twelfth-century period when Jerusalem was actually in Christian hands and the religious orders and the liturgy and rituals of the pilgrimage flowered. The authors of accounts surviving from this period, such as John of Würzburg, were typically ecclesiastics and their concentration was overwhelmingly on the Holy Places as such. Secondly, there is the still more abundant literature of the period after the mid-fourteenth century when Christendom seemed resigned to the loss of the Holy Land and the Franciscans had the task of overseeing Christian pilgrimage under the eye of the Muslim rulers.

Numerous personal narratives and guidebooks survive from this later period. Josephie Brefeld has argued that the latter, which exist in numerous versions, both manuscript and printed, probably stem from a common prototype which was available from the Franciscans in the Holy Land and perhaps also at Venice, where so many pilgrims embarked. By computer-assisted analysis she has tried to establish which existing example most resembles the prototype, coming down in favour of an early printed specimen now in the New York Public Library. The number and identity of Holy Places included in different guides, the order in which they appear and what is said about them, all provide clues to family resemblances and interdependence, as well as suggesting that these books may reflect actual guided tours. Many of the 'personal narratives' in fact depend so closely on the 'guidebooks' that Brefeld includes them in her sample, as evidence for what the 'prototype' was like. The amount of free-form personal reminiscence, that is to say, is variable and often limited, which is perhaps not unnatural as many of the pilgrims concerned, while anxious to leave an individualised record of their experiences, were not professionally accustomed to writing discursive prose.

Narratives of this later period, particularly but not solely when written by laymen, often contain a greater proportion of secular matter than earlier accounts and may also be more personal and autobiographical in character. This does not of itself indicate that the motives for actually undertaking so arduous and dangerous a pilgrimage were secularised, consciously at least. Pilgrimage as devout adventure did not remain the exclusive property of the clergy and the noble or fighting man, any more than the enjoyment of chivalric literature did. The late medieval literature of Holy Land pilgrimage was enriched by merchant pilgrims, who in their accounts of their travels fused an unquestioning religious sensibility with interests and attitudes derived from a way of life that was neither ecclesiastical nor aristocratic. Professionally literate and to some degree at least familiar with books, they were new entrants into the social, economic and cultural elite. Among the uses to which they put their literacy was the description and evaluation of commodities, and much that they saw in the east fitted with that professional concern as well as with the appreciation of the exotic, which they shared with their contemporaries both lay and clerical. They had good reason to become acquainted with camels while on pilgrimage, but many other phenomena, from giraffes and leopards to bananas, also attracted their attention.

No other pilgrimage created a comparable literature, although there are of course Roman guidebooks and, unsurprisingly, a great deal of incidental reference to Roman pilgrimage in a wide variety of sources. The twelfth-century *Mirabilia Urbis Romae* and the work of Master Gregory, with their concentration on the classical remains, contrast with the guidebooks to come out of northern Europe in the late fourteenth and fifteenth centuries, whose authors focus all but unwaveringly on the Christian antiquities of Rome and (like their Holy Land counterparts) on the indulgences to be had there. One of the most entertaining must be the doggerel English verse *Stacions of Rome*, of the late fourteenth century, which was also produced in a shorter prose version, and expatiated on the wondrous qualities of remission to be obtained at Rome. The author subscribed wholeheartedly to the now current belief that a host of indulgences had been granted by the early popes, such as Gregory the Great, who would have been most surprised by this intelligence. Later English guides were produced by the East Anglian Augustinian friar John Capgrave (*Ye Marvels of Rome*, 1450) and by William Brewyn, who was there in 1469.

The Roman pilgrimage afforded less scope for the writing talents of the Italian merchant, for whom Rome was altogether familiar territory. Pilgrimage to Compostela was a slightly different matter. The literature of the pilgrimage to Santiago has been dominated by the celebrated *Pilgrim's Guide*, to which reference has been made several times, but, as already noted, there is no evidence that it was known or used by medieval pilgrims. There was, however, a late medieval flowering of Compostela pilgrimage narratives, mostly fairly brief, written by pilgrims from different parts of Europe. Three anonymous accounts by Italian pilgrims, one by a Venetian who made the pilgrimage in the early fourteenth century and two by Florentines who went in the later fifteenth, within their limits complement the Holy Land narratives we have already touched on. Whether they were clerks or laymen, they encountered little, on taking the road to Spain, for which they did not have easy comparative measures, and they betray none of the ferocious disdain that the twelfth-century author of the *Pilgrim's Guide* evinces for the subhuman Basques and Navarrese.

The Venetian is brief. Like a number of other late medieval pilgrims he basically records only the distances between stopping places and the currencies and rates of exchange encountered along the way; on entering the kingdom of Navarre, he explained, one had to testify on oath how much gold one was carrying and pay twopence for every gold coin. He was, however, sufficiently impressed by the perilous forest around Grasse to remark on it. The format adopted by the two Florentines is not dissimilar but their comments are much superior in quantity and quality. This is especially true of the account dated 1477. The other, which is not precisely dated, devotes a great deal of space to the breathless enumeration of relics and the works of art which accompanied them. A crucifix at Burgos, which the writer believed to be the work of Nicodemus, he thought the most beautiful thing he had ever seen; it was miraculous and everyone came to see it. Nicodemus was evidently both prolific and versatile, for at San Salvador de Valdediòs there was another crucifix, in ivory, attributed to him. This was however surpassed by a fresco of the crucifixion with Mary and St John. The painter had gone to lunch leaving the heads unfinished, only to find them completed when he came back: 'And these three heads are beautiful, especially that of our Lord, and it seems that they talk with you.'

This writer was struck by Toulouse, 'a fine rich city, big and well-supplied and full of artisans'. This appreciation of urban amenity, which one might perhaps expect from an Italian observer and which is also to

be found in Holy Land memoirs, is still more strongly marked in the
1477 account. The author of this itinerary added to its usefulness by
noting where inns and hostels were good, numerous, or both, where
provisions were abundant and where there was evidence of vigorous
craft activity. He carefully distinguished degrees of urbanisation by
applying the words *città*, *villa* or *castello* to different types of settlement,[7]
and noted the existence of bridges in wood or stone, and paved roads.
St Jean de Maurienne, for example, was a large and fine *villa*, with many
craftsmen and many good inns, rich in bread and wine. Grenoble was
'a fine big *castello*', well off for craftsmen of every kind and with good
inns; it was also completely paved and in the middle a stone bridge
crossed the Isère. Pont St Esprit on the Rhône had similar amenities, but
Toulouse took the palm (albeit its bridge over the Garonne was only of
wood). To the Florentine this was 'a fine big city'; it was also commer-
cially well-developed (*molto merchantile*).[8] Carcassone was fine and clean.

This traveller was correspondingly, and negatively, sensitive to landscapes such as he observed on the way to St Antony at La Motte: 'a bad
country, the most frightening and the worst there is between here and
Florence, and the wildest'. The country was bad too between St Jean-Pied-
du-Port and Roncesvalles, all forest and mountain. In Spain, Burgos was
fine, large and well populated; but Leon was 'not very fine'. In compensation, the Florentine thought that the church of St Mary there was
the finest he had seen since Florence and he greatly admired the main
altarpiece, which showed the Assumption. This was 'a wonderful thing'
and so, too, was the choir of the church, inlaid with three tiers of figures
in relief; he had never seen the like. Compostela itself was not highly
rated simply as a town. It was small and dirty (literally, 'piggish', *porci-
nosa*) within, but the church of St James was fine by the standards of the
place.

This narrative sheds light on the sensibilities which one fifteenth-
century observer exercised in the course of a journey through an environment which was not exotic, but worth describing, if only because the
description might be of use or interest for others. Pilgrimages to Canterbury or Cologne were less likely to merit this degree of attention. The
accounts of pilgrimage which are included in the famous *Book* of
Margery Kempe of Lynn are at a different extreme of subjectivity: they
are much more about Margery, her reactions to what she saw and her
experiences and travails on the journey, than they are about the places
themselves. In some respects, although not in her constant laments
about the way she was treated by her fellow-pilgrims, she belonged to a

great and ancient tradition, recently represented by Birgitta of Sweden, whose pilgrimages, though real enough, are in a sense visionary experiences, announced by visions, interpreted through visions and productive of visions. Margery, as we have seen, knew about Birgitta. Both took the way of pilgrimage as a path to salvation, which (even if they believed implicitly in the objective value of indulgences) had to be personally experienced as part of a relationship with Christ, an imaginative act of participation in His life and sufferings. Richard of St Vanne's tears in the garden of Gethsemane and his identification of himself with Mary Magdalen, four hundred years before Margery, belonged to the same essential tradition.

NOTES

Chapter 1: Medieval Pilgrimage

1. See E. D. Hunt, 'Were there Christian Pilgrims before Constantine?' in J. Stopford (ed.), *Pilgrimage Explored* (Woodbridge, 1999).
2. For the wider context in which early Christian pilgrimage developed see the writings of Peter Brown and also R. A. Markus, *The End of Ancient Christianity* (Cambridge, 1990).
3. This derives much of its point from the Latin pun on *vidisse* (to have seen) and *vixisse* (to have lived).
4. The term *memoria* was still used to describe a saint's shrine a thousand years later.
5. Because Christ had been circumcised, it was possible to claim that His foreskin had been preserved; this was exhibited at St John Lateran in Rome, where there was also a piece of His umbilical cord. There were relics of the blood Christ shed at the crucifixion, and also of the Virgin's hair, tears and breast milk.
6. For Willibald's travels, see the translation in T. F. X. Noble and T. Head, *Soldiers of Christ: Saints and Saints' Lives from Late Antiquity and the Early Middle Ages* (London, 1995).
7. The Saxon *schola* may have been the oldest of them; later English chroniclers attributed its foundation to Ine of Wessex, who died at Rome in 726, or to Offa of Mercia. It was rebuilt after a fire in 817.
8. Simeon had previously been at Rome, and that some people at Rome may have known about the cult of St James is suggested by a letter written in 956 to Pope John XIII by Cesarius, bishop of Tarragona, who said he had been consecrated to his see at Compostela, described as James's 'apostolic see'.
9. The battle of Clavijo was in fact fought by Ordoño I (850–66) in 859.
10. Odo's *Life* of Gerald is translated in Noble and Head, *Soldiers of Christ*.
11. North of the Alps the most celebrated was Mont St Michel in Normandy, which may well have been an offshoot of the Apulian shrine.
12. In the fourteenth century, Elizabeth, the mother of King Louis the Great, promoted pilgrimage to Martin both at the royal palace at Buda and at a church at Hatvan, for which she obtained papal indulgences.
13. This is the point of the inscription over the gates of Hell imagined by Dante (*Inferno* III, 9): 'All hope abandon, ye who enter here.'

14. *Veneranda Dies* is translated in *The Miracles of St James*, ed T. F. Coffey, L. K. Davidson and M. Dunn (New York, 1996).
15. A quarantine was a period of forty days, recalling the duration of Lent and Christ's ordeal in the wilderness.
16. These were little vessels made of cheap metal (lead, tin). The ampullae made centuries earlier in the Holy Land and elsewhere in eastern Christendom had been ceramic. The very first containers for 'Becket water' were wooden, which had obvious disadvantages.
17. This misreading has been much quoted in works on pilgrim badges, apparently following J. Sumption, *Pilgrimage: An Image of Medieval Religion* (London, 1975), p. 161.
18. The nickname 'de la Calzada' means 'of the paved road'.
19. Benevento was a common stopping place for travellers making south from Rome, to Sicily or to take ship for the Holy Land. The apostle Bartholomew was venerated there.
20. This was two to three times the population of Florence itself around 1300. The 'twenty hundred thousand' which Guglielmo Ventura of Asti said was the current estimate among the Romans themselves perhaps suggests the same figure misheard or mistranscribed.

Chapter 2: Motives for Pilgrimage

1. The author's translation. The Latin word *speculor*, here rendered as 'explore', has strong connotations of inquiry and investigation.
2. This was believed to be the staircase which Christ descended after his interview with Pilate, and was installed at the church of St John Lateran.
3. Christianity became the official religion of Iceland in the year 1000.
4. Gucci calculated that the total cost of the trip, for one person and his servant, including the return journey to Florence, was more than 300 gold ducats.
5. That Francis had in fact obtained a plenary indulgence from Honorius III in 1221, as pious legend has it, is highly improbable.
6. This was a misunderstanding in so far as the *culpa* was remitted only by the prior repentance of the sinner and absolution by the priest. The confusion was harmful if it led the ignorant to suppose that indulgences mechanically disposed of 'guilt' without the need for both true repentance and sacramental confession.

Chapter 3: Varieties of Pilgrim

1. A cockle-shell (not the true scallop) was found with him, but no badges, although there is a remote possibility that they may have been accidentally destroyed, along with the head of the skeleton and perhaps a hat, during previous works which were carried out in ignorance of the burial.

2. These occurred when St James's Day (25 July) fell on a Sunday and plenary indulgences were available. On the sea-route to Santiago, see Wendy Childs, 'The Perils, or Otherwise, of Maritime Pilgrimage to Santiago de Compostela in the Fifteenth Century', in J. Stopford (ed.), *Pilgrimage Explored* (Woodbridge, 1999).

Chapter 4: The Geography of Pilgrimage

1. The name, a Gallicisation of Altopascio, recalls its connection with the hospital and order of Altopascio itself on the Via Francigena south-east of Lucca. The order possessed properties and hospices all along the roads to Santiago; its collectors were to be found raising money throughout Christendom.
2. The lists used by the inquisition of southern France in the thirteenth and fourteenth centuries worked on quite different principles. The inquisitors distinguished between major and minor pilgrimages, which were imposed according to the gravity of the offence. The major pilgrimages were to Rome, Santiago and Canterbury, and also to Cologne; the Holy Land constituted a category on its own. With the exception of the shrine of St Dominic at Bologna, added in the fourteenth century, the minor pilgrimages were all in France.
3. Peter Rieter of Nuremberg too went to Montserrat in 1428.
4. One extraordinary testimony to the fame of the Purgatory is a fourteenth-century fresco in the small central Italian town of Todi.
5. The cortege took an easterly route back to Sweden, pausing (in March–May 1374) at Gdansk. Dorothea of Montau, one of the many holy women to feel Birgitta's influence, was a resident of the city at the time, aged twenty-seven.
6. For information on Polish pilgrimage I am indebted to Professor Halina Manikowska, to whom I am most grateful.
7. The present arrangement below the lower church at Assisi, which makes possible a one-way circulation of pilgrims to view the shrine, is not the medieval one.
8. The citizens had hoped, but failed, to appropriate the body of St Francis.
9. This is of course connected also with the contemporary revival of the pilgrimage, which is undertaken for a wide variety of reasons and supported by national and regional societies.
10. The cult generated a miracle collection, compiled by Johannes von Ellrungen in 1442. The chapel (now incorporated in the rebuilt church) boasts an altarpiece of the Last Supper by the great sculptor Tilman Riemenschneider.
11. Peter was made cardinal and bishop of Metz in 1384 at a very young age, resigned his see a year later, and went to Avignon where he died in 1387.

Chapter 5: Pilgrimage in Medieval Culture

1. Thorpe's diatribe is translated in the Introduction to Erasmus, *Pilgrimages to Saint Mary of Walsingham and Saint Thomas of Canterbury*, trans. J. Nichols (London, 1875).

2. When the Volto Santo was transmogrified in more northerly climes such as Bavaria and Switzerland into a bearded lady known as St Wilgefortis she took on the patronage of musicians.

3. The French song which was composed in the eleventh century on the basis of the popular Latin life of Alexius had such a dramatic effect on Valdes, a merchant of Lyon, when he heard it sung a century later, that he abandoned his worldly existence and became, inadvertently, the founder of the Waldensian heresy.

4. The pilgrim's staff is mentioned in the tenth-century story of a knight, Otger, who was seeking the best place to adopt the monastic life.

5. A recent study has calculated that more scallops have been found in graves in Denmark (122) than in any other part of medieval Christendom.

6. Master Larke is not certainly identified, but may have been Thomas Larke, Wolsey's confessor, a chaplain to Henry VIII and Master of Trinity Hall 1520–5.

7. *Città* may be translated as 'city' or 'town', *villa* more or less as 'village'. A *castello* was a fortified settlement.

8. Although this pilgrim was on the way to Compostela he believed that the head and body of St James the Great and the body of St James the Less were at Toulouse, as he was doubtless told when there; he credited Galicia only with the head of the latter.

SUGGESTIONS FOR FURTHER READING

The first section of this bibliography includes a few works on modern and non-Christian pilgrimage as well as some suggestions for reading on sanctity, relics and miracles. English translations of sources are listed in the appropriate section. There are several modern English versions of well-known works cited in the text, such as Dante's *Comedy*, Bede's *History of the English Church and People*, the *Anglo-Saxon Chronicle*, Langland's *Vision of Piers Plowman*, Chaucer's *Canterbury Tales*, etc.; therefore no particular editions are specified here. More information on saints mentioned in the text can be found in works listed here (e.g. Vauchez, Weinstein and Bell) and in standard reference works such as the *Oxford Dictionary of Saints*.

General

Barber, R., *Pilgrimages* (Woodbridge, 1991).

Bhardwaj, S., *Hindu Places of Pilgrimage in India: A Study in Cultural Geography* (Berkeley, CA, 1973).

Coleman, S. and J. Elsner, *Pilgrimage Past and Present in the World's Religions* (London, 1995).

Dillon, M., *Pilgrims and Pilgrimage in Ancient Greece* (London, 1997).

Eade, J. and M. J. Sallnow (ed.), *Contesting the Sacred: The Anthropology of Christian Pilgrimage* (London, 1991).

Gauthier, M. M., *Highways of the Faith: Relics and Reliquaries from Jerusalem to Compostela* (London, 1983).

Graham-Campbell, J. (ed.), *Archaeology of Pilgrimage*, Special issue of *Medieval Archaeology*, 26 (1994–5).

Holm, J. and J. Bowker (ed.), *Sacred Place* (London, 1994).

Kedar, B. Z. and R. J. Zwi Werblowsky, *Sacred Space: Shrine, City, Land* (London, 1998).

Krötzl, C., *Pilger, Mirakel und Alltag: Formen des Verhaltens im skandinavischen Mittelalter* (Helsinki, 1994).

Nolan, M. L. and S. Nolan, *Christian Pilgrimage in Modern Western Europe* (Chapel Hill, NC, 1989).

Ohler, N., *The Medieval Traveller*, trans. C. Hillier (Woodbridge, 1989).
Stopford, J. (ed.), *Pilgrimage Explored* (Woodbridge, 1999).
Sumption, J., *Pilgrimage: An Image of Medieval Religion* (London, 1975).
Turner, V. and E. Turner, *Image and Pilgrimage in Christian Culture* (Oxford, 1978).
Ward, B., *Miracles and the Medieval Mind*, 2nd edn (Aldershot, 1987).
Webb, D., *Pilgrims and Pilgrimage in the Medieval West* (London, 1999).
Weinstein, D. and R. Bell, *Saints and Society: The Two Worlds of Western Christendom, 1000–1700* (Chicago, 1982).

The Earlier Middle Ages

Boniface, St, *The Letters of Saint Boniface*, trans. E. Emerton (New York, 1940).
Crook, J., *The Architectural Setting of the Cult of Saints in the Early Christian West, c.300–c.1200* (Oxford, 2000).
Geary, P., *Furta Sacra*, revised edn (Princeton, 1990).
Gregory of Tours, *see* Van Dam, R.
King Harald's Saga, trans. M. Magnusson and M. Pálsson (Harmondsworth, 1966).
Njal's Saga, trans. M. Magnusson and M. Pálsson (Harmondsworth, 1960).
Noble, T. F. X and T. Head, *Soldiers of Christ: Saints and Saints' Lives from Late Antiquity and the Early Middle Ages* (London, 1995).
Orkneyinga Saga, trans. H. Pálsson and P. Edwards (Harmondsworth, 1978).
Sheingorn, P. (trans.), *The Book of Sainte Foy* (Philadelphia, 1995).
Sigal, P.-A., *L'Homme et le miracle dans la France médiévale* (Paris, 1985).
Suger of St Denis, *Abbot Suger on the Abbey Church of St.-Denis and its Art Treasures*, trans. E. Panofsky, 2nd edn (Princeton, 1979).
Van Dam, R., *Saints and their Miracles in Late Antique Gaul* (Princeton, 1993). [Includes translations of Gregory's *Lives* of St Julian and St Martin.]
The Vinland Sagas: The Norse Discovery of America, trans. M. Magnusson and H. Pálsson (Harmondsworth, 1965).
Webb, D., 'Raimondo and the Magdalen: a Twelfth-century Italian Pilgrim in Provence', *Journal of Medieval History*, 26 (2000), pp. 1–18.
Webb, D., 'The Holy Face of Lucca', in *Anglo-Norman Studies*, IX: *Proceedings of the Battle Conference, 1986*, ed. R. A. Brown (Woodbridge, 1987), pp. 227–37.

The Later Middle Ages

Angela of Foligno, *Complete Works*, trans. P. Lachance (Mahwah, NY, 1993).
Birgitta of Sweden, *Life and Selected Revelations*, ed. M. Tjader-Harris (Mahwah, NY, 1990).
Boeren, P. C., *Heiligdomsvaart Maastricht: schets van de geschiedenis der Heiligsdomsvaarten en andere Jubelvaarten* (Maastricht, 1962).
Bornstein, D., *The Bianchi of 1399: Popular Devotion in Late Medieval Italy* (Ithaca, NY, 1993).

Dorothea of Montau, *Vita Dorotheae Montoviensis Magistri Johannis Marienwerder*, ed. H. Westpfahl (Cologne, 1964).
Kempe, Margery, *The Book of Margery Kempe*, ed. B. Windeatt (London, 2000).
Kempe, Margery, *The Book of Margery Kempe*, trans. R. B. Windeatt (Harmondsworth, 1985).
Klaniczay, G., *The Uses of Supernatural Power* (Cambridge, 1990).
Mirakelen von Onze Lieve Vrouw te 's-Hertogenbosch, ed. H. Hens, H. Van Bavel, G. van Dijck and J. Frantzen (Tilburg, 1978).
Tate, R. and T. Turville-Petre, *Two Pilgrim Itineraries of the Later Middle Ages* [Purchas's Pilgrim and Master Robert Langton] (Santiago de Compostela, 1995).
Vauchez, A., *Sainthood in the Later Middle Ages*, trans. J. Birrell (Cambridge, 1997).
Webb, D., 'Saints and Pilgrims in Dante's Italy', in *Dante and the Middle Ages*, ed. J. Barnes and C. Ó'Cuilleanáin (Dublin, 1995), pp. 35–55.
Wunderli, R., *Peasant Fires: The Drummer of Niklashausen* (Bloomington, IN, 1992).

The Holy Land (including the Crusades)

Biddle, M., *The Tomb of Christ* (Stroud, 1999).
Brefeld, J., *A Guidebook for the Jerusalem Pilgrimage in the Late Middle Ages* (Hilversum, 1994).
Egeria, *see* Wilkinson, J.
Glaber, Ralph, *Historiarum Libri Quinque*, ed. and trans. J. France (Oxford, 1989).
Grabois, A., *Le Pèlerin occidental en Terre sainte au Moyen Age* (Paris and Brussels, 1998).
Hamilton, B., 'The Impact of Crusader Jerusalem on Western Christendom', *Catholic Historical Review*, 80 (1994), pp. 695–713.
Hill, J., 'From Rome to Jerusalem: an Icelandic Itinerary of the Mid-Twelfth Century', *Harvard Theological Studies*, 76 (1983), pp. 175–203.
Housley, N., *The Later Crusades: From Lyons to Alcazar, 1274–1580* (Oxford, 1992).
Hunt, E. D., *Holy Land Pilgrimage in the Later Roman Empire, AD 312–460* (Oxford, 1982).
Kopp, C., *The Holy Places of the Gospels* (Freiburg and London, 1962).
Lanza, A. and M. Troncarelli, *Pellegrini Scrittori: Viaggiatori toscani del Trecento in Terrasanta* (Florence, 1990).
Mitchell, R. J., *The Spring Voyage: The Jerusalem Pilgrimage in 1458* (London, 1964).
Ousterhout, R. (ed.), *The Blessings of Pilgrimage* (Urbana and Chicago, 1990).
Peters, E. (ed.), *The First Crusade* (Philadelphia, 1971).
Peters, F. E., *Jerusalem: The Holy City in the Eyes of Chroniclers, Visitors, Pilgrims and Prophets from the Days of Abraham to the Beginnings of Modern Times* (Princeton, 1985).
Prescott, H. F. M., *Jerusalem Journey: Pilgrimage to the Holy Land in the Fifteenth Century* (London, 1954) [based on the journals of Friar Felix Fabri].
Prescott, H. F. M., *Once to Sinai: The Further Pilgrimage of Friar Felix Fabri* (London, 1957).
Riley-Smith, J., *The First Crusaders, 1095–1131* (Cambridge, 1997).

Röhricht, R. and H. J. Meisner, *Das Reisebuch der Familie Rieter* (Tübingen, 1884).

Wilken, R., *The Land called Holy: Palestine in Christian History and Thought* (New Haven, CT, 1992).

Wilkinson, John (ed.), *Egeria's Travels* (London, 1971; 3rd edn, Warminster, 1999).

Wilkinson, John, *Jerusalem Pilgrims Before the Crusades* (London, 1977).

Wilkinson, John, *Jerusalem Pilgrimage, 1099–1185*, Hakluyt Society, 2nd Ser. 167 (London, 1988).

Rome and the *Via Francigena*

Birch, D. J., *Pilgrimage to Rome in the Middle Ages* (Woodbridge, 1998).

Brewyn, William, *A XVth Century Guide-book to the Principal Churches of Rome*, ed. C. E. Woodruff (London, 1933).

Capgrave, John, *Ye Solace of Pilgrimes: A Description of Rome circa AD 1450*, ed. C. Mills (London, 1911).

Kessler, H. L. and J. Zacharias, *Rome 1300: On the Path of the Pilgrim* (New Haven, CT, 2000).

Magoun, F. P., 'The Pilgrim-Diary of Nikulas of Munkathvera: the Road to Rome', *Medieval Studies*, 6 (1944).

Magoun, F. P., 'The Rome of Two Northern Pilgrims: Archbishop Sigeric of Canterbury and Abbot Nikulas of Munkathvera', *Harvard Theological Review*, 32 (1940).

The Marvels of Rome: Mirabilia Urbis Romae, ed. and trans. F. M. Nichols (reprinted New York, 1986; first published London and Rome, 1889).

Master Gregory, *The Marvels of Rome*, ed. and trans. J. Osborne (Toronto, 1987).

Quintavalle, A. C., *La strada Romea* (Milan, 1976).

Springer, O., 'Medieval Pilgrim Routes from Scandinavia to Rome', *Medieval Studies*, 12 (1950), pp. 92–122.

The Stacions of Rome and the Pilgrims Sea-Voyage, ed. E. Furnivall, Early English Text Society, 25 (1867).

Stopani, R., *La via Francigena: storia di una strada medievale* (Florence, 1998).

William of Malmesbury, *A History of the Norman Kings (1066–1125)*, trans. J. Stevenson (Llanerch reprint, 1989).

Santiago de Compostela

Davies, H. and M.-H. Davis, *Holy Days and Holidays: The Medieval Pilgrimage to Compostela* (Lewisburg, 1982).

Dunn, M. and L. K. Davidson, *The Pilgrimage to Compostela in the Middle Ages* (New York, 1996).

Fletcher, R., *St James's Catapult: The Life and Times of Diego Gelmírez of Santiago de Compostela* (Oxford, 1984).

190 Suggestions for Further Reading

Frey, N. L., *Pilgrim Stories: On and Off the Road to Santiago* (Berkeley, CA, 1998). [The modern pilgrimage experience.]
Kendrick, T. D., *Saint James in Spain* (London, 1960).
Künig von Vach, Hermann, *The Pilgrimage and Path to Saint James*, trans. J. Durant, Confraternity of Saint James Occasional Paper, no. 3 (London, 1993) [translation of itinerary published in Strasburg *c*.1495].
The Miracles of Saint James, ed. T. F. Coffey, L. K. Davidson and M. Dunn (New York, 1996) [translation of parts of Book I of the *Codex Calixtinus*].
The Pilgrim's Guide to Santiago de Compostela: Critical Edition, ed. A. Stones, J. Krochalis, P. Gerson and A. Shaver-Crandell, 2 vols (London, 1998).
Shaver-Crandell, A. and P. Gerson, *The Pilgrim's Guide to Santiago de Compostela: A Gazetteer* (London, 1995) [includes translated text].
Tate, B. and M. Tate, *The Pilgrim Route to Santiago* (Oxford, 1987).
Webb, D., 'St James in Tuscany: the Opera di San Jacopo of Pistoia and Pilgrimage to Compostela', *Journal of Ecclesiastical History*, 50 (1999), pp. 207–34.
Williams, J. and A. Stones (ed.), *The Codex Calixtinus and the Shrine of St James* (Tübingen, 1992).

The British Isles

Adair, J., *The Pilgrims' Way: Shrines and Saints in Britain and Ireland* (London, 1978).
Adomnan of Iona, *Life of St Columba*, trans. R. Sharpe (Harmondsworth, 1995).
Dickinson, J. C., *The Shrine of Our Lady of Walsingham* (Cambridge, 1956).
Duffy, E., *The Stripping of the Altars: Traditional Religion in England, 1400–1580* (London, 1992).
Erasmus, *Pilgrimages to Saint Mary of Walsingham and Saint Thomas of Canterbury*, trans. J. Nichols (London, 1875).
Finucane, R., *Miracles and Pilgrims: Popular Beliefs in Medieval England* (London, 1977).
Harbison, P., *Pilgrimage in Ireland: The Monuments and the People* (London, 1991).
Haren, M. and Y. de Pontfarcy, *The Medieval Pilgrimage to St Patrick's Purgatory: Lough Derg and the European Tradition* (Clogher, 1988).
Jancey, M. (ed.), *St Thomas Cantilupe of Hereford: Essays in his Honour* (Hereford, 1982).
Knox, R. and S. Leslie, *The Miracles of King Henry VI* (Cambridge, 1923).
Lubin, H., *The Worcester Pilgrim*, Worcester Cathedral Publications, 1 (1990).
Nilson, B., *Cathedral Shrines of Medieval England* (Woodbridge, 1998).
The Tale of Beryn, ed. F. J. Furnivall, Early English Text Society, extra series, 105 (1887).
Valente, C., 'Simon de Montfort, Earl of Leicester, and the Utility of Sanctity in Thirteenth-Century England', *Journal of Medieval History*, 21 (1995).
Wall, J. C., *Shrines of British Saints* (London, 1905).
Webb, D., *Pilgrimage in Medieval England* (London, 2000).
Yeoman, P., *Pilgrimage in Medieval Scotland* (London, 1999).

Pilgrim Badges and Souvenirs

Andersson, L., *Pilgrimsmärken och vallfart*, Lund Studies in Medieval Archaeology, 7 (1989).

Bruna, D., *Enseignes de Pèlerinage et Enseignes Profanes* (Paris, Musée Nationale du Moyen Age–Termes de Cluny, 1996).

Cohen, E., '*In Haec Signa*: Pilgrim-badge Trade in Southern France', *Journal of Medieval History*, 2 (1976), pp. 417–35.

Spencer, B., 'Medieval Pilgrim Badges: some General Observations Illustrated Mainly from English Sources', Rotterdam Papers: *A Contribution to Medieval Archaeology*, 1 (1968), pp. 137–53.

Spencer, B., *Medieval Pilgrim Badges from Norfolk* (Norwich, 1980).

Spencer, B., *Pilgrim Souvenirs and Secular Badges: Medieval Finds from Excavations in London* (London, 1998).

Spencer, B., *Salisbury and South Wiltshire Museum, Medieval Catalogue*, pt 2: *Pilgrim Souvenirs and Secular Badges* (Salisbury, 1990).

Van Beuningen, H. J. E. and A. M. Koldeweij, *Heilig en Profaan: 1000 laat-middeleuwse insignes*, Rotterdam Papers, 8 (1993).

Van Heeringen, R. M., A. M. Koldeweij and A. Gaalman, *Heiligen uit de Modder: in Zeeland gevonden Pelgrimstekens* (Utrecht, 1988).

INDEX

Barbara, St, 148
Barcelona *see* Montserrat
Bari *see* Nicholas, St
Bartholomew, St *see* Benevento
Bavaria, Bavarians, 11, 134, 143
Beaulieu, Bernard abbot of, 16
Becket, St Thomas, 24, 61–2, 123–4,
    131, 150, 167
    see also Canterbury
Bede, the Venerable, 4, 6, 11, 49,
    85, 92, 176
Benedict of Nursia, St, 82
    see also Fleury
Benedict Biscop, St, 6, 11, 85
Benevento, 40, 118, 123, 133, 146,
    183 n.19
Bentivoglio, Giovanni, 50
Bernard of Angers, 33, 156, 167–8
Bernard of Aosta, St, 130
Bernard of Beaulieu, abbot, 16, 17
Bernard of Clairvaux, St, x, 73, 89, 170
Bernardino of Siena, St, ix, 42
Berthold of Regensburg, 64, 172
Beverley, John of, St, 100, 124
Bianchi of 1399, 75–6, 155
Birgitta, St, 79, 95, 119, 120, 122,
    145, 146, 160, 181
    shrine at Vadstena, 60–1, 63,
    120, 136, 153
Black Prince, 33, 101
Blaise, St, 150
Bobo (Bovo), St, 130
Bohemia, Bohemian pilgrims, 76,
    120, 144
    Sviatopulk, duke of, 131
Bollezeel (Flanders), 36
Bologna, 37–8, 116, 133, 134, 151
Bona of Pisa, St, 92, 124
Boniface of Wessex, St, 10, 11, 45,
    49, 55, 82, 90–1
Boulogne, Our Lady of, 127, 142,
    150, 165
Boxley Abbey, 29, 65

Boxtel, 142
Boys, Sybil, 97
Bratislava, 120
Bremen, 137
Brendan, St, 48
Brewyn, William, 133–4, 137, 178
Breydenbach, Bernhard von, 161
Bridget, St *see* Birgitta; Brigid
Bridlington, John of, St, 102,
    124, 149
Bridlington Priory, 74, 142
Brigid of Kildare, St, 7, 119
Brindisi, 133
Bromholm Priory, 102, 149, 174
Broni, 130
Bruges, 134
Brunswick, 137
Brussels, 137, 138, 139–40
Budapest, 117, 182 n.12
    Synod of (1297), 32–3
Bunyan, John, 154
Burgh (Lincs.), 109
Burgh, Elizabeth de, lady of Clare, 97
Burghersh, Bartholomew, 103
Burgos, 179, 180
Bury St Edmunds, 10, 34, 84, 102
    Samson, abbot of, 32, 84

Cadiz, 119
Calais, 134, 137
Canterbury, 6, 24, 30, 35, 44, 78,
    115, 146, 149, 153, 171
    Becket's shrine, xi, 63, 84, 102,
    126, 148, 166, 170
    Eastbridge Hospital, 38, 41
    see also Chaucer, Geoffrey; souvenirs
Capgrave, John, 178
Capua, 133
Carcassone, 180
Chad, St, 8
Charlemagne, 11–12, 124
Charles IV, Emperor, 33, 102,
    135–6, 137